I've Had to Think Up a Way to Survive

AMERICAN MUSIC SERIES

Jessica Hopper and Charles L. Hughes, Series Editors

Bruce Adams, *You're with Stupid: kranky, Chicago, and the Reinvention of Indie Music*

Margo Price, *Maybe We'll Make It*

Francesca Royster, *Black Country Music: Listening for Revolutions*

Lance Scott Walker, *DJ Screw: A Life in Slow Revolution*

Eddie Huffman, *John Prine: In Spite of Himself*

David Cantwell, *The Running Kind: Listening to Merle Haggard*

Stephen Deusner, *Where the Devil Don't Stay: Traveling the South with the Drive-By Truckers*

Eric Harvey, *Who Got the Camera? A History of Rap and Reality*

Kristin Hersh, *Seeing Sideways: A Memoir of Music and Motherhood*

Hannah Ewens, *Fangirls: Scenes from Modern Music Culture*

Sasha Geffen, *Glitter Up the Dark: How Pop Music Broke the Binary*

Hanif Abdurraqib, *Go Ahead in the Rain: Notes to A Tribe Called Quest*

Chris Stamey, *A Spy in the House of Loud: New York Songs and Stories*

Holly Gleason, editor, *Woman Walk the Line: How the Women in Country Music Changed Our Lives*

Adam Sobsey, *Chrissie Hynde: A Musical Biography*

Lloyd Sachs, *T Bone Burnett: A Life in Pursuit*

Danny Alexander, *Real Love, No Drama: The Music of Mary J. Blige*

Alina Simone, *Madonnaland and Other Detours into Fame and Fandom*

Kristin Hersh, *Don't Suck, Don't Die: Giving Up Vic Chesnutt*

Chris Morris, *Los Lobos: Dream in Blue*

John T. Davis, *The Flatlanders: Now It's Now Again*

David Menconi, *Ryan Adams: Losering, a Story of Whiskeytown*

Don McLeese, *Dwight Yoakam: A Thousand Miles from Nowhere*

Peter Blackstock and David Menconi, Founding Editors

I've Had to Think Up a Way to Survive

ON TRAUMA, PERSISTENCE, AND DOLLY PARTON

Lynn Melnick

University of Texas Press

Austin

The names and identifying details of some individuals have been changed to protect their privacy.

Requests for permission to reproduce material from this work should be sent to:
Permissions
University of Texas Press
P.O. Box 7819
Austin, TX 78713-7819
utpress.utexas.edu/rp-form

♾ The paper used in this book meets the minimum requirements of ANSI/ NISO Z39.48-1992 (R1997) (Permanence of Paper).

Library of Congress Cataloging-in-Publication Data

Names: Melnick, Lynn, author.
Title: I've had to think up a way to survive : on trauma, persistence, and Dolly Parton / Lynn Melnick.
Other titles: I have had to think up a way to survive
Description: First edition. | Austin : University of Texas Press, 2022. | Series: American music series | Includes bibliographical references.
Identifiers: LCCN 2022000739
ISBN 978-1-4773-2267-3 (cloth)
ISBN 978-1-4773-2599-5 (PDF)
ISBN 978-1-4773-2600-8 (ePub)
Subjects: LCSH: Melnick, Lynn. | Parton, Dolly. | Parton, Dolly. Songs. Selections. | Women poets—Biography. | Women country musicians— Biography.
Classification: LCC PS3563.E4436 Z46 2022 | DDC 811/.54 |
[B]—dc23/eng/20220128
LC record available at https://lccn.loc.gov/2022000739

doi:10.7560/322673

I think friends can literally save your life.
—Dolly Parton

This book is dedicated to my friends.

CONTENTS

I've Had to Think Up
a Way to Survive

Seven Bridges Road

Little Sparrow, 2001, 3:29

THE FIRST TIME I REMEMBER hearing a Dolly Parton song start to finish was in the triage room of a hospital, as I waited to be admitted to a drug rehabilitation program in West Los Angeles. I was fourteen. It was 1988, and Dolly and Kenny Rogers were singing 1983's "Islands in the Stream" across LA's KOST-FM. I knew her voice, of course. It would have been hard to be anywhere near a radio or television in the last fifty years without getting to know Dolly's warm, clarion soprano. But while I grew up on folk songs—basically country for blue states—music like Dolly's was often scorned in my parents' home, and by my friends. My friends and I spent our time chasing down heavy metal bands on the Sunset Strip and would not have given Dolly the time of day. Many people of my generation—or at least those born outside the reign of country radio—first knew of Dolly as a straight-talking goofball on *The Tonight Show,* a set of giant tits, someone your grandma got a kick out of, someone who, my father would say with derision, was "famous for being famous." Meanwhile, Dolly had been churning out hits for decades, possessed of a preternatural talent for writing and for singing authentic emotion into every song. Class and gender stereotypes could not and would not obscure her absolute genius or stop her from going where she wanted to go.

I don't remember my parents in the moment they signed me into rehab, not their probably weary faces—younger than my own now—or much of what they said, only that the high cost of hospitalization was mentioned, and a joke made about hitting the annual insurance deductible in one night. March 3. A date I have marked every year in the thirty-plus years since. As a parent of a teenager myself now, I assume there was significant pain involved, some bewilderment, but also perhaps some acknowledgment of this predictable next step in the falling-apart sequence I'd been slowly enacting since I was raped by a teenage boy on overgrown 1970s carpeting before I'd turned ten years old. Now halfway through ninth grade, I had already been expelled from school twice; reckless behavior, followed by variously successful attempts to cover it up, was how I spent my free time while other kids studied or kissed or participated in team sports.

I welcomed the stay at Glen Recovery Center. If I couldn't just be given an entirely new self, at least I wanted to make it clear to the world that the one I inhabited was wrecked. Being in rehab seemed like a rubber stamp to that effect. Less fond of cocaine and whiskey than of the exhilaration of forgetting, I craved the fresh environment. My parents filled out intake forms, and I was asked to create a list of people I approved to visit me. I sat with the lined sheet of paper on my lap even though I knew I didn't want to see anyone. Outside, on Pico Boulevard, the Santa Ana winds blew through the tops of the palm trees visible from the windows of the triage room. I could hear the traffic flow east toward the tall vacant buildings of Downtown after dark and west toward Twenti-eth Century–Fox Studios and eventually the Pacific Ocean. It was a relief to abandon whatever promise I'd held as a curious, shy girl in my brother's hand-me-down Sears dungarees and a cherished Strawberry Shortcake turtleneck shirt, the outfit

I'd worn to school on picture day a couple months before my body was violated on that deep pile of beige shag carpet.

I'd worked hard since then to convince the outside world to join me in giving up on my potential. But Dolly's voice from the hospital's ceiling speakers held a different kind of promise than that which I'd failed to meet. It was a release, a renewal, euphoric. When I heard Dolly's voice over the four-plus minutes of "Islands in the Stream," I knew I needed to hear it again. Though it would be a few months before I purchased a *Greatest Hits* cassette tape from the bargain bin at a Thrifty Drugs, the multifaceted clarity of her voice hooked me instantly. I needed to feel that euphoria in my body again. I needed to believe in that bright precision, in an artistry as unstoppable as Dolly herself.

Resilience. Longevity. Outlast those who would doubt you. Just keep going. In my darkest moments, that's been the light she shone on me. With over one hundred singles, fifty albums, 160 million records sold, more than four hundred television appearances, and scores of awards, Dolly has become even more of an icon in recent years, claimed and reclaimed by fans across a startling number of demographics and featured prominently and with due reverence everywhere, from memes and kitsch merchandise to awards shows and a Ken Burns PBS series. Dolly is an icon of feminine strength and yet also an objectified caricature of womanhood. She's super savvy while often playing the rattlebrain—a deflection, perhaps, a feint of self-protection in a world where big talent and business acumen prove threatening when coming from a woman. She's a phenomenally accomplished artist who giggles it off as she keeps marching forward (in five-inch heels) through the life she wants. She's an American Dream.

My husband, two daughters, and I arrived in Dolly-wood—a theme park in Pigeon Forge, Tennessee, that is partly owned by and fully named after Dolly—in the middle of the worst year of my adult life. A year so horrible that we were pretty sure Dollywood would be a disaster, a fairly expensive disaster, this dream vacation paid for with the remains of a fellowship from the New York Public Library—money I'd earned for once, maybe for always, with my poetry. I'm not great at desks, so I spent that year with my ass on the industrial carpet of the very posh offices of the New York Public Library's Cullman Center for Scholars and Writers, fielding phone calls and texts of crisis more than I spent it working on poems. My grandmother died. My husband's best friend died. My beloved father-in-law had emergency open-heart surgery. I suffered with whooping cough for months. My daughter Ada, in seventh grade, was melting down in ways both predictable and terrifying. I was trying to promote my just-released book of poems about my own trauma, which in effect kept retraumatizing me. I needed a break.

The afternoon we arrived in East Tennessee, I stood in my rainbow wedge heels on the deck of our rental log cabin overlooking the Great Smoky Mountains and I let the landscape lap over me. I had never really grasped the rightness of their name, which is derived from the Cherokee "shakonage," or "place of blue smoke," until just that moment. Dense green, hawks soaring toward the sun, then erased by the low, thick clouds that create the illusion of another world: I felt desperate to lose myself in it, and to find myself there as well.

One of twelve children, Dolly was born in the hills of East Tennessee to Avie Lee and Robert Lee Parton in January of 1946, and grew up in poverty. I grew up the daughter of a college professor and a second-grade teacher; my older brother, Cliff, was my only sibling. Now my brother's family and mine were sharing one of the priciest cabins you can rent at Dollywood—"High Hopes." How could I learn to be more Dollylike, rising again and again from the embers of expectation? What did it mean to be a forty-four-year-old woman, survivor, mother of two young daughters? A woman with years of missteps and recovery behind me? As a diehard

Dolly fan, what did it mean to have finally made it there? I needed the escape of a completely new environment, but I also felt desperate to breathe in the backdrop that had formed the woman who in many ways formed me. I knew it would connect me back to myself, and to Dolly.

"I had to get rich in able to sing like I was poor again," said Dolly about her bluegrass albums. It took me finding safety to be able to write about violence. And it took writing about rape culture to find my way through it, and toward joy. Rape culture—the environment in which sexual assault, harassment, coercion, and misconduct are ignored, diminished, and allowed to flourish without repercussion—is rampant in the United States and around the world, and it too often originates from the very language we use to describe and define events and actions. From casual rape jokes traded among friends, to "boys will be boys," to journalists calling the many assault and harassment allegations against Hollywood figures a "sex scandal," to women my age being told they should appreciate street harassment because it means they've "still got it"—these everyday microaggressions and flat-out aggressions keep women and other victims from feeling safe, and often also keep them from achieving their career and personal goals.

And what if Dolly—with her outsize hair and curves and heels—epitomizes the kind of woman who is "asking for it," all while using this very stance to full-steam-ahead on her artistic ambitions, and to spread her message of kindness and joy and charity? What if she's using rape culture against its own damn self?

Beginning in the 1960s, Dolly wrote and sang scores of memorable country and pop hits, charting on one list or another in every decade since her career began in earnest. Early hits like "Jolene" and "I Will Always Love You" brought her critical acclaim and commercial success, which she solidified by churning out about an album a year throughout the 1960s and 1970s; these were thoughtful and well-produced records despite the relentless pace, and they thrived on country radio each time. By the 1980s, Dolly was in her thirties, and country radio had benefitted from her crossover success. Hooky, irresistible songs like "Islands in the Stream" and "Here You Come Again" appeared on both the pop charts and the country charts, and she began to enter the public consciousness as a celebrity as well as an artist. By the mid-1990s, however, she suddenly wasn't contemporary, mainstream, or young enough for either chart. "Nobody plays artists like me on country radio anymore," Dolly said in an interview in *Goldmine* in 2002, "because they assume people my age are over. But artists like me hopefully never are. Because I've lived so many lifetimes."

Dolly's later-career roots albums of bluegrass, country gospel, and Appalachian folk—namely, 1999's *The Grass Is Blue* and 2001's *Little Sparrow*—brought her back to her beginning and reinvigorated her career. This music of her youth finds her unbound by commercial considerations, and also serves to remind anyone who might have forgotten her impeccable talent. *Little Sparrow* was, until very recently, unavailable for download, and I no longer own a CD player, so I listened to its songs on YouTube, most frequently the title track and also "Seven Bridges Road." I listen to "Seven Bridges Road" via my laptop's dinky sound system whenever I need inspiration or cheering up—which, because I am human and frantic and overwrought inside the demands of womanhood and motherhood, and the work demands of late capitalism, is near daily. "Seven Bridges Road" is a deep Dolly cut, one of my very favorites because of its unchecked, almost cosmic exuberance. It starts off my playlist.

I created my Dolly playlist in 2012 to celebrate my first non-hand-me-down laptop, just months before my first book would be published. I felt a rush trying to remember all my favorites, as they tumbled too quickly through my head. Why do people make playlists? To weed out the filler? To create their dream album? Control? To me, making a playlist is like ordering a book of poems; the story changes depending on how you arrange it—where it begins, where it ends, and all the little feats of magic that happen in between. My playlist (entitled, imaginatively, "Dolly") was the story I wanted to tell with her music. This book is also that story; it follows the order of my playlist.

Dolly Parton is unquestionably one of the greatest American songwriters of all time, though she didn't write "Seven Bridges Road." It was written by "outlaw country" singer and songwriter Steve Young in the 1970s and made famous by the Los Angeles–formed band the Eagles. Young moved to Los Angeles from Alabama as a young man, didn't know what to make of it, and quickly moved back to the South. Even though I never knew what to make of LA, I still long for it in a way that appalls me. But not the city as it is now, airbrushed and grown-up. I long for LA as I knew it, with its glam and booze and bad ideas, its wide, bright boulevards and how the light bounced off the sidewalks in a way that almost hurt. The whole time I lived in Los Angeles I failed to notice the escape hatches around me. I met one bad idea after another—drugs, brutal men, LA's darkest corners—in search of someone to touch me gently, to point me to the wildflowers I couldn't still my head to notice, to move me past the ordinary as I knew it.

Jim Mills's banjo on Dolly's "Seven Bridges Road" is sublime, extraordinary, bubbling under the surface of winding arrangements and simple nostalgia until the end, where the mandolin and the banjo and Stuart Duncan's always brilliant fiddle and Becky and Susan Isaacs' complex harmonies finish at a peak; the song doesn't blink. And it is Dolly's voice that holds us with her passion and longing, holds every entry in a dictionary of feelings. Her voice is subtext and primary text; it says more per note than I have said in whole books. I'm exaggerating. I'm proud of my books.

In the early 1990s, when I was twenty years old, my then boyfriend pulled a tall, full bookcase down on top of me. He was furious about my reading and my writing. Shelves of Alice Walker, Emily Brontë, and poetry anthologies I'd found at thrift stores; fat Nortons and community college textbooks on anthropology and United States government; lurid dime-store paperbacks I'd inherited from an old woman who handed them to me in a McDonald's bag at the laundromat: all of these collapsed on top of me, along with the oak shelves, and pinned me to the floor.

He didn't start off angry. When I met him he was worshipful, couldn't get enough of me. He touched me so tenderly I felt made of lace, and when I was handled like lace, he made me forget I was blighted. I felt instead lovely, decorous, *his*, and so I also forgot the strength I'd learned surviving everything I'd endured before him.

He had some books of his own. Carlos Castaneda, *The Tao of Pooh*, a handful of field guides to the fauna of California. He used Dr. Bronner's soap and alternated between Taco Bell and being vegan. He wasn't strictly beautiful—his eyes were wild like a splenetic animal. Early on in our courtship, I called him frightened from a gas station telephone because a man had threatened me, put a knife to my ribs on a city bus. It was decided that I shouldn't take the bus anymore, that he should drive me everywhere in his always shiny car. This is how I became his to worship, to teach, to protect, to harm.

My cassette of Dolly Parton's *Greatest Hits* from Thrifty was long lost by then but I had the CD—already the soundtrack to my own hoped-for resilience—which I slipped into the player while the man who'd just thrown a bookcase on me went to 7-Eleven to buy me yet another package of apology candy, always Red Vines, which are still my favorite. I left the books all over my floor, my bed—they'd even bounced well into the hallway. My body hurt. I couldn't cry. I started a poem whose words and sounds and placement on the page held my whole story, some of which I couldn't speak out loud without vomiting until I was in my forties. My body was covered in bookcase bruises for weeks and the marks shamed me, but I didn't stop writing, trying to tell my story.

"I think it's just simple ways of telling stories," Dolly recently said about country music, "experiencing and expressing feelings. You can dance to it, you can cry to it, you can make love to it, you can play it at a funeral. . . . It really has something in it for every body"—she emphasizes these words separately—"and people relate to it."

Dolly Parton left her hometown in Sevier County, Tennessee, in 1964. "I graduated on a Friday night and hurried to get to Nashville, so I came down on Saturday mornin'." At her graduation ceremony, she announced to her class and their families that she was going to be a star, and the audience laughed. "They don't know," she thought. "They don't know." The next day she left for Nashville, which was what I would soon do, only now it was 2018 and my family would be heading to the airport there to go back home to New York City.

I buckled my rainbow wedge heels and sipped my coffee. My visit to Dollywood would take some months to process, but it left me feeling more certain than ever of my strength and ability to create and to shine on my own terms. If you want the rainbow, Dolly says, you gotta put up with the rain. But now there was only sun, as far into the mountains as I could see, as I stepped onto the back deck of the cabin one last time. Like Dolly, the light in Tennessee dazzles. It glints and shifts. It thrums, it astounds, it is nothing but itself.

CHAPTER ONE

Why'd You Come in Here Lookin' Like That

White Limozeen, 1989, 2:32

AFTER DOLLY ENJOYED SEVERAL YEARS of crossover success, her 1987 album, *Rainbow*, released not long before I was released from rehab, was a relative flop. Despite heavy promotion on Dolly's short-lived variety show (also a flop), it didn't have a single hit. *Rainbow* is slick and unremarkable, so quintessentially 1987, with its overprocessed drum machine and a producer whose earlier credits include work on the *Breakfast Club* soundtrack. It's hard not to cringe while listening to it. Even Dolly—who can make the tritest sentiment come urgently to life—seems bored and disconnected while delivering the songs on *Rainbow*. The first release from a deal with Columbia Records that was supposed to have her alternating between pop and country albums, *Rainbow*'s failure sent Dolly back to her roots for the rest of the contract. Her 1989 album, *White Limozeen,* is straight-up country. The cover features Dolly in neck-to-toe sparkly white, a fluffy white stole around her shoulders. Her hair is permed and her arms are up as if to say, see? All of this—white limousine, paparazzi, adoring crowd, name on marquee—is mine! Meanwhile, the look on her face is pinched.

"I think the timing is perfect for me to do country music again," Dolly told William Stadiem in *Interview* magazine in July 1989, when she was forty-three years old. "It's kind of come back again to that traditional sound that it had when I could make a living at it years ago and wanted to get out and expand." *White Limozeen* was produced by industry veteran and noted bluegrass artist Ricky Skaggs, who also plays fiddle like a door slamming at the finish of "Why'd You Come in Here Lookin' Like That," the album's most enduring hit. There are steel guitars and banjos, a mandolin, and even a Pedabro—and no drum machine in sight. The song reached number one on the *Billboard* Hot Country chart in August of 1989, helping to keep *White Limozeen* on the Top Country Albums chart for one hundred weeks, where it peaked at number three. The same year, Dolly starred in the popular movie *Steel Magnolias*, which highlights her not inconsiderable acting skills.

"Why'd You Come in Here Lookin' Like That" is a song that objectifies men the way men's songs objectify women— "Why'd you come in here lookin' like that / In your cowboy boots and your painted-on jeans"—basically blaming the man for the fact of his body in his clothes and its ability to distract. I scoured articles about the songwriters, Bob Carlisle and Randy Thomas, but could find no evidence the song was written with a male singer singing about a woman in mind. The songwriters are two Christian music songwriting veterans, best known now for the 1997 song "Butterfly Kisses," a sappy, patriarchal song about a girl coming of age and getting married but still loving her daddy. It is as different from "Why'd You Come in Here Lookin' Like That" as a girl being handed from dad to groom is different from Dolly ditching her small town on her own the day after she finished high school.

The year 1989 was a good one for Dolly and not the worst one for me. It was the first year I actually enjoyed sex with a man, a beautiful young man named Jason whom I loved but for whom I think I was ultimately a torment. Before that I'd thought sex with boys or men was just for the pleasure of boys or men. I wasn't at all aware of "Why'd You Come in Here Lookin' Like That" when it came out—likely only played on stations I didn't listen to—but I had seen *Steel Magnolias* in the movie theater where Jason worked, and I loved the whole thing, every complicated middle-aged woman centered in the story. That Dolly's husband in *Steel Magnolias* is played by Sam Shepard, whose absurd, gritty, cerebral plays Jason explained to me between rounds of kissing at the park, only made her seem cooler. I likely never spoke of Dolly to Jason, as she was a rather private passion still. I was afraid of not being sophisticated enough, although Jason would have loved anything I loved—such was his heart. I wish I could say my whole life looked up from there, from his full lips hovering on mine in the burst of the Los Angeles sun, but you already know it didn't.

To promote *White Limozeen*, Dolly went on *Saturday Night Live*, as both host and musical guest, and sang "Why'd You Come in Here Lookin' Like That" as well as the album's rags-to-Hollywood title song. After *Rainbow* and her ill-fated variety show, this appearance was a return to form—celebratory and a bit kitsch. I have a very vague memory of watching it as it happened, and thirty years later her performance is as impressive as ever. She near flawlessly delivers the opening monologue, a camera panning to a close-up of her famous chest as we hear her chirp about how respectful everyone in New York City has been to her. She participates in a sketch—originally written for, but rejected by, guest host Raquel Welch in 1976—about a planet where women have such gigantic breasts that those with Dolly-size breasts are thought to be defective. Another sketch has her spinning folksy yarns, unaware that the detailed stories her mom told her as a kid were just paraphrases of episodes of television shows like *Bonanza*. Dolly knows how to laugh at herself, knows how to let us laugh at her, knows how to sell both a record and herself. She looks trim, her waist impossibly tiny in an NBC peacock–inspired, spangly spandex jumpsuit.

In the late 1980s I also wore a lot of spandex. I wore it to my first job, babysitting a rabbi's son on Saturday nights in the upscale Westwood area of Los Angeles. I was finished with my dramatic high school freshman year, and feeling pretty good about myself. Sometimes my father would say I looked like a hooker and insist I change before going to babysit, and then I'd wriggle out of my long, flowy skirts at the bus stop. Did you ever have anyone tell you what to wear? I mean, outside of school and work uniforms? Have you ever wanted to placate someone enough that you wear what they tell you to? The man who threw the bookcase on me put me in outfits, one of which included a chunky cotton sweater in Pepto pink and baggy blue jeans. He was embarrassed by my spandex and he was embarrassed by my midcentury thrift-store dresses. He wanted so desperately for me to be publicly mainstream and unsexy because I was a prize just for him, an object he liked to slam his dick into. At the time, I felt his dressing me was an act of love. When I left him, still asleep, I left most of my clothes behind.

Years later, when I was in my early twenties, I was in a grad school program for writing, and two men at a department party in a drab classroom decided to tell me they couldn't take me seriously because of how I dressed. I would never be a serious poet because I liked to wear dresses and sometimes bright colors and would I like another drink? Would I like to go to their apartment for more? In a 1977 interview with Dolly, Barbara Walters rudely says, "You don't have to look like this, you're very beautiful, you don't have to wear the blond wigs, you don't have to wear the extreme clothes, right?" In a demure, almost melancholy voice, Dolly offers one of her canned Dollyisms: "I would never stoop so low

to be fashionable, that's the easiest thing in the world to do."
Walters keeps coming at her, though, even more aggressively:
"Do you feel like you're a joke, that people make fun of you?"
Dolly keeps her composure, her affable lilt, her measured
words, while she refuses this typecasting so hard I hollered
with vindication when I first watched the clip.

"Oh, I know they make fun of me, but all these years the
people have thought the joke was on me, but it's actually on
them. I am sure of myself as a person. I am sure of my talent.
I'm sure of my love for life and that sort of thing. I am very
content, I like the kind of person that I am. So, I can afford
to piddle around and do-diddle around with makeup and
clothes and stuff because I am secure with myself."

The rabbi and his family lived in a fancy condo with two
floors and black leather couches and what seemed—in its
almost glittering whiteness—to be very expensive carpeting.
In retrospect, I think I read "expensive" where I should have
read "tacky," but it was the 1980s so it was probably both.
Having grown up in a series of "dingbat" apartments built in
the '50s and '60s, with low popcorn ceilings and tiny windows, I was especially taken with the floor-to-ceiling windows in the condo, and on summer evenings before sunset the
exceptional Los Angeles light cloyed its way around the walls,
the numerous houseplants, our faces, in a way that seemed
both life giving and somehow also dangerous. Sunset marked
Havdalah service on Saturday evenings, the end to the weekly
Sabbath observance. I'd stand politely at their dining room
table as the rabbi recited prayers, but I'd already stopped
believing. I knew early on that the Judaism I'd met had no
equal place for girls or women, though a lot of bones were
thrown. Still, I was young and I felt a bit of awe for the posi-
tion of rabbi, and the authority it conveyed, and for the rabbi's
wife, who seemed very chic. She also wore spandex, and so
I thought she was cool because, wow, a rabbi's wife wearing
short skirts and black tights. She was small and curvy like me

and didn't hide it, and she wore very high heels. I was still in (knockoff) Keds, the shoelaces removed, as was the trend.

They'd leave and I'd put their toddler, Isaac, to bed after a bit of play, and then it got really good because I was being paid five dollars an hour to lie on the leather couches in my little spandex skirt, not as high quality as the rabbi's wife's and probably stolen from friends or the mall, but I still felt sexy with their expensive, tacky carpeting all around me while I read as many of their books as I could. Like my own parents, the rabbi and his wife had the Jewish canon on their shelves: Philip Roth, Henry Roth, Isaac Bashevis Singer, Saul Bellow. There were few women. The couple always returned home noticeably buzzed, the rabbi's wife glowing, reminding her husband she'd still be up when he came back from driving me to my apartment, several miles east of there. They almost always asked if I wanted to borrow whatever book I was reading and I always said no, because I didn't want to owe them anything. The first time I traded my body for money, it was to the rabbi.

It's Dolly lore, how she modeled her look on the local sex worker. "There was this woman, we won't call her names, but she was beautiful. . . . I had never seen anybody, you know, with the yellow hair all piled up and the red lipstick and the rouge and the high-heeled shoes, and I thought, 'This is what I want to look like.'" This exaggerated idea of femininity made a big impression on young Dolly, the way the rabbi's wife's miniskirts and high heels—waltzing right in there looking like that—made a big impression on me.

Musically, "Why'd You Come in Here Lookin' Like That" is exhilarating: fast-paced, raucous, and graced with the irresistible, transcendent joy of a late-in-the-song a cappella key change. The rugged throat rattle on the "why'd" that follows is bordering on heroic. Women country artists have been brandishing this particular weapon for decades, from Brenda Lee's 1957 hit "Dynamite" to Carrie Underwood's 2006 hit

"Before He Cheats." The throat rattle is an exclamation point, a defiant rale buoyed by its own unstoppable vivacity. It gives no fucks. Sprung in spirit from the depths of the body, it remains risky for the real damage it might do when born in the throat. The sound is tough, emphatic, and employed just briefly enough in "Why'd You Come in Here Lookin' Like That" to demand our full attention throughout.

Dolly took the song all over the 1980s TV landscape and beyond. She performed it on multiple talk shows and, of course, at Dollywood. On *The Arsenio Hall Show* she's in top form in a black-and-silver spangled jumpsuit and dangerously high heels, her throat rattle on "why'd" so spectacular we can see her feel it like we feel it. Meanwhile, on *The Pat Sajak Show*, Dolly is just kind of phoning it in. Maybe it's hard to keep selling yourself. I know this on a small scale; I've been on book tours. I've dressed myself in the morning with an eye toward selling my books. In her conversation in *Interview*, Dolly states she's about to go out on the road for *years* to promote *White Limozeen*. Maybe you can't have a throat rattle on "why'd" every single night.

One evening, in a fancy black car in the basement garage of his building, the rabbi handed me a copy of the classic 1981 self-help book *When Bad Things Happen to Good People*. He said he had an extra copy and he knew I liked to read. I thanked him. Then, as he spoke about the book, he took my hand and put it on his crotch, over his dress slacks. He owed me twenty dollars for the babysitting and he handed me two twenties. You deserve this, he said. I pulled out his cock. He handed me a handkerchief. I jerked him off and he told me it was great. He drove me home, talking more about the book that was sitting between us. Harold Kushner, also a rabbi, wrote the book to try to keep his belief in God after the death of his fourteen-year-old son. He was only around your age, the rabbi told me, with gravity. He had his whole life ahead of him, he said. Like you, he said. But I felt like my life had already ended when I was nine years old and pinned on a shag carpet. "In the final analysis," wrote Kushner, "the question of why bad things happen to good people translates itself into some very different questions, no longer asking why something happened, but asking how we will respond, what we intend to do now that it has happened."

I still don't believe in a God or gods, but I do, from my middle-aged vantage point, understand the truth of a lot of the messages in Kushner's book. At the time I received it, I thanked the rabbi, who looked forward to seeing me again next week (and he did), went upstairs to the room I shared with my brother, and put my money into the little brown faux-leather coin purse I'd had since I was not much older than Isaac. I threw the book on the floor. Its title stared at me for weeks, taunting me in and out of spandex, until it got buried under more clothes and whatever else, and I don't know what happened to it after that. I don't know what happened to the rabbi either. I can't even remember his first name let alone his last, and after a few months of what was a very lucrative and easy arrangement, his wife called and said they wouldn't be needing me anymore. "Get with it, Clairee," Dolly's Truvy tells Olympia Dukakis's character in *Steel Magnolias*. "This is the '80s. If you can achieve puberty, you can achieve a past."

The music video for "Why'd You Come in Here Lookin' Like That," which is staged as a casting call for itself, is wild. After a parade of men whom Dolly's meant to evaluate based solely on their looks, there's Dolly too, at the end of the song, in her own high-heeled boots and painted-on jeans, self-objectifying as she always is—preemptively, and with an eye toward what's good for business. Yet she's also taking her hotness and using it both to distract us and to remind us who is in charge. We don't know "real" Dolly so we can't slobber over made-up Dolly in any meaningful way, in any way that can get to her. She's always been in on the joke; she created the joke in the first place.

When I came to Dollywood at forty-four, deflated but
defiant in my rainbow wedge heels and curve-hugging dresses,
I came to try to find the real Dolly, or a piece of the real Dolly,
or a piece of the construct, or myself, in any case. I didn't put
a lot of thought into what I'd wear to Dollywood, which was
odd for me, as envisioning outfits is a real pleasure of mine. I
had just tossed about seven dresses that let me feel like myself
into my suitcase back in Brooklyn, without designating one
as *the* Dollywood dress, singled out for the momentous day
I'd spend in her world. Day of, I chose a maxi dress with blue
and red flowers on a white background (it was July 3, after
all). It hugged me well and didn't scream—only Dolly can
scream in Dollywood, I'd soon learn—but I knew I stood out
in East Tennessee. Pale skin, thick glasses, dark wavy hair. I felt
radioactively Jewish.

The heart of Dollywood, or so it is to a Dollyologist like
me, is Chasing Rainbows, the Dolly memorabilia museum.
One of her tour buses sits out front, but the bus was closed on
the day we visited, to my not inconsiderable disappointment.
Across from the museum is a store called Dolly's Closet, for
which I'd earmarked a rather sizeable chunk of money. "Step
inside this fashion boutique representing all of the unique
styles of Dolly herself," reads the blurb on Dollywood's website. "You will find a unique blend of clothing, accessories
and jewelry showcasing Country Western Dolly, Romantic
Dolly and of course Glamour Dolly. . . . This is a shopping
experience you will not want to miss." I did not find a unique
blend of clothing. I found a Chico's, if Chico's let a crafty but
prudent class parent loose with a Bedazzler. I knew I wasn't
Country Western Dolly, and my maxi dress did say Romantic
Dolly, but Glamour Dolly was why I'd set aside those dollars. I'll admit, I almost cried. I'd imagined myself arriving
back at LaGuardia Airport with a form-fitting minisuit and
some sky-high heels. Or at least a form-fitting country dress
(okay, yes, I will be Country Western Dolly, okay), but I sorted

through a lot of dull, drapey, poly-blend fabrics in what the mom who once helped me organize Wellness Week at my girls' elementary school called "forgiving" styles, which seems to mean styles that don't form in conversation with the body but with the aim to shut it up.

Dolly loves to tell the story of entering a drag contest and losing: "They had a bunch of Chers and Dollys that year, so I just overexaggerated—made my beauty mark bigger, the eyes bigger, the hair bigger, everything." She knows she's an exaggeration, and that there's power in that. I just watched videos of both Frank Fine and Willow Pill lip-syncing to "Why'd You Come in Here Lookin' Like That," Pill in all denim with a skirt cut up to there, and Fine in a more Dolly-esque blue-and-white ensemble. I can report, however, that I spotted, regrettably, no clothes for drag queens at Dollywood.

My husband, Timothy, who is by nature a problem solver, rescued my mood, quickly darkening in Dolly's Closet (I had to buy *something*), by finding a black lace cover-up that I could imagine wearing quite a lot between seasons, with late-night drafts or summer in the city and its overachieving air-conditioning. Months later, though, I still haven't worn it, because it feels like something I bought at an airport, from nowhere in itself.

Why is Dolly's Closet trying to convince me that Dolly would ever have any Chico's hanging in hers? Is it a token thing? We can have one painted lady we respect, but good lord, that's it! The rest of respectable womanhood can admire Dolly, but heavens no, they won't dress like her! Dolly understands objectification and sexism, sharply. She knows how to resist it but she also knows how to go with it for money. She knows her body and clothes sell records, but she also knows that her fans have little intention of making a joke or spectacle of their own selves.

Most every woman has had a Barbara Walters slut-shame her or render her invisible or ridiculous. Most every woman knows what her body is really worth and to whom. I watch my daughters, now fourteen and ten, to see how much of this they already know, in spite of how much I've tried to surround them in light, tell them all bodies are good bodies, give them the tools they will need when alone on any sidewalk. My fourteen-year-old has been through middle school with her body, and it was as rough as expected, but my ten-year-old is still ebullient inside hers. In rape culture, this seems like a victory. Every day that I dress myself is a calculation of *confidence* × *safety* + *courage* ÷ *rape culture*. Every day is an answer to Dolly's titular question. I have used my body almost my whole life to get me noticed or to keep me paid—sometimes it backfired and sometimes it got me what I wanted—and now I'm staring at this music video and I guess I'll watch it again. It's not quite empowering what Dolly is doing. But there's that throat rattle, and it sounds like survival.

CHAPTER TWO

Steady as the Rain

The Grass Is Blue, 1999, 3:05

DOLLY APPEARS ON THE COVER of 1998's *Hungry Again*, her thirty-fifth studio album and her final on Decca Records, wearing a loose braid and overalls, sitting on a porch swing. Considered a "heritage" artist by country radio and television stations by the time of that album's release, Dolly, then fifty-two, admitted to *Billboard* magazine, "I know what it's like in country music now for an artist my age." She continued, "But being the artist I like to believe I am, I wasn't about to give up trying. So I decided to do something that really comes from my heart—the more organic stuff that I do best—and go back home. I wanted to get back in touch with that part of the country and who I was and not necessarily be commercial or tailor-made or riding on other people's coattails but at least be appreciated by those who appreciate where I come from."

While *Billboard* called *Hungry Again* Dolly's "best stuff in years," they also note in their review that her first single from the album, "Honky Tonk Songs," flopped on radio, rejected by "young women listeners [who] no longer welcome such overt drinking songs told by a woman aiming to get drunk and dance." This is a bewildering misread of the song, which is sung from the perspective of a woman left by a man for a woman half her age—and left wondering why more women don't sing down and dirty songs about men who've wronged them. Still, the review isn't mistaken that young country music fans in 1998 were far more interested in LeAnn Rimes's album of inspirational songs (a chart-topper that year) and Shania Twain's more slickly empowered single "That Don't Impress Me Much" (a chart-topper in 1999).

"Until the Gucci arrival of Shania Twain, Dolly Parton was country glamour," wrote *Rolling Stone* in early 2000 in a very positive review of Dolly's first bluegrass album, *The Grass Is Blue*, released in fall of 1999. "Curled tongue abandon" is how they describe her singing. Earlier in 1999, Decca Records had closed their Nashville office, leaving Dolly without a record label. It was then that her longtime producer, Steve Buckingham, suggested she make a bluegrass album, which couldn't have seemed like a far leap from what drove her to record *Hungry Again*. "I thought," she told *Billboard*, "since I manage myself now and have my own label and can do what I want, why not do it?"

Coming just before the popular Coen brothers movie *O Brother, Where Art Thou?* would make bluegrass unexpectedly trendy, *The Grass Is Blue* wasn't reviewed very widely and its chart success was only middling; still, it went on to win a Grammy for Bluegrass Album of the Year, and in throwing it back, Dolly found a way forward for herself. *The Grass Is Blue* is emotional, rowdy, scary, and *fun*. I love the title song, love the cover of Johnny Cash's "I Still Miss Someone," and although "Steady as the Rain" is not, and was likely not meant to be, one of *The Grass Is Blue*'s breakouts (it was never released as a single), it has always been one of mine. Mandolin, dobro, and fiddle all make an appearance, all those string instruments leaping in before Dolly's urgent voice announces itself. The music is busy, buoyantly relentless.

Dolly Parton wrote "Steady as the Rain" in the 1970s, but her younger sister Stella was the first to record it, for her 1979

album *Love Ya.* "This is another song I wrote in the basement," Dolly recently shared in her book *Songteller,* "when my
house was being built forty years ago. . . . I remember when
I was singing it, my sister Stella said, 'Oh, I love that song.
I'm gonna record that someday.' And, sure enough, she did.
And she had a hit with it. I was really proud of her record of
that song." A story of grief and coming to terms with a lover
falling out of love with you, "Steady as the Rain" contains
some of my favorite Dolly lyrics and hooks, but the feeling in Stella's version gets lost in the busy production, in the
way many songs of that era did. Dolly wrote the song on a
banjo—"That's why it has that steady rolling sound," she told
Bluegrass Now in 1999—but you'd never know it from Stella's
version; the music, though with a country tinge, definitely
sounds trapped in its peak disco era.

Still, some of Stella's phrasing is particularly compelling
in its straightforwardness; it suggests a kind of hardened pain.
Her voice is deeper, possibly even richer, than her older sister's, but she doesn't carry the same stirring heft, doesn't possess whatever magic it is that Dolly has. When Dolly sings
"Steady as the Rain" on *The Grass Is Blue,* it reminds us how
talent works. Not just star power, which is one piece, but
sheer ability, which is the other. The song isn't Dolly's best,
but her voice is so tinged with yearning it's impossible to
ignore. Shout-out, too, to the nostalgic horniness with which
Dolly sings, "Once you lived for rollin' me / And then your
feelings changed," and to the gentle syncopation that nevertheless adds a weighty tension there. This particular line barely
registers in Stella's version. It's unsyncopated and undemand-
ing. She's fine, but she's not magic.

In 2019, Stella Parton—the sixth of the twelve Parton
siblings and the sister closest in age to Dolly—lashed out at
her famous sibling on a podcast for country music fans. Long
an advocate for victims of abuse and violence, and a survivor

herself, Stella said she felt "ashamed of my sister for keeping her mouth shut [about #MeToo]. This is the first time I've really publicly called my sister out. But it's high time that some of these older women speak up and speak out. They've all gone through all kinds of abuse in this industry so: speak up!"

I know this exhaustion, and I understand wanting others to pick up the slack. "There is no silver bullet, no one person, no one way," said Tarana Burke, the founder of the #MeToo movement—aimed at empowering women and femmes to share their stories of abuse and harassment and at holding men accountable for these actions. "It is literally going to take all of us all doing all that we can at capacity to move the needle just a little bit."

I wrote a book of poems about rape culture, *Landscape with Sex and Violence,* and it had the odd timing of launching on the very same day that the #MeToo hashtag broke huge on Twitter, in October 2017, ten days after the *New York Times* published sexual assault and harassment allegations against Hollywood mogul Harvey Weinstein. Two weeks prior, *Publishers Weekly* complained in a review that my book depicts men as "undeserving" and "suspect," and the review bemoaned the "parade of *I*" throughout. I thought, well, okay then: this is always what happens when you call men out on their shit, call rape culture out on its very existence. Which is to say, I felt stomped on but not at all surprised by it.

Then suddenly #MeToo was the thing and we were all supposed to be sharing our stories. We were supposed to be shouting about men who were undeserving and suspect, and my work was now brave and timely. The *San Francisco Chronicle* called my collection "vital reading for the #MeToo era," and I used the hell out of that in the promotion of the book, which meant commodifying my own trauma history (something I've been accused of multiple times), but why shouldn't a writer want to stand confidently behind their work? Why shouldn't a person who has undergone hard experiences want to tell their story? I live every day with the physical and emotional consequences of the violences that have happened to me; they are the story I have to tell.

There are things in *Landscape with Sex and Violence* that I'd never spoken out loud to anyone; writing trauma doesn't make trauma easier to voice intimately to another. Traveling around the country throughout 2018 reading about rape and other violence is not the kind of triumphant book tour I'd ever fantasized about as a writer. I sat on a stool in Manhattan, a bright light on my face, when a young man asked me, "Would you say it was ultimately beneficial to have gone through your struggles, because they gave you an edge on other poets?" A man in Illinois came up to me after I read and asked me if I still did "that kind of work" and if my kids knew about it. A woman in Tampa asked me exactly how old I was the first time I was raped. It was massively retriggering; I began having nightmares again.

When the hearings to confirm Brett Kavanaugh to the Supreme Court took place in the fall of 2018, and he was ultimately confirmed despite the testimony of Christine Blasey Ford that he'd tried to rape her at a party in the 1980s, friends and acquaintances kept seeking my thoughts on the matter. But I felt done. Done with sharing my stories and opinions. "I wrote a book about me too," I texted to friends when they wanted to know how I felt about the moment. "That's all I want to say." I'm tempted to defend Dolly against her sister's call-out. It's fucking exhausting being asked to speak. But what if it's not exhaustion? What if her silence is savvy?

I think about how Dolly is, as ever, all things to all people. Feminist to the feminists and not feminist to those who conflate feminism with, say, communism. In an interview with the *Guardian*, Dolly weaves everywhere, expertly: "I don't think . . . I mean, I must be if being a feminist means I'm all for women, yes. But I don't feel I have to march, hold up a sign or label myself. I think the way I have conducted my life and my business and myself speaks for itself. I don't think of it as being feminist. It's not a label I have to put on myself. I'm just all for gals." Almost anyone can see their side of the story in that. I see mine for sure: Dolly is a feminist (she's appeared in *Ms.* magazine on more than one occasion) but also a savvy career woman. Still, when Stella Parton says, "Speak up about injustice, Dolly Parton. Speak up. And speak out. Defend women, and don't just do it in a little song. Speak up," well, I hear that too. Dolly's platform is huge. Dolly can speak to the Right and the Left, and they will listen. So does she owe us her voice here? I'm not sure. Would I like her voice here? Yes, it would mean a lot to me.

It's tough with siblings. You're so close in proximity, genetics, memories, and yet often entirely apart. Still, the whole time we were growing up, my older brother, Cliff—who shares our mother's mild temperament—got angry at me twice that I can remember. When I was three or so I knocked over his castle in a sandbox in Indiana (can't say if it was accidentally or on purpose) and he hit me and I cried. Several years later, I broke a radio he prized, a radio designed to look like a robot. He told me I ruin everything, which is something like truth, or would be soon, because much of our youth was spent dealing with my crises while Cliff just toed the line and likely felt ignored. But this was before all of that. He probably didn't realize how I adored him, admired his ability to take whatever was dealt to us without incident. We never had much in common, but I spent a lot of my youth playing *Star Wars* games or going to the baseball card store just to be around him. Our two-family trip to Dollywood was only the third or fourth time we were sleeping under the same roof since we were teenagers, and we probably did more talking that week than we'd done in the almost thirty years prior combined.

The earlier risers, we'd take our coffee out onto the back deck and watch broad-winged hawks and turkey vultures swoop toward their morning meals as we ate our grocery store pastries. All that week I tried to find a way to bring up our childhood, but mostly I reverted to the silence of our youth and stayed on easier topics. Although we were only in our forties, Cliff kept bringing up his retirement plans and wishes, which I guess seemed kind of within reach so far from home and with the day mild and bright and wide open. It was nice to see we could both exist in the quiet, outside the family tension, that we could maybe have a relationship without baggage. "Maybe I'm thankful I have a brother," a line from a Sally Delehant poem, kept going through my head that week.

My daughter Ada was three when she asked for a sister, and she got one (I was already pregnant when she asked). Like Dolly's, Ada's little sister is Stella. Stella attended the first of many Ada dance recitals when she was just three weeks old. Stella spent much of her first year and a half on my lap on a bench at a playground, happily watching Ada play. Ada learned to read by reading to Stella. Every morning when we'd drop Ada off at kindergarten for the day, toddler Stella would pout, then cry, then say, "I want Ada!" (which she'd pronounce "ee-dah"). Once, when a game machine refused to spit out Stella's earned tokens at the Chuck E. Cheese, Ada, maybe nine, marched right up to one of the game attendants and demanded justice. Stella had an ally in the world who seemed unshakeable. They were each other's favorite person. People told us how lucky we were that they never bickered.

And then, in 2018, seventh grade struck hard. Ada was twelve and experiencing anxiety and suffering from undiagnosed ADHD and also experiencing homophobia and misogyny amid coming out as bisexual and existing while female in supposedly progressive Brooklyn. She grew angry and selfish and even mean, which was not like her. And she broke Stella's heart, crushed it day after day with her short temper and, more so, her indifference, her promises of attention and her repeated breaking of those promises. Stella knew Ada was suffering; she cried under the oppressive weight of all the tension at home. She was scared for Ada and for herself. But the seemingly unbreakable bond between them had slowly and yet all of a sudden broken and none of us knew what to do. Stella, only eight, then nine, didn't want to talk about or even acknowledge any of it, even once Ada was better and trying hard to repair and connect. Stella bristled, or was—though normally very empathetic and tenderhearted—even herself outright mean, probably crushing Ada's heart right back. In "Steady as the Rain," when Dolly sings regret at no longer being important in her beloved's life, the poetic economy of Dolly's lyrics cuts right to a painful reality that feels familiar. Every corner of our apartment, our neighborhood, New York City, seemed a finger-pointing trigger of hurt feelings.

Last night I watched Ada open a window during a rainstorm and just stand there for a bit, feeling the drops on her cheek. Last night I watched a 1992 episode of the Vicki Lawrence show *Vicki!*, as she hosts a number of "celebrity siblings," which led me to watch a cooking segment in which Roger Clinton—troubled brother of Bill—helps Stella Parton make "Dolly's Dill Dumplings." Earlier she sat next to Clinton, who looks on with an eager sympathy as Stella insists she's earned "my own self and my place in this world." Stella looks a bit like Dolly, though less, well, dolled up, and her speaking voice is eerily similar and similarly compelling in its vacillation between demure and folksy. While the show clearly wants some scandalous tidbits from its star siblings, the most Stella will disparage Dolly is to recount how she'd banish Stella to the front of the school bus while she told dirty jokes in the back. In her autobiography, Dolly shouts her sister's praises in a myriad of ways, and also goes on to worry if she's been a hindrance to her, if she's hogged the spotlight. "She has had a lot of well-deserved success," Dolly writes, "and deserves to be known as Stella Parton—period, end of sentence. The second man to walk on the moon left footprints every bit as deep as Neil Armstrong's, and yet how many of us know his name?" I wonder in what way their relationship will survive the rift over #MeToo. It figures that rape culture splits sisters while men usually go unpunished.

After the horrific school year, flying my family to a cabin in the Smoky Mountains at the crest of 2018 was a very good idea. Sometimes you just want to sit and stare at something beautiful and feel your body relax. Like Dolly in braids and overalls on a porch swing on the cover of *Hungry Again*, sitting on the porch swing behind our cabin at Dollywood simplified everything, let the cruel complications and violences of the world float into the clouds between the mountains. What trauma doesn't afford you is stillness. If you're not actively reacting, you're being asked to react or you're biding your time between your body's outsize responses. "The damage done to me is real and debilitating," speaks comedian Hannah Gadsby at the end of her revelatory smash stage show *Nanette*, concerning the many gender-based violences she's suffered in her life. "I will never flourish."

Nanette was released just weeks before our trip to Dollywood, and my friend Hafizah kept urging me to watch it throughout the summer of 2018. I was afraid to, and I was afraid to precisely because of my expected reaction: as I finally watched it in the fall, I felt overwhelmed by someone mirroring my own traumatized marrow—inside of a comedy special. Yet that's a circumstance I so enjoy in music. Dolly's "Steady as the Rain" maybe doesn't particularly stand out on *The Grass Is Blue*, but it falls into my favorite category of song, characterized by happy music and sad lyrics. "Sad bangers," the kids are calling them these days, a mode of song construction that absolutely floors me.

"A sad banger requires this combo," explained David Levesley in *British GQ* in 2019: "It needs surface-level cheer that quickly gives way to a story of deep melancholy on closer inspection." Think the Pretenders' "Back on the Chain

Gang," or Smokey Robinson and the Miracles'"The Tears of a Clown," or "almost any Kinks song," my oldest and closest friend, Jess, messages me from Vermont when I ask for examples, or "'8TEEN' by Khalid," Ada texts me from photography class when I ask her the same. Think "Steady as the Rain." I'm a sucker for that brand of resilient but wide-awake optimism, maybe because I am holding it together for everyone around me yet am often unbearably sad. I cried just now when I wrote about my children, even as they are in their bedroom laughing together (together!) about some silliness. I cried when I had to read week after week from a book of my own trauma. Sad bangers, Levesley goes on to say, capture "a very important human sensation: catharsis, the feeling of triumph in the face of adversity." Triumph is what Dolly's voice was made to do, and why I listen to "Steady as the Rain" so frequently. The sure bet of hope.

CHAPTER THREE

The Seeker

Dolly, 1975, 3:14

I WASN'T TERRIBLY FAMILIAR WITH the 1975 *Dolly* album until the 2003 compilation cover album, *Just Because I'm a Woman: Songs of Dolly Parton*, came out and I fell in love with Shelby Lynne's version of the earlier album's most successful song, "The Seeker." Lynne's bluesy, tough expression of the overtly religious lyrics—she has a deeper, somewhat sexier voice than Dolly—strides above the groovy guitar and languid piano, both compelling and keeping at arm's length. I have sometimes dismissed Dolly's religious songs pretty immediately and knee-jerk, as I tend to dismiss all religious things pretty immediately and knee-jerk, but when Lynne sings Dolly's words, "I am a vessel that's empty and useless," it feels not so much like the need to be filled by God as to be filled by the validation that *yes*, I have felt empty and useless. For such a spiritual song, God or Jesus are never mentioned by name in the lyrics. What if it's a hymn to depression and self-annihilation but then also resilience? This seeker is a kind of bad seed I know, not a sinner in the broad religious sense of weakness of the flesh, but in the living-hard sense of having ever been on the wrong side of a bottle or a fist.

An October 1975 review of *Dolly* in *Cashbox*, a music-industry trade magazine, describes the album as a collection of love songs, and Dolly describes the same in her liner notes, with "The Seeker," then, presumably, being a love song to God. "A poor sinful creature," the speaker describes herself. There is no one weaker, she believes, but she also believes that God will reach out and rescue her. This idea of God as *the one* who can save you feels at odds with my Jewish upbringing. I'll say it a million times that the Old Testament God is toxic and bullying and really a straight-up asshole, but he also allows us to make our own mistakes. If the Torah (the first five books of the Jewish bible) is the rule book, the guidelines for living, then the Talmud (the main text of Rabbinic Judaism and the primary source of Jewish religious law and theology) is where we question and untangle these guidelines continuously; Jewish practice encourages endless questions.

"What kind of a God would create the weak? What kind of a God would create empty and useless vessels?" my aunt Barbara—my father's youngest sibling and only sister—responds to me when I ask for her Jewish take on this God from "The Seeker." I email Timothy, raised Catholic, for his take on these lyrics and he emails back (he's at home, I'm at a coffee shop), "I don't know how other people raised Catholic feel, but I don't identify with what's going on here. I wasn't raised to think of myself as 'a poor sinful creature' or 'bad seed' and in need of God to fix me, but that I was intrinsically good and God would protect me from evil. However, I don't know where religion stops and my own psychology takes over—maybe no one does."

Dolly's voice in "The Seeker," clear and heartfelt as always, is also forceful, and even hopeful, part of what poet Patricia Spears Jones referred to as Dolly's "Southern Hopeful Christian aesthetic." Imagine being hopeful as you literally sing that you're a loser! What kind of faith is that? I have hope, irrational hope, hope that drives my family and friends bananas sometimes. But also I'm Jewish: I know how to plan for the worst. My aunt Barbara and I refer to the czar-led pogroms in the Russian empire—large-scale, frequent anti-Jewish rioting that began in the nineteenth century and continued through the twentieth—all the time in our many text chats. We talk about the trauma of being Jewish, of inherited generational trauma and the current trauma of living in the United States amid the rise in anti-Semitism. When I mentioned with envy how gentle my brother, Cliff, is, Barbara said, "The Czar looks for that kind of thing." Part of surviving as a Jewish person is always being aware of the terrible.

Recently Dolly has released several Christian songs, including the dance song "Faith" with the Swedish group Galantis, and "There Was Jesus" with Christian singer Zach Williams. The latter single reached number one on the Christian charts in 2020, making Dolly—at seventy-four—the first artist to have topped the adult contemporary, Christian adult contemporary, Christian airplay, country airplay, dance or mix-show airplay, and Hot 100 charts. "I don't even know hardly what to say about all the No. 1s in all the different fields of music," she told *Billboard* magazine. "Thank you God, thank you fans and thank you everyone who has worked so hard to make this possible." Another song, released in April of 2019, was called "God Only Knows," a collaboration with Christian pop duo For King & Country, two brothers from Australia with early-1990s style, fancy-but-masc fashion, and serious locks. "God Only Knows" is an insipid, patronizing, synthesizer-heavy song about people who have sinned being redeemed and not judged by others. It's a pat on the back for inclusion and kindness that, I would argue, should be the starting point. In the video, Dolly plays herself, and she also plays a woman who may be a sex worker, or possibly just old-fashionedly "loose," flopped on a bed in fishnets, probably regretting all her choices. Because fishnets equals sinful. (Dolly looks *great* in fishnets.)

"A lot of people can't even understand their own suffering, much less try to look and see somebody else's," Dolly recently said. "So that's where I, as a Christian person, [come in]." "The Seeker," suggests music journalist Nancy Cardwell, in her 2011 book, *The Words and Music of Dolly Parton*, comes closest of any of Dolly's songs to what her religious philosophy really is: the dailiness of her conversations with him (Dolly assumes always that God is a father figure), the admitted imperfection of her decisions and behaviors, the love. Dolly occasionally speaks of a fear of God, but it is the love of God—"The Seeker" on an album of love songs—that defines her Christianity, and her unwillingness to make her belief system anything other than particular to herself. Certainly, with her extensive charitable endeavors, Dolly adheres to the compassionate side of the Christian faith, but she is patently unwilling to adhere to its more hard-line tendencies. "I hate those Christians that are so judgmental," she tells Jad Abumrad on his podcast, *Dolly Parton's America*, and she's specifically referring to so-called Christians being judgmental about gender and sexuality. "All my life," she writes in her autobiography, "I have been driven by three things; three mysteries I wanted to learn more about; three passions. And they are God, music, and sex. I would like to say that I have listed them in the order of their importance to me, but their pecking order is subject to change without warning. In my heart of hearts, I always know that God comes first. But in my body of bodies, some other urges can be absolutely irresistible."

Dolly grew up in the Church of God, an evangelical, fire-and-brimstone kind of congregation where her maternal grandfather was the preacher. Her nonbelieving father would wait in the car until services were over. What Dolly loved about church was, no surprise, the music. "The preacher would say, 'Does anybody have any special songs?'" recalls Dolly in Alanna Nash's 1978 biography of the singer. "Course everybody did, so we took turns. People'd bring tambourines, guitars, banjos, fiddles. And we would *sing*." Since leaving the congregation of her youth, Dolly hasn't regularly attended any organized church, but she's had a chapel built on her property. She has a very personal relationship with God, she often says, an open dialogue. In her 1994 autobiography, she describes a rather mystical experience she had at an abandoned church where boys and men would come to fight, couples would come to fuck, and sometimes young Dolly would play the old piano and enjoy the spectacular acoustics in between studying all the dirty drawings etched onto the walls. "Here in this place of seemingly confusing images, I had found real truth," Dolly writes. "I had come to know that it was all right for me to be a sexual being. I knew that was one of the things God meant for me."

Dolly describes "The Seeker" as being her talk with God, even if God doesn't appear in the song. I still don't know what I would say to God, should there be one, except, How do you live with yourself amid the untold suffering you presumably oversee? Really, I would like to know. I would like to know how to believe.

My father, a stern ruler in a very heteronormative nuclear family, grew up a reasonably observant Jew but became more and more of a believer as Cliff and I grew. In his head, I think, my dad wanted something like the religion he encountered in the 1967 book and then 1981 movie *The Chosen*, about a Hasidic Jewish community in New York City—a euphoric, communal, all-laid-out path—but without the sexism or quite all that socializing. Though sometimes interesting, with the rhythms of the prayers caught in my poet ear forever, it could be very lonely, this kind of religion. Dolly forges a solo prayer path, but unlike Dolly, who is Christian in a Christian-dominant country—so even alone, she isn't alone—our Jewish community was often just my family of four. We went to a synagogue attended by mostly elderly congregants. We didn't go to Jewish day schools or summer camps. I didn't have any observant Jewish friends. It was hard for me to know a God in the isolation.

Saturday afternoons spent with my father sitting between my brother and me on the couch reading us random laws from the Talmud or even mystical passages from the Kabbalah—as if we'd get it!—when what I wanted to do was finish *Jane Eyre* and Cliff wanted to play basketball; endless, wordless songs before Shabbat dinner based on Hasidic songs that must have seemed like a place where one could feel sacred and a part of something bigger, except we were just four people, sometimes only one enthusiastic, around the dining room table in our small second-floor apartment; the time my father told me he'd consider me dead if I married a non-Jew, which was like something out of *Fiddler on the Roof* (which finds its characters fleeing the czar in a nineteeth-century shtetl) but without all the show tunes: this was my Jewish practice, and it came to seem to Cliff and me like the place joy went to die, not least of which because my father, in his wish for the perfect spiritual setup, was repeatedly disappointed by reality, and us.

Yet I often think about a primary thing that kept him from going full Orthodox, the reason he didn't send us to Jewish day schools or synagogues, where we would be separated by gender while the men went off to have their collective religious ecstasies. That thing was me. He believed in my equality, my humanity. In his lifelong refusal to go along with the crowd and go along with trends, he could sometimes get it wrong, of course, but he got it very right by teaching me to follow my own instincts. That mine are so different from his is a testament to that important lesson.

I might sometimes want, but will likely never have, a Jewish community, beyond the cultural connection we inherently share with one another. My brother and his family were able to join a synagogue and find joy and community there, a kind of Jewishness I think he craved growing up. Both my niece and my nephew have been bat/bar mitzvahed and have gone to Jewish camp many summers. I am nothing if not Jewish, and I carry that collective trauma, anxiety, world view with me every day. But I bristle so hard at praying to a toxic God, to thanking an unseen being for what I have been given and what I have earned. I envy people their faith, though, and always have.

"I think people try too hard," Dolly told Jad Abumrad. "I talk to God like he's my best friend." "A man is born into this world with only a tiny spark of goodness in him," the character Reb Saunders says in *The Chosen*. "The spark is God, it is the soul; the rest is ugliness and evil, a shell. The spark must be guarded like a treasure, it must be nurtured, it must be fanned into flame."

When I got out of rehab in 1988, I was given a list of AA meetings to attend. A shy girl, especially when sober, I hated the AA meetings because I'd spend the whole time dreading the possibility that I might be called upon to speak, although speaking was never mandatory. The other attendees scared me, especially the old-timers, with their decades-long series of horrors. Self-destruction on that scale seemed impossible to fathom. But I did like AA for its access to cigarettes I could bum from older men creepily eager for my attention; I started smoking cigarettes in rehab when a counselor with a skinny-tail braid down the back of his neck gave me one of his Capri Slims. I did, as a very insecure and goofy teen in taped-up eyeglasses, like having a bit of cool with my friends, some kind of adultlike sophistication, or so it felt, for being required by my school to go to AA meetings as a prerequisite for being unexpelled.

A couple of my friends liked to go with me to the meetings on Sunset Boulevard in Hollywood (a "Terrace of Trauma," according to Dolly in her 1982 song "Hollywood Potters"), because often that's where you'd see the hair-metal musicians in full regalia—not looking unlike the dudes from the "God Only Knows" video—and often high or drunk. I'm writing a whole book about a celebrity whom I don't know and have never even met, but my ever-growing distaste for celebrity culture is real, and it started on Sunset. Sometimes the hair-metal guys prowled for teen girls, and we felt pretty hot about it because they were grown-up and they were *somebody*. LA is about scrounging to be near anyone who is considered *somebody*. AA was a must-have accessory that spring!

Rehab was where I first heard that corny yet moving "foot-prints" story about the Lord carrying us when we can't walk on our own. AA was where I first experienced the notion of "letting go and letting God," of giving up one's power to an unseen higher being. I was fourteen but I'd already given up enough power on shag carpeting at age nine, and had been tumbling on down from there ever since, so even at that young age I could not shake the idea that this higher power they spoke of wasn't my God, my Jewish God of order and vengeance and don't-fuck-this-up-you-absolute-schmuck. But—God—it must feel so good to hand it all over, I would love to hand it all over, and after all, it was Deuteronomy, in the Old Testament, the Jewish Torah, that tells us, "There you saw how the Lord your God carried you, as a father carries his son, all the way you went until you reached this place."

When I arrived at my career- (if not life-) changing fellowship at the Cullman Center of the New York Public Library in fall of 2017, I was expecting to write a book of poems about the anti-Semitism of the past, specifically the 1980s in which I grew up. The reality of living in Trump's United States changed all that. "Are Jews People?" asked a banner under CNN's daily pundits. White men marched in Virginia chanting, "Jews will not replace us!" the August before I arrived at the library. All my life my grandparents seemed to half expect the Nazis to come back for us, and I thought it was sad, what trauma does, but not a thing to worry about. This is how we get complacent, right? The book I ended up writing was about the failures of God, of religion, of the United States; showing up to Dollywood on July 3, 2018—flags a-waving everywhere—was a mindfuck. As soon as you get through the gates of the park's entrance, you'll find the Southern Gospel Hall of Fame Museum to your left. We didn't go in. We only had one day and—having LA's Disneyland in our heads—we expected the park to be a lot larger and longer to get through than it ended up being. Southern gospel was not the priority.

The night before we left East Tennessee I lay in bed with Timothy, nine-year-old Stella asleep between us in the king-sized bed in the second-floor bedroom in the High Hopes cabin, and, perhaps because of all the countryness of the past few days, I said, "Do you remember square-dancing in school? It just popped into my head!" Do you remember square-dancing in school? Once a year lining up in the gym to learn to do-si-do and swing your partner round and round? What a random thing to teach children in early '80s Los Angeles. I looked it up on my phone. Henry Ford—notorious anti-Semite and rousing American success—and his wife, Clara Jane, created a concerted campaign in the 1920s to bring square-dancing back into the culture via children in school in order to combat and counteract what they believed to be the Jews' embracing of Black culture—jazz and jazz dancing specifically—to corrupt the white youth of the United States.

Said Ford, "Many people have wondered whence come the waves upon waves of musical slush that invade decent homes and set the young people of this generation imitating the drivel of morons. Popular music is a Jewish monopoly. Jazz is a Jewish creation. The mush, slush, the sly suggestion, the abandoned sensuousness of sliding notes, are of Jewish origin." White Jews are white, I will never not believe. We benefit from that privilege, but we are also other, astonishingly other—or at least astonishing to me, a comfortably fourth-generation American in a very blue state. Forgetting is seductive and dangerous.

When I allowed myself to forget all the reasons I went to

rehab in March of '88, I found myself in late fall of '88 skipping school and snorting a line in my friend's bathroom because it was there, and I felt better when I did that, until I didn't feel better. What I'm saying is, pretty soon after I started, I stopped going to those AA meetings, and to the God that lived there. I always remembered the "footprints" poem though, a poem whose ownership was claimed by three different authors and that, naturally, caused a lawsuit. God bless America. That last night in Dollywood country, Timothy went online and found me a copy of a 1926 book, *Good Morning: After a Sleep of Twenty-Five Years, Old-Fashioned Dancing Is Being Revived by Mr. and Mrs. Henry Ford*, which would arrive at our apartment building's small lobby when we landed back in Brooklyn. "I could totally turn this whole thing into an essay," I said to him, before putting my phone down and going to sleep. That's how this book was born. It was going to be an essay on Dollywood and America and anti-Semitism.

Recently I emailed my uncle Ralph (another of my dad's siblings) and mentioned I was writing a book about Dolly and Dollywood. He wrote back that he knows little about her, except for her "twangy" singing and a slightly anti-Semitic comment he remembered her making several years back. My heart sank a bit, the way it sank when another hero, Alice Walker, was quoted in the *New York Times* supporting conspiracy theorist David Icke, who believes, among other things, that the Jews funded the Holocaust and that the world is funded by alien lizard people, many of whom are Jewish. I didn't know what comment of Dolly's Uncle Ralph was talking about, so I went in search of it.

In February of 1994, Dolly told *Vogue* magazine, in regard to her proposed TV show about a gospel-singing country music star, "Everybody's afraid to touch anything that's religious because most of the people out here [in Hollywood] are Jewish, and it's a frightening thing for them to promote Christianity." She apologized to the Anti-Defamation League: "I know from personal experience how stereotypes can hurt, and I regret that my words could have conjured up an impression of Jewish 'control' of Hollywood." The apology was accepted. Later that year, in her autobiography, Dolly recounted the incident a little differently. "I said something like, 'I can imagine how hard it would be for a Jew to write this. It would be like a hillbilly trying to write the story of Judaism.'" Received notions about whole groups are hard to shake because they are ingrained in us as fact; water is wet, Jews control Hollywood. People don't always stop to think that what they need to do is rethink. I'm glad Dolly finally stopped and did, even if it took a bit of blowback. Surely it hurts that my hero othered my people, but I do not doubt her heart. I also do not doubt that I've othered people, and I would like to imagine I could apologize with sincerity and acceptance.

In a July 2015 performance at Nashville's Ryman Auditorium to benefit a local music school, Dolly introduces a performance of "The Seeker" first by poking fun at the Pentecostals of her upbringing—her grandfather the Pentecostal, "Holy Roller" preacher—as she often does before she performs this particular song. Later she adds that no one believes in God more strongly than she does. "I believe," she says, "that God judges us on the content and intent of our hearts." Dolly has so many religious songs, and so many of them feel akin to the heavy-handed God for which she would have side-eyed her Pentecostal family. But the best of them are contagious. "He's Alive." "Shine." "Raven Dove," whose joy makes me tear up every time I listen. The joy in "The Seeker" is for sure contagious, the kind of experience I think my father was after in his study of mystical Jewish texts. "If you think too much about something, you're not feeling it," Shelby Lynne said in an interview with NPR, "and that's just the way I approach music." Her version of "The Seeker" is my daughter Stella's favorite. "It's the coolest," she tells me.

In her famous essay "Poetry Is Not a Luxury," Audre

Lorde says, "The white fathers told us, I think therefore I am. The black mother in each of us—the poet—whispers in our dreams: I feel therefore I can be free." And I think this is, in her way, what Dolly is trying to tell us about religion, to get out of our heads the musts and the judgements of men. In "The Seeker," the relentlessness of the bass line underscores God as an emotional backbone to the singer. And it's a comfort, even if I don't think I'll ever believe in a God, possibly because I can't get out of my brain's way. Which is to say, What kind of God is this, that allows so much pain? But what kind of God is this! That allows so much joy! In her 2018 song "Red Shoes," which she wrote for the feel-good, coming-of-age movie *Dumplin'*, Dolly sings that if she gets to heaven she'll "walk the golden streets" in her red shoes. This is a kind of religion to which I already subscribe. (Though, and not to harp on this, there were no red high heels at Dolly's Closet.) Dolly recently wrote that "The Seeker" "is for those people who are struggling for some kind of truth. It could even be about people who are not religious. People look for whatever that meaning of life is, whether you call it science or whether you call it 'higher power,' or whether it's just seeking that better part of you."

"The Seeker" reached number two on the US country singles chart in 1975, and the *Dolly* album peaked at number fourteen on the US country album chart. Dolly rerecorded the song for her 1995 album, *Something Special*, which also featured new versions of "Jolene" and "I Will Always Love You." For such a God-full song, Dolly's updated version of "The Seeker" is soulless, owing in large part to the overproduced sound, which stomps on the authenticity of the stripped-down original. "The drummer is swinging more in the new version," my friend and former coworker Paul—a drummer—messages me back when I send him both versions. "He's throwing in eighth notes on the hi-hat . . . the original is just straight ahead quarter notes. The beat is more straightforward in the original." *Something Special* is not over-produced in quite the way of 1987's egregious *Rainbow*, but still, the addition of an electric guitar and the overcomplicated rhythms lose the more focused celebration. Dolly's outsize faith feels unusually rote and dull.

In her original version of "The Seeker," the religious ecstasy is bubbling under the surface and boils over at the end, cathartic. What if it turns out I need the joy Dolly finds in her Lord? What if that sense of hope that at first confused me now keeps me listening? Pop singer Nelly Furtado's 2011 version of the song does not hold back with production but also just full-on goes for the gospel of it, and it left me in tears listening over earbuds in a Midtown coffee shop. Furtado's "The Seeker" is a love song, as it was originally intended to be. I am actually writing this paragraph on Valentine's Day, wearing the tights with multicolored hearts on them that Timothy bought for me, so praise God, here's to love.

CHAPTER FOUR

Here You Come Again

Here You Come Again, 1977, 2:53

SPEAKING OF LOVE, LET ME tell you this story about my marriage. In spring of 2018, at the height of the mess of seventh grade, and in the midst of some hard losses, we all felt raw and stunned and I was spending most of my weekdays not writing much poetry at the Cullman Center at all and instead caretaking everyone but myself, my phone right beside me for whatever might pop up next. One day, Timothy and I remembered we had theater tickets to see Edward Albee's *Three Tall Women*, starring Glenda Jackson and Laurie Metcalf and Alison Pill. The idea of leaving for an idle afternoon, of ever escaping from the panicked fog we were all in, of taking a fraction of a day to enjoy something we would have easily enjoyed years before, before kids, before books, before our Monday afternoon wedding at Borough Hall (me in a pink Betsey Johnson dress with red velvet flowers and beads at the bottom), before we'd hurt each other in all the inevitable ways spouses hurt each other—it seemed near impossible. But Timothy said, "Let's just go," so we took the F Train to Forty-Second Street and sat in good mezzanine seats for three hours and listened to extraordinary sentences. Sometimes you just need extraordinary sentences.

The three tall women are the different ages of the same

woman—twenty-six, fifty-two, and ninety-two—and modeled after Albee's mother, who had an unhappy marriage and a difficult relationship with her son amid a life of privilege. The first act ends with the eldest of the three women saying, "I think they all hated me, because I was strong, because I *had* to be." And then she has a stroke. The lights went back up and I cried because of the sentences, and 2018, and Timothy, whose shoulder I had leaned on in the dark, because I was tired of having to be strong.

Assuring me that everything will be okay is one of Timothy's best skills, and there is nothing I can think of that he wouldn't do for me if I just asked. He said to me, after it had been a few months and Ada was feeling more at ease and was getting back to herself, that our marriage survived that year of hell—when we'd heard of some that had not—because he, who normally likes to be very much in charge of his own actions and decisions, just followed my lead. When I asked him to do something, whether practical or emotional—call the school guidance counselor, go to Rite Aid, give me a hug—he'd do that thing. And he let me be how I am, which is sometimes stormy and probably always too intense. In turn, as much as I could (I am by nature very demonstrative with my affection), I tried not to invade his space, physical or emotional, and gave him a lot of it. He likes space. When he was a kid, he thought the Eric Carmen song "All by Myself" was a celebration, mistaking the lyric "*don't* want to be all by myself" for "I *want* to be all by myself."

I joked with him earlier that I'm about to start writing on Dolly's song "Here You Come Again," while he—a poet like me—has written a poem about the Whitesnake song "Here I Go Again," about a loner. I don't know; somehow this works. Sylvester Stallone gave an interview in *Ain't It Cool News* where he talks about trying to get Whitesnake to record a song for his 1984 movie with Dolly: "The most fun I ever had on a movie was with Dolly Parton on *Rhinestone*. I must tell everyone right now that originally the director was supposed to be Mike Nichols, that was the intention and it was supposed to be shot in New York, down and dirty with Dolly and I with gutsy mannerisms performed like two antagonists brought together by fate. I wanted the music at that time to be written by people who would give it sort of a bizarre edge. Believe it or not, I contacted Whitesnake's management and they were ready to write some very interesting songs alongside Dolly's." *Rhinestone* is the worst movie I have ever had the most fun watching. Those two have some really enjoyable chemistry, sparking rumors of an affair. There were always rumors of affairs at that point in Dolly's career, maybe because her husband was never at events with her. He also likes to be alone.

In over fifty years, there have been only a handful of photos of Dolly with her very tall, very handsome, very independent husband, Carl Dean. We don't know too much about him. He's a farmer, a landscaper, a driveway paver? He approached Dolly when she was standing outside a laundromat in 1964 and told her she'd get a sunburn in an outfit like that, and he drove away just to circle right back. On *The Tonight Show* in 1977, Dolly describes the moment she met Carl, and Johnny Carson says, "If you see a man go into a laundromat with clothes, it's not a bad assumption," and Carson finishes the sentence, "that he's single," while Dolly says at the same time, "that he'll do the washing for you."

Dolly and Carl were married two years after they met at the Wishy Washy, also on a Monday, and three weeks before my parents were married in spring of 1966. Early on, Carl accompanied Dolly to an industry event after which he swore off them, preferring quiet. In a 2020 interview with *People* magazine, Dolly talks about how Carl still brings her daffodils in early spring, and he writes her poems. "He is my home and my heart," she's said. They go on picnics or hop in their camper and drive anonymously about. "We just do our little things like that," she says. "Or I'll do a candlelight dinner. We don't make an issue of it. It's like certain days, you feel a certain way. And I'll say, 'I'm going to surprise him. And we're going to have real cloth napkins and real crystal. I'm going to put the real china out instead of the paper plates we usually eat on because we don't want to have to wash dishes.'"

Although Timothy is more public, more gregarious, and utterly charming in social situations, like Carl he holds his cards close, while even now I'm laying so many of mine on the table for you. "What is it about him that attracted you?" asks *Playboy*'s Lawrence Grobel in 1978. "His honesty," answers Dolly. "His decency. His earthiness. I like the way he loves me. I do. The way he lets me be free. And lets me be me." I relate to all of this, except the earthiness. In my marriage, I'm the earthy one, bound to have several to-do lists going at once and to have everyone's schedule memorized and emotional needs accounted for. Timothy fell for me in the mid-'90s when we were in grad school together. He was the handsomest man I'd ever seen, so it took me a while to realize he was attracted to me too. He fell for my sexy twenty-something midriff, for my affection, for how talented he felt I was, long before anyone else noticed my words. Even now, almost a quarter century and a few books later, there is so much about me only he will ever know.

"I'm a very private person," says Dolly, in the middle of an interview in which she talks about watching porn at a sketchy theater in pregentrified New York City and about how performing onstage turns her on. I get this, this kind of privacy. I'm happy to talk to you about how writing turns me on or my history with drugs or the time a guy I briefly dated gave me a black eye because I made fun of his love for Steely Dan. But please don't ask me about the other stuff that the man who threw the bookcase on me did. Because of course it got worse, and I can't speak that stuff in person or on the page.

Timothy grew up in a middle-class suburb of Rhode

Island. His parents hadn't gone to college, nor did they know how to advise him to apply, but he found two schools, got into both, and chose Johns Hopkins in Baltimore because his parents were too nervous about him moving to New York City. I grew up the daughter of an academic from New York City in a house full of books. To the end, my grandmother believed that writing a book was the highest possible human achievement. That I flunked out of high school and later went to community college was a fucking crisis. I clawed my way back but I missed a lot of learning, so even two-plus decades later, when I showed up for my fellowship at the buttoned-up Cullman Center in the New York Public Library, a history of violence on my body and a record of oft-derided feminist activism behind me, I did not feel like I fit in—not in how I spoke (like a sailor), not in how I dressed (heels and colorful dresses, all the time), not in what I believed words could do (make us better).

My office at the library was right next to that of the fiction writer Melinda Moustakis, and this was a fortune, because neither of us quite fit in with that particular NYC literati, with the folks whose conversations rise and fall based on what's in the current issue of the *New Yorker* or the *New York Review of Books*, who have friends in all the important places, who can network a party like a smartly choreographed dance, rather than hide in the corner working on a puzzle with one of the other fellow's kids (yeah, I did that). Melinda had ties to Alaska and to Bakersfield, California. I came up in a literary world more likely to publicly criticize the aforementioned prestige publications for their shocking white maleness than to get excited about their content. Imposter syndrome brought Melinda and me together, possibly, or the fact that our offices were right next to each other's, and in any case I was grateful for the company.

Melinda saw me cry over patriarchy, and poetry, and seventh grade. What I'm getting at is that not a lot of people have seen me full-on cry, save for Timothy and my kids, but that's how bad 2018 got. I never gave Melinda the full extent of the endless piles of 2018 shit, but I learned to share a bit. For my birthday in November, she bought me an enormous poster of Dolly to put in my office, from the 1977 album cover for *Here You Come Again*: Dolly in a red blouse with white polka dots, wide-legged jeans, and white heels, smiling broad under a round bouffant wig. It's an iconic Dolly image. Safe, inviting, playful. Sitting at the lunch table at the other end of the center one afternoon, I looked up and spotted it from across the room. "Oh! You can see my Dolly poster from here!" I happily exclaimed. "Dalí?" asked the Cullman Center's director, an affable man who really did try to get me, if only because it was his job to connect. It was clear that fitting in to the literary mainstream was going to take a little more practice.

Much as 2017–2018 was my crossover year, 1977, the year "Here You Come Again" came out, was Dolly's crossover year. Written by the songwriting team of Barry Mann and Cynthia Weil, initially with a kind of Burt Bacharach swinginess, the song was first recorded by B. J. Thomas (famous for "Raindrops Keep Fallin' on My Head") and then by Dolly, for whom it would be her first pop hit, reaching number three on the pop chart in January of 1978—behind Player's "Baby Come Back" and the Bee Gees' "How Deep Is Your Love." It was a very mellow moment in pop history. Nervous that her original fan base would abandon her, Dolly insisted the song feature a steel guitar. "She wanted people to be able to hear the steel guitar, so if someone said it isn't country, she could say it and prove it," album producer Gary Klein told Tom Roland in *The Billboard Book of Number One Country Hits*. "She was so relieved. It was like her life sentence was reprieved." Still, the song was recorded in Hollywood and leaned "heavily on the new novelty of synthesized keyboard," as Nancy Cardwell wrote.

"It's All Wrong, but It's All Right," a Dolly-penned song

about having ill-advised yet very necessary sex, was another hit single from the *Here You Come Again* album. It stayed for several weeks at the top of the country singles chart, despite being pretty risqué contentwise. Maybe the late '70s was a moment where you could be a little daring, but I don't remember. I was a young child in a rather conservative household. It was for sure a moment where Dolly could basically all but admit to some kind of extramarital experience within her marriage, and for that disclosure to be fine; Dolly insists in her *Playboy* interview that neither she nor Carl would want to know about any infidelities. Seems functional. Secrets, passion, trust. These all deepen with the years or they blow up and you call it quits. In the summer of 2021, Dolly delighted the internet by dressing in her *Playboy* outfit from 1978 and presenting Carl with an updated bunny photo for his seventy-ninth birthday. Dolly and Carl are in this life together. As are Timothy and I.

"Here You Come Again" is Timothy's favorite Dolly song. It goes down easy, but it is not without its pathos. There's lust, lies, some bad decision-making. As in "Why'd You Come in Here Lookin' Like That," the woman is transfixed by the beauty of the love object, and isn't herself the object, but the bouncy brightness of Dolly's singing on this one— *Billboard* magazine questionably called this "little girl sounding vocals"—makes the outright fuckery of the love object seem inevitable and maybe even . . . okay. The lover shows back up, and it's all over for her heart.

For the 2018 movie *Dumplin'* Dolly recorded a duet of the song with young singer Willa Amai, and the latter singer sings it slow, with desolation, in the same way Shelby Lynne darkens "The Seeker." The singer lamenting a lover's return right when she's beginning to get over them isn't so much an *oh shucks, I can't resist you*, but more like an *oh fuck, I can't get away from this endless toxicity*. I relate to this. The man who threw the bookcase on me liked to storm out, drive to the beach in a huff over whatever it was I was said to have done, swim out into the darkness—"You'd better hope I don't drown!"—then return home to me right when I'd moved on from panic and into some kind of feeling of freedom or relief. Dolly sings in the background of Amai's "Here You Come Again," and the timbre of her voice serves almost as a warning, as a has-been or might-have-been, a super clear echo of what perhaps the lead singer isn't sure they can say.

Songwriters Mann and Weil, both Jewish, both from New York City, could well have been my people, what with that typically Jewish, czar-fleeing tangledness with which they wrote songs, including the Animals' "We Gotta Get Out of This Place" and the Righteous Brothers' "You've Lost That Lovin' Feelin'" (cowritten with Phil Spector, and a song that would go on to be the most spun of the twentieth century). *Billboard* listed "Here You Come Again" at number one on a 2015 list of their favorite Dolly songs, pointing to that instantly identifiable keyboard intro as the key. Timothy says it sounds like it could be a song from the Muppets, and he's not wrong—it was even performed on *The Muppet Show*, we recently learned, in a feature with Leslie Uggams in 1979. The sweet stomp of the keyboard is soothing, reliable, and for sure memorable. People who didn't grow up with country radio, like myself, stood a chance of coming across "Here You Come Again" via Top 40 in the '70s, and then Lite FM stations for a long time after. It's just a solid pop song, so good that Dolly told *Playboy*, "A monkey could have made it a hit. Well, you're looking at a million dollar monkey."

Dolly is famous for saying outrageous things—"Dolly-isms," as both she and we call them—but if you read her interviews, starting with her first with a major country music publication, *Music City News*, in 1967, and through to today, there is a distinct change in what she is willing to say, or, more importantly, what she stops herself from saying. The word I always use for her 1978 *Playboy* interview is "bananas." I think it would be hard to imagine any celebrity giving an interview like this today, let alone a celebrity whose fan base has no small number of conservative listeners. She talks about all the sexual exploration that happened in her family's barn as a kid. "How old were you the first time?" asks *Playboy*. "Now I can't tell you that," Dolly answers. "Because that would be real perverted. As little kids, we were *always* experimenting." She talks about being mistaken for a sex worker in Times Square before chasing the potential client off with her gun. She flirts with the interviewer! After a series of cagey sentences about whether or not Dolly has ever had an affair, Dolly says perhaps an affair could make someone a happier person. The interviewer follows up with, "But couldn't it also lead to complications in your life?" "Well, kiss me, we'll see," Dolly shoots back.

In a journal entry from 1956, the poet Sylvia Plath imagined the private thoughts of confident people at parties. Among them: "Kiss me, and you will see how important I am!" Plath, like me, was a poet married to a poet. The first time Timothy kissed me was on a navy blue futon mattress in my oddly shaped, first New York City apartment. It was all hallway, that place. The morning after the first time Timothy kissed me, we sat out on my fire escape writing a collaborative found poem from a vintage "teach yourself German" book we'd bought from a street vendor for a dollar on Broadway and 111th Street. It was midsummer, and midsummer is where I thrive. "Is a cup of tea or black coffee better against thirst?" the poem ended. It was the only time Timothy and I collaborated on a poem, although now I'm wondering what it would be like to do it again. Cynthia Weil and Barry Mann wrote dozens of songs together yet no other with quite the magic of "Here You Come Again." And none with the magic that Dolly further brings to it. In a live version of the song, performed several years ago for a Muscular Dystrophy Association telethon, Dolly adds the word "darlin'" to the end of the song. Adding that one word erases some of the perceived toxicity of the comer and goer. As a poet, I love what one word can do, and I love how Dolly is a poet.

Halfway through my crossover year writing poetry at the New York Public Library, in about January of 2018, it occurred to me that I had more disposable income than I'd ever had in my life, thanks to the generous stipend that came with the fellowship. It's rare that I spend money on myself and completely out of left field that I would drop thousands to go on my dream trip to Dollywood. I didn't know at the time how necessary the trip would prove, but as my colleagues planned work and leisure trips to Europe or Cape Cod, I ordered a Dollywood guidebook and traded texts with my sister-in-law, Jessica, who is the most efficient travel planner I know. A year later, 2018 finally behind me, I decided I was exhausted from writing poetry about rape culture and my own trauma and I wanted to write about joy. I wanted to write about Dolly. In prose. Which is how I'm here. "I'm not going to limit myself just because people won't accept the fact that I can do something else," Dolly wrote in the "Wit and Wisdom of the Dolly-Mama" section of her 2012 inspirational book, *Dream More*. Dolly says the things I need to hear. Dolly dared to cross over. And it worked.

By early February 2019, with the disasters of the prior year (more or less) behind us, Timothy ordered food from the diner and the four of us sat on the floor in front of the TV to watch the Grammy Awards. Brandi Carlile performed "The Joke." Janelle Monáe performed "Pynk." And Dolly was honored as the "MusiCares Person of the Year" for her artistic and philanthropic contributions over the course of her long career. At the awards show, pop fluff Katy Perry and rising country star Kacey Musgraves started the tribute with a wonky (I'm being kind) version of "Here You Come Again"—wonky, that is, until Dolly comes onstage and rescues it with her particular brand of ease. Then she takes over the tribute for the duration, in the most congenial but determined way. On Twitter, feminist writer and activist Feminista Jones quipped, "Dolly told EVERYONE to sing back-up and she would pay tribute to herself and y'all . . . I am now 115% committed to my life as a Dolly Parton stan." There is something about watching a woman do it her way.

Toward the end of my fellowship year, a fellow fellow at the Cullman Center excitedly came up to me in the office's kitchenette. She'd recently met people at a literary event who knew me and my work as a poet. "I didn't realize you were somebody!" she exclaimed. "Everyone is somebody," I said. "Crossover is unfortunate, because it makes definition hard," KENR disc jockey Ric Libby told *Billboard* in 1977, in an article that otherwise celebrates the addition of more pop sounds to the country waves. Well, screw definitions, no? *Here You Come Again* was Dolly's first platinum album *and* the biggest country album she'd ever had. Her *Playboy* interview—subtitled "A Candid Conversation with the Curvaceous Queen of Country" and running between a pictorial of a topless girl on rainbow roller skates and an early ad for Apple computers—came out right at that apex moment, and she ends the interview with, "I want to be somebody who extremely shines. A star shines, of course, but I want to be really radiant."

CHAPTER FIVE

Jolene

Jolene, 1974, 2:42

OF ALL OF DOLLY'S RECORDS, "Jolene" has most endured— her best-known and most beloved hit. It is the one people recognize and remember, the one people meme and tweet about, the one my primary care doctor told me he covers with his weekend band, the one that inspired an avant-garde art installation in 2007 in New York City, the one Nelson Mandela is said to have played from his prison cell, the one that prompts response and parody songs. "Jolene" is almost inescapable; the iconic guitar riff, the beseeching repetition. But it's not my favorite of Dolly's songs, probably not even in my top five. Why is this *the one*? Timothy can't stand it. "It's the kind of oppressive sound that if you heard it coming from a machine you'd be like, 'Stop that sound!'" he said when I asked him to tell me why. "If that song was a person at a party, I would avoid that person." I laughed because I love a strong opinion on pop culture, even when it's wrong. He googled "Why do I hate 'Jolene'" and reported, "Nope! Everyone else seems to love it."

For a song that's seemingly simple, with so few words, there is an astonishing complexity to "Jolene." It is a song of desperation, pleading, and obsessiveness. Its chorus climbs an octave, then climbs back down, ending right where it started, then starts again, repeating the name of the singer's rival over and over. It is haunting. It is relentless. The opening riff is so instantly recognizable that it might challenge the opening notes of the Rolling Stones' "Satisfaction" or Nirvana's "Smells Like Teen Spirit" in the public consciousness. *The Boot*, a popular online country music news site, ranked the riff in "Jolene" number two in their article "Country Music's Top Ten Guitar Riffs," just behind Johnny Cash's beloved "I Walk the Line." "It's a great chord progression—people love that 'Jolene' lick," Dolly told NPR in 2008. "It's as much a part of the song almost as the song." As it continues, the chord progressions differ between the song's verses and the chorus, a move perhaps hardly noticeable except that the music shakes us up, makes us listen harder and again.

Dolly wrote "Jolene" in 1972, the year my brother, Cliff, was born, and she released it as a single on October 22, 1973, a few weeks before I arrived. Although nominated for two Grammys at the time, it didn't win one until it was nominated again as part of Dolly's collaboration in 2016 with the hokey a cappella group Pentatonix, one of the more recent of the hundreds of acts to cover the song over the decades. Olivia Newton-John did it disco. The Sisters of Mercy went goth with it. Chiquis Rivera and Becky G recorded a Spanish-language, cumbia-pop take. The White Stripes cover made it cool with a hipster crowd. Lil Nas X performed a slow, urgent, acoustic version in 2021. Mindy Smith recorded a version for the 2003 Dolly tribute album, *Just Because I'm a Woman*, and the breakthrough song of Smith's career was said by Dolly to be her favorite cover of the song. Smith's intense relationship to its vulnerability might also make it mine.

Per an interview with *Music City News* in 1967—Dolly's first in a major music publication and published about three years after she arrived in Nashville the morning after high school graduation—Dolly had, by her own estimate, already written hundreds of songs. Dolly wrote "Jolene" and "I Will

Always Love You" at the same time. In a radio interview on *The Bobby Bones Show*, Dolly says, "That was a good writing day." She pauses before "day." "That was a good writing . . . day." In 2020 in an interview with *Time*, she mentions finding a cassette with the two songs back to back. "We were just shocked," she says. Dolly's songwriting skills get overshadowed by her vocal talent, as does her ability to play multiple instruments, and overshadowed all the more by the lore and the (often self-) objectification. But imagine writing one song—one song!—that still resonates with hundreds of thousands of listeners more than fifty years after you wrote it. Imagine writing two. On the same day (or thereabouts). Near the end of her life, Marilyn Monroe asked of an unnamed interviewer, "Please don't make me a joke. End the interview with what I believe." Think again of Barbara Walters asking Dolly, another blond bombshell, "Do you feel like you're a joke?" No matter how many brilliant hits Dolly wrote in one day in 1972—"Some of my very best songs I've written within thirty minutes' time," she told *Music City News*—perception of her so often comes down to how she looks.

The raw candor in Dolly's "Jolene" vocals is a departure from her earlier work on songs like 1967's "Dumb Blonde" and 1969's "I Don't Believe You've Met My Baby." In these, Dolly's voice is reminiscent of singers in the Patsy Cline tradition, clear as ever but so highly stylized it's difficult to uncover the emotion that is Dolly's signature. "Jolene" turns that almost aggressive reserve on its ear and brings us a sincerity that is painful and impossible to ignore, a sincerity that is her trademark, a sincerity and vulnerability that is, to this moment, I think, mostly unmatched. In a 2008 NPR interview about "Jolene," Dolly speaks of the titular subject in typically animated and self-deprecating sentences: "She had everything I didn't, like legs—you know, she was about six feet tall. And had all that stuff that some little short, sawed-off honky like me don't have. So no matter how beautiful a woman might be, you're always threatened by certain . . . you're always threatened by other women, period." "Jolene's a mess," Mindy Smith told NPR's *All Things Considered* in 2008. "She steals things."

Jealousy is enmity prompted by fear; *envy* is enmity prompted by covetousness. In her book *The Possession*, which is about the aftermath of a love affair, Annie Ernaux writes, "It wasn't the other woman, in the end, whom I saw in my place—it was me, the way that I never would be again, in love and sure of his love, on the threshold of everything that hadn't yet taken place between us." To be always threatened by other women is to suggest other women are always out to take what's yours and recognizably yours, that they even want it, that they are never true to you, or themselves, that they are reduced to a *thing* that is *sexy* and will *take*. The speaker pleads with Jolene that her happiness rests on what Jolene decides.

In March of 2018, after a cruel but mercifully short battle with cancer, Timothy's best friend, the celebrated poet Lucie Brock-Broido, died. Grief over Lucie hit Timothy hard: crying-all-the-time, falling-apart-at-the-funeral, making-irrational-decisions hard. Lucie had been his mentor, his friend, his confidante, his foil, his love, since they first met in the early '90s. They were hysterical together, in their own world, absurd. When I began spending the night at Timothy's sometimes, in the mid-'90s, I got used to hearing his clangorous landline at 2 a.m., and the sound of his voice quietly next to me in bed in his tiny bedroom, and Lucie's voice through the line. Twenty years later, and from the second floor in our apartment, I'd often wake to the sounds of that same chatter, laughter, into the earliest morning, when Timothy would come to bed, and I'd soon get up and get our kids ready for school. Our schedules have always been staggered. He's a night owl and I thrive on light.

Lucie died in the spring, and her public memorial service was held in the fall, in the Miller Theatre at Columbia

University. Almost seven hundred people filled the room to hear Lucie's friends discuss her quirky brilliance and the particular pleasure of being in her circle. Her poems were read, voices choked up, a slide show on which Timothy carefully worked with his typical obsessive precision ran during a recording of Lucie reading her poem "Infinite Riches in the Smallest Room":

What if I were gone and the wind still reeks of hyacinth, what then.

Lucie's scent is still with us in a shirt Timothy lovingly folded into a plastic bag as he was cleaning out her New York City apartment. At the memorial, Timothy spoke of their Gemini gifts for gab, of talking all night, of his deep love for her. "I feel like I'm still on the phone with Lucie Brock-Broido, and I'm never hanging up," he said. Oh, how I want her back for him. "I miss you. It is May," Lucie wrote in a steno pad she left on their shared desk at the university, and which we came across in a stack of papers and books on our table at home, months after she died. After the memorial service, there was a reception under tents and string lights, at which her hordes of current and former students attacked the wealth of free food so quickly that by the time Timothy and I got to the tables they were mostly bare. Timothy kept busy accepting all the condolences. I kept busy worrying that he would not be okay, because he was not okay. At the memorial reception two women came up to me, separately, to ask if I had been jealous. I didn't even understand the question the first time. Jealous of what?

Most anyone with whom I regularly chat has heard from me in recent weeks about jealousy. One friend asked, Wouldn't you be jealous if Timothy was friends with a lot of beautiful women? And my answer was, He is! And no. Maybe it's because I always feel like I'm on borrowed time with any of the good fortune I've had, but it's also because I know that love doesn't necessarily exist single file. Timothy and I have found and clung to each other in this life, together, no matter. What's more: a gruesome end is inevitable for everything. "Ruin hath taught me thus to ruminate, / That Time will come and take my love away. / This thought is as a death, which cannot choose / But weep to have that which it fears to lose" (Shakespeare, Sonnet 64). "In all of country music, there's nothing quite like the sense of accelerating dread that propels Parton's great 'Jolene,'" Tom Carson wrote in *Rolling Stone* in 1978. Enmity prompted by fear. Maybe I don't let myself have fear to lose.

I have never felt romantic or sexual jealousy. I've never doubted that the people I'm with want me, and won't stray; I've never felt threatened by other women because I have always gotten the lovers I wanted. "No lover had ever left me," Melissa Febos writes in her book *Abandon Me*. "I had spent enough years in therapy to know this was not something to brag about." Some wouldn't let me go. The man who threw the bookcase on me followed me to New York City and showed up at my apartment building, where I ran and hid behind the worn rows of mailboxes, and then he showed up at my workplace; he grabbed my arm near the same library at which I'd hold my fellowship years later. He walked with me up Fifth Avenue and then stood us on the famous lion-guarded steps of the Forty-Second Street branch, telling me that pigeons are really rock doves. My heart beat out of my chest with fear. A woman I'd kissed, once, harassed me for years, one evening trapping me in a bathroom at a party—Gloria Gaynor's "I Will Survive" and the sounds of enthusiastic dancing muffled through the blocked door—demanding to know why I was so obnoxious, daring not to desire her back. She hates me so much I still hear from her from time to time.

The speaker in "Jolene" is begging, literally begging, obsessively saying the name of the thing that would harm her most.

But why is it Jolene who harms her and not the man who would cheat? Why are women doing all the emotional labor? The singer's man is just happily going about his business, fucking or not fucking Jolene, maybe just flirting, clearly talking about her in his sleep, but, I mean, I once dreamt that the actor Laurence Fishburne took me ice-skating in Central Park. Maybe he's just being friendly, maybe his subconscious is hot for Jolene and that's okay, isn't it, and meanwhile the speaker is losing her shit and Jolene is like, I don't even know him.

Enmity prompted by covetousness. Here are some things of which I've been envious: people whose infants slept through the night, people who can digest cheese, every fashion trend my family couldn't afford or chose not to buy me from about 1982 to 1987, anyone who lives debt free, people who can fall asleep right away, bodies that don't feel the everyday residual pain of a history of being knocked around.

I have been disappointed. I have *wanted* things. I have wanted people. I have wanted pain to stop. I have wanted pleasure. I have wanted skin on skin, new. The speaker of "Jolene" is putting her whole life in another woman's hands, a woman we don't even know has any interest in the speaker's man, but I guess appealing to the man is not an option here. While catching up at a local bar, my friend Shelly suggests this is a feminist response. If the genders were reversed, and the woman was shut out of the conversation, it would be problematic, she says. But to shut out the man from the discussion over his own situation, to speak to only the other woman, could seem kind of revolutionary. Written the year Helen Reddy's "I Am Woman" was released (a song many radio stations refused to play), "Jolene" may be Dolly's own second-wave-feminist anthem. But Dolly, I know—and you will see—is all things to all people, fiercely feminist and repeatedly unwilling to identify as such. That's a reason she's lasted. Sure, Dolly said all women are jealous of other women, but forty-plus years later, Shelly—one of the most confident and staunchly feminist women I know—is saying, well, maybe she's shutting the man out because who needs 'em.

Two redheads inspired "Jolene." The first was a bank teller of whom Dolly felt her husband, Carl, was just a little too fond. "She got this terrible crush on my husband. And he just loved going to the bank because she paid him so much attention. It was kinda like a running joke between us—when I was saying, 'Hell, you're spending a lot of time at the bank. I don't believe we've got that kind of money.' So it's really an innocent song all around, but sounds like a dreadful one." And then there's the other redhead, who is so innocent she's a literal child: "One night, I was on stage, and there was this beautiful little girl—she was probably eight years old at the time. And she had this beautiful red hair, this beautiful skin, these beautiful green eyes, and she was looking up at me, holding, you know, for an autograph. I said, 'Well, you're the prettiest little thing I ever saw. So what is your name?' And she said, 'Jolene.' And I said, 'Jolene. Jolene. Jolene. Jolene.' I said, 'That is pretty. That sounds like a song. I'm going to write a song about that.'" Again, from *The Possession*: "It seemed to me to put a name to this woman would allow me to construct, out of what is always awakened by a word and its sounds, a personality type: to hold an image of her—even a completely false one—inside me. To know the name of the other woman was, in my own deficiency of being, to own a little part of her."

In 2012, an internet phenomenon known as "Slow Ass Jolene" showed up, when a DJ called Good Little Buddy slowed down the 45 rpm of the original "Jolene" to 33 rpm, making Dolly's voice sound markedly deeper, less feminine, more of a trudge. Friends kept sending me the link, tagging me in their excited Facebook posts about it. Twitter was obsessed. People argued in the comments of YouTube about whether this was or wasn't actually Dolly Parton singing. Andrea DenHoed, writing in the *New Yorker*, remarked that Dolly, her "baby-high soprano" slowed, comes to a "reasonable alto range."

It irks me still that this legendary song had to be stripped of its femininity in order to be seen as the masterpiece of songwriting and performance that it is by those unfamiliar or unappreciative of Dolly's work, to be seen as *reasonable*, the way it irks me when my daughter Ada, überfeminine right out of the womb, often has to do twice the work to prove to teachers, and other adults, that she's smart and creative. Dolly's songwriting is undeniably genius, so why did it take "Slow Ass Jolene" to prove this?

And yet, let's take "Slow Ass Jolene" as the success the internet believes it to be, let's take it as a way to showcase, for those who can't keep up with her pace, Dolly's incredible songwriting and vocal prowess. Country songs of the "Jolene" era tended to be in major keys, still tend to be in major keys, but "Jolene" is sung—baby-high soprano!—technically on a modal scale (that in-between state, like so much church music), and definitely veering toward a minor key. In her book *Unlikely Angel: The Songs of Dolly Parton*, scholar Lydia R. Hamessley writes that this "unusual modal harmony seems to propel us into another time." Studies have suggested that humans prefer minor keys. But isn't it like us, here in the United States, to pretend to lead with optimism? To fear and suspect women? What if Jolene doesn't even want the man but has to suffer everyone's assumptions? She makes sense in a minor key.

In 2017, Cam, a contemporary country singer originally from California, cowrote and performed a song called "Diane," a response song to "Jolene." "In true country fashion," she told *Rolling Stone Country*, "I've set the whole raw story to upbeat music, so you can dance while you process it all." This sad-banger setup—happy music, sad lyric—is a huge reason I've long been so soft on country music. In "Diane," the singer, the Jolene, apologizes to Diane, the long-suffering spouse of the straying man. The video portrays a conventionally good-looking white man as he goes on a series of amazing dates with Jolene, while Diane is home with the kids, crying. It is for sure one of the more touching "Jolene" response songs. The worst of these songs—and also named "Jolene"—is by an Estonian band called Ewert and the Two Dragons, in which the male singer suggests Jolene is the pushy problem and asks her to understand that "I'm someone else's man." The best of the answer songs is by Sugarland's Jennifer Nettles. Called "That Girl," it finds the singer arriving at the realization that her man has another woman at home, despite his trying to keep it a secret. Nettles is trying to course-correct the trope of women as competitive man stealers, but the noxious stereotype endures.

Maybe sometimes it's easier for women to fuck with other women because there's no real messing with men in patriarchy and rape culture. Men are rarely blamed, and Dolly gets—even exploits—that. But I don't feel threatened by other women any more than I feel threatened by a universe that would cause me untold loss in untold forms. Maybe this is what jealousy is, then—guarding against loss and grief, until loss and grief arrive, inevitably. Because Lucie died and it left me sobbing in bed when I thought I'd been asleep. Lucie died and it wrecked Timothy because he loved her profoundly, with all the messiness of true love. "Whether it's a love affair or not," Dolly said of her relationship with her early-career music partner Porter Wagoner, "you're all in, in the relationship. Whether it's sexual or whether it's passionate, you are connected. . . . It is a marriage of sorts." Maybe there are Jolenes everywhere, but not actually, just imagined, maybe actually. Jolene as heartbreak. Jolene as betrayal, disappointment, disillusionment. Jolene as death.

Time will come and take my love away.

What if I were gone and the wind still reeks of hyacinth, what then.

I sort of lied to you, I suppose I should admit. More than a year before he threw the bookcase on me, the man who threw the bookcase on me broke up with me to pursue my friend. And I was outraged. I felt if anyone broke up with anyone, it should be me breaking up with him! He wasn't so great. He couldn't keep a job and he had a temper and was already so controlling, telling me what to wear (that horrible Pepto-pink sweater). But he was mine. In the beginning, he put me first, he rose and fell on my every word and gesture. And then he didn't. I set about making myself so irresistible that of course he had to come back to me, and he did, and it was among my worst mistakes—never again did I hang the moon for him, he had successfully put me in my place—all sprung from a baffled jealousy. I don't want to mention the man who threw the bookcase on me anymore in this book, but the fact is my body can't forget him, it flinches when even my own child startles me, so I probably will.

Still, I need you to know that I never once blamed my friend for why my ex strayed, or for my desperation to get him to return, or for the harm I found myself in not infrequently once he did. I did not have to have this talk with you, Jolene.

I am you, Jolene. So many women are. You see, I walk through New York City as I walked through Los Angeles, dodging and cringing from the many assumptions and crude comments that the mere fact of my body creates. Ada was dress-coded in middle school for wearing a tank top in a ninety-plus-degree classroom because her body made the garment too distracting. I once sat across a table from a friend and her husband, whom I'd just met that evening, and my friend said, I will get jealous if you even look at my husband. I can't help it, she said. And so I sat staring at my plate throughout the meal. Jolene, I'm sorry.

In footage of Dolly singing "Jolene" triumphantly at the Glastonbury Festival in the UK in 2014—where, Rebecca

Nicholson gushed in the *Guardian*, "the sun briefly glistened on that infamous peroxide wig [and] there were moments of incredible beauty"—Dolly, then sixty-eight, sings to an audience of two hundred thousand with a voice as plaintive and concerned about the fact of Jolene as it ever was. It seems that everyone in the audience knows the words. "Well," Dolly tells the crowd when she's done. "Thanks for singing along with me! I heard ya out there!" A whole field of people calling out the name Jolene as the placeholder for whomever Jolene is in their own lives: a collective cry, a collective warding off of what could destroy us. "People don't come to see me be me," Dolly once said about performing. "They come to see me be them." We'd best name what could destroy us.

CHAPTER SIX

The Grass Is Blue

The Grass Is Blue, 1999, 3:45

DOLLY CLAIMS IT WAS DIVINE intervention that led her to compose "The Grass Is Blue" during a thirty-minute lunch break while filming the 1999 Lifetime movie *Blue Valley Songbird*, about a woman trying to escape an abusive spouse. The song, she says, just poured out of her, like the album did. Recorded in August, it was released in October. In an interview late that year with *No Depression*, a roots music magazine, it's noted that four of Dolly's scratch vocals on *The Grass Is Blue*—vocals usually recorded just as a guide for the backing music and not intended to be final—went on the finished album, including the title song. "There was like this perfect magic between these great musicians and me singin'," Dolly recalls, "and they really seemed to be enjoying what I was doin'; I was certainly enjoying what they were doin'. It sort of created this very magical moment at times that I think that this brought us all sometimes to tears."

The Grass Is Blue appeared just before bluegrass was to have a small moment in the larger pop culture. The vocals on the title track—a song in which the reality of heartbreak is so unbearable that the singer can carry on only by denying one truth after another—were recorded live, and Dolly's voice sings the pain so that we feel the impossible but necessary alternate universe where she and her lover are still together. The intricate harmonies of the backing vocals came later, performed by Alison Krauss—whose band, Union Station, was also about to enjoy the renewed interest in bluegrass—and Dan Tyminski, a guitarist, member of Krauss's band, and, notably, George Clooney's singing voice in the soon-to-be-hit movie and best-selling soundtrack for *O Brother, Where Art Thou?*

Almost every band member on *The Grass Is Blue* was at the time of the recording already an accomplished solo artist in the bluegrass world. Sam Bush on mandolin. Stuart Duncan on fiddle. Jim Mills on banjo. Jerry Douglas on dobro. Dolly referred to this assemblage as "God's Bluegrass Band." The music "hit a chord in me that just rang real spiritual and real true," she's said of their work together. Dolly won Best Female Country Vocal Performance at the 2000 Grammys and *The Grass Is Blue* won Best Bluegrass Album; to her utter surprise and delight, it also won Album of the Year at the 2000 International Bluegrass Music Awards. It worked, to go home again.

In the early '80s, in Los Angeles and feeling very far from her Tennessee home, separated from a man with whom she'd at least had an emotional affair ("a special friend, an affair of the heart, which just about killed me"), suffering from increasingly difficult gynecological problems, unhappy with her body size, and forced to cancel her tour because of telephoned death threats from unstable "fans," Dolly, deeply depressed, feeling overexposed—"my face was everywhere, my boobs were everywhere"—contemplated suicide. Check in on your friend who seems so okay. Check in on your friend who can perform for thousands with an ebullient smile on her face, cracking folksy jokes while hiding the darkest thoughts. In a 1986 interview with *Ladies' Home Journal*, Dolly remembers, "I was sitting upstairs in my bedroom one afternoon when I noticed in the nightstand drawer my gun that I keep for burglars. I looked at it a long time, wondering and saying to myself, 'Well now, this is where people get the idea of suicide, isn't it? Guns around the house and people sorrowing and all.'"

Dolly felt her low moment to be a humbling before God—"I kind of think it was God's way to bring me to my knees long enough to pray"—a reset on her attitude and drive. In her 2007 song "Better Get to Livin'," Dolly advises, "All healing has to start with you," so we'd better stop whining. Part of me bristles at the whole "Buck up!" attitude toward mental health. It can be dangerously isolating; some people never escape depression, and it's not because they're not trying hard enough. In the late '90s, I was so depressed I could barely leave my apartment except to go to work. I couldn't pick anything up off the floor of my studio. I watched numbly as two mice feasted on an open box of Entenmann's glazed donuts in the middle of the room. I'd finally gotten my life where I wanted it, where it seemed normal—man who loved me, *kind man* who loved me, steady aboveboard office job that provided health insurance, the city I love, surrounded by poets and poetry—and it was then that I plunged, forced to come to terms with all the trauma that had come before.

Maybe you don't realize you're surviving until you're done doing it. It all hit me at once. Like Dolly, I had to recalibrate to figure out how I could go on. I'm grateful for what Dolly knows about survival, how she spins pain into art; a song like "The Grass Is Blue" is so effective because the pain of which she's singing feels authentic. When I was first pregnant with Stella in 2008, very sick and worried about miscarriage (I was bleeding a lot), I listened frequently to both "The Grass Is Blue" and "Better Get to Livin'," and they helped, in part because I know what Dolly went through to bring them to the world. Her words are arguably cloying, but not empty.

When I first showed up at the Cullman Center, two decades past that worst depression and almost a decade past my last pregnancy, I found myself listening to songs that pointed to particularly resonant, if not always nostalgic, moments for me. I listened to the Indigo Girls, whom I fell in love with when I fell in love with Jason as a teenager, and who accompanied me as I began to write. I listened to Tori Amos, whose *Little Earthquakes* album soundtracked the brief moment of empowerment I felt as a successful community college student before I allowed the man who threw the bookcase on me to take over my life. I listened to *The Grass Is Blue*, which I had kept on constant rotation at my office job in 1999 as I tried to overcome post-traumatic-stress-disorder-related depression and panic. I'm not sure why I needed all of those albums again in my first month at the Forty-Second Street library, stone lions nicknamed Patience and Fortitude keeping watch out front, but perhaps I needed to subtly remind myself who I am and from where I'd come.

Sitting on the floor of my library office, a poem poured out of me, a poem that—like the musicians working on "The Grass Is Blue"—brought me to tears while I created it. I wrote it in January 2018, before we were able to address Ada's ADHD, and in the midst of her deep suffering. I'd never written a poem in the eye of a crisis before. Most of my prior book was about trauma from decades earlier, written in hindsight. I had thought time and distance were crucial, but this poem arrived as the feelings were as fresh as any feelings I'd ever had. The new poem was called "Twelve," and I wrote it the morning after I had skipped the yearly New York Public Library gala, an opportunity to dress up fancy (which I quite enjoy!), and instead stayed home with Ada and Stella to do their laundry and know that Ada was home, and that I was there if she needed me for anything at all (Timothy was out of town).

I didn't realize at the time that Ada's inability to even sort her laundry was a sign of her crumbling. I sat against the cabinets in my work space, my coffee reliably to my right, and I wrote everything I remembered about being twelve. I wrote about a basement reception at my parents' shul where an old man pinched my cheeks because I was so adorable; I wrote about sneaking into a bar the next weekend with friends to buy them cigarettes from the vending machines, where an older man walked by and pinched my ass. It's a weird, weird age, suspended between personae. I wrote about wanting to save Ada from everything I learned the hard way. I'm not sure why I thought that was possible. I forgot about what patriarchy does to girls. I thought it would be simple, since she hadn't suffered the trauma I'd suffered. Absence of x equals avoidance of y, I thought in my faulty math. I sat on the floor typing through big tears falling in front of me. When Melinda came in to do one of our daily morning check-ins, I was still crying.

TWELVE

When I was your age I went to a banquet.
When I was your age I went to a barroom

and bought cigarettes with quarters
lifted from the laundry money. Last night

I did all your laundry. I don't know why
I thought this love could be pure. It's enough

that it's infinite. I kiss your cheek when you sleep
and wonder if you feel it.

It's the same cheek I've kissed from the beginning,
You don't have to like me.

You just have to let me
keep your body yours. It's mine.

When I was your age I went to a banquet
and a man in a tux pinched my cheeks.

When I was your age I went to a barroom
and a man in a band shirt pinched my ass.

There is so much I don't know about you.
Last night I skipped a banquet

so I could stay home and do your laundry
and drink wine from my grandmother's glass.

When I was your age boys traded quarters
for a claw at my carcass on a pleather bench

while I missed the first few seconds of a song
I'd hoped to record on my backseat boombox.

When I was your age I enjoyed a hook.
You think I know nothing of metamorphosis

but when I was your age I invented a key change.
You don't have to know what I know.

I've put "Twelve" in my most recent book of poems, and
I dedicated it to Ada. It is maybe the most honest and complicated love poem I've written. I taught Carmen Giménez
Smith's poem "Daughter" last week in my feminist poetry
class at Columbia University. "Sometimes she's a stranger
in my home because I hadn't imagined her. / Who will her
daughter be?" One of my twentysomething students said they
found it offensive, a mother not being able to see her daughter as an autonomous being with agency. "I hear you," I said,
kind of rote, because I felt a bit sheepish about how much I
related to Smith's lines. I've been twelve but I've also been the
parent of twelve. How did I dare to imagine my kids could
grow up without struggle? I worry all the time that I failed,
that my anger and frustration and PTSD clouded my ability

to save Ada from what maybe would not have been inevitable. "The Grass Is Blue" is about the end of a love affair, and "Twelve" is too, in its way.

In "The Grass Is Blue," the narrator is basically hoping for what we used to call in grade school "opposite day." If the grass is blue, then anything is possible, then love might return. The paradoxical structure of the song is pretty singularly terrific and inventive. Scholar Lydia R. Hamessley says of the song, "No matter how many opposites the singer tries, the sorrow does not cease, and the song ends on *blue*. These exquisite lyrics alone would be enough to place this song among Dolly's best. But her musical setting is outstanding in the way it sets the lyrics and embodies their meaning, and her performance intensifies the song's emotional effect." This is classic Dolly, imbuing every word with pathos.

Aughts pop darling Norah Jones recorded the song twice, once in a smooth jazz vibe for the *Just Because I'm a Woman* album of covers in 2003 and again in 2019 as part of the alt-country trio Puss N Boots, with Catherine Popper and Sasha Dobson. Dobson told online magazine *uDiscoverMusic*, "I think what makes it shine is the lyrics. You can tell she's feeling a lot of loss for someone. We actually all sat around, looking at each other and just talking about the lyrics with our jaws open." The genius of Dolly is that, yes, the lyrics make this song shine, but so does her singing of the lyrics. Dolly's voice elevates songs that might otherwise hold less meaning. Think again of Stella Parton's merely okay interpretation of the lyrics of "Steady as the Rain." When talking about *Hungry Again*, the album prior to *The Grass Is Blue*, Richie Owens, Dolly's cousin and a musician himself, says, "A lot of records she's done have been great records with great production—but that's the thing, it's all great production instead of Dolly Parton."

I saw Dolly perform "The Grass Is Blue" live in Forest Hills, Queens, in 2016 and I cried through the whole thing (though, full disclosure, I cried through that whole concert). I have since watched Dolly perform the song in videos uploaded to YouTube, recorded in Nashville, in London, and at the same show I caught in Queens. When she sang the song as a duet with Norah Jones at the 2003 Country Music Association Awards, Dolly serves as a haunting, high-pitched echo to the velvety sadness with which Jones delivers her words. Dolly starts out the performance with just a guitar and a banjo in the background, adhering closely to the album's bluegrass version. As Dolly walks over to the piano, Jones takes it away in a more bluesy style. Since Jones's version came out, Dolly tends to perform the song on the piano, with the cover arrangement. Lately, Norah Jones, with Puss N Boots, performs the song in a modern country style, backed by electric guitars. I love how artists transform one another.

For Valentine's Day 2019, I took part in a theater production around the subject of love, part of a performance series, now called Poetry Well, in which actors read poems ordered into a narrative arc. I sat at a table—a "table read"!—and explained my poem "Twelve" to Jeanine Serralles, the actor assigned to read it. "When I was your age I enjoyed a hook," she read. What do you mean by that, she wanted to know. I mean, I liked songs with music that easily snags us. I mean, I wasn't opposed to an anthem. I mean, I knew suddenly my body was worth something, a twisted knowledge that would come in handy later, hook like hooker, see. Like sex worker.

By the night of the show, I sat in the crowded Caveat theater on the Lower East Side listening to my own words in a new way, a certain weariness on display, whereas I had been performing the poem kind of defiantly, because I'm angry that my daughter has to suffer the same patriarchy and make the same mistakes I did, regardless of everything I know, everything I thought I taught her. I'm angry that Stella probably will too, and I see her adolescence coming up like a train about to run away and I don't know where it will go. Like

Dolly taking on a jazziness in "The Grass Is Blue," thanks to
Norah Jones's interpretation, when I read "Twelve" to audiences now, I take on the weariness, thanks to Serralles. After
the show, I texted Timothy on my walk back to the train
station and mentioned how intense my poem felt, hearing
someone else read it. "Duh," he wrote back.

In a performance of "The Grass Is Blue" at Nashville's
Ryman Auditorium in 2015, Dolly introduces the song: "I
think almost everybody has had a broken heart. And if you
ain't, you're gonna have one. We all think, when we have our
first broken heart, that it's just gonna kill us. Well, a broken
heart won't kill ya, but it can make you wanna die." To avoid
these dire feelings, the song's narrator refuses to acknowledge,
or perhaps cannot even see, reality, and so her pain is less-
ened by this refusal. Obviously this is a fallacy, this myth of
blissful insanity, perhaps representing the magical thinking of
grief, the mental smoke screens and human defenses of living
post-trauma.

> I've had to think up a way to survive
> Since you said it's over, told me goodbye

This is what words can do! Dolly doesn't write, "I've had to
think *of* a way to survive." That "of" would imply that ways to
survive trauma exist. "Up" implies survival methods will need
to be invented from whole cloth, that survival is a creative act.

In 2002 Dolly released a song on her *Halos & Horns*
album called "Raven Dove" that closely mirrors much of the
melody from "The Grass Is Blue." Dolly does this not infrequently, one song echoing or even banging against another,
years or decades later. Written post-9/11, "Raven Dove" is
a call toward God but one that isn't about Old Testament
vengeance or the kind of patriotism that seeped into religion in the George W. Bush era of the aughts. It's about survival, redemption, God transforming hate to love. While "The

Grass Is Blue" winds down sorrowfully at the end—no climax, just more of the sad, sad same—at the end of "Raven Dove" Dolly's voice rises, "Hallelujah! Hallelujah!" in a way that mirrors religious catharsis, and with the original song hanging around in the background, it seems to offer even more hope, not in God, or at least not for me, but in survival. Maybe even after everything feels hopeless, there is a future with ecstasy. Hallelujah.

After I was raped as a child, it took me quite a while to tell anyone. I came from a secret-keeping family even before I had big secrets of my own to keep, so it was almost like I knew on some biological level to keep my pain to myself. "Scholars of intergenerational trauma tell us," writes Rabbi Tirzah Firestone in her book *Wounds into Wisdom: Healing Intergenerational Jewish Trauma*, "that the silence shrouding a family's untold stories paradoxically becomes the strongest form of transmission." I put my bloody underwear in my book bag and threw it away at school the next day, in the trash bin on the far side of the playground, past the slide and the baseball diamond and the handball court, the piercing sun of California probably pinning into me, because it was always there, doing that. I don't think I knew the words for what had happened; I didn't even know what sex was, really. I was in the fourth grade.

Some survival ideas I came up with: obsessive concern with the feelings and needs of others at the expense of my own, crying all night into my pillow, "I am going to turn around and when I turn back around I will be a whole new person," alcohol, marijuana, cocaine, promiscuity, Dolly Parton, abusive men, poetry, poetry, poetry, New York City, Zoloft, image rehearsal therapy, candy, friendships, high heels, poetry, Xanax, feminist activism, Timothy, Ada, Stella.

After her near-suicidal breakdown, Dolly hopped in a camper (no wig, no makeup) with her best friend from childhood, Judy Ogle. "For weeks on end," *Ladies' Home Journal* tells us, "she swam, soaked, strummed a guitar, wrote songs and read everything from self-help to poetry." She made it through. Poet Wallace Stevens said, "It is a violence from within that protects us from a violence without. It is the imagination pressing back against the pressure of reality." Which is another way to say, I've had to think up a way to survive.

――――――――| CHAPTER SEVEN |――――――――

Coat of Many Colors

Coat of Many Colors, 1971, 3:04

IN DECEMBER OF 1984, I received a bit of Hanukkah money from my grandparents and I used it to purchase a pair of white overalls decorated with a paint-splatter pattern in Day-Glo colors. Florescent fashion had been all the rage at the start of sixth grade, a year that found me a little out of step with my peers. Suddenly everyone was concerned with what they wore and with TV shows I didn't watch and with the latest gossip of who liked whom. Shy and nerdy, it was a while before I noticed I was being left behind socially, that I didn't have any of the right clothes or hairstyles. My parents never spent money they didn't have, and that didn't leave a lot for brand fashions. So when that December I had twenty dollars to spend on anything I wanted, I wanted overalls with florescent-colored paint splatter. I returned to sixth grade triumphant in January of 1985 until, on my way to my homeroom class, blond, confident Desirée—probably wearing an oversized Oxford shirt cinched casually, but with perfection, by a chunky leather belt—stopped me and said, "Oh my God, florescent is *way* out. Even Katherine knows it, and she brought it into this school." I never wore the overalls to school again; I stayed hopelessly uncool for quite a while.

Dolly's well-known "Coat of Many Colors" tells the story

of a coat that Dolly's mother sewed for her out of used scraps of cloth she'd received as charity. "I never seen a picture of myself," Dolly recounted to the *Great Speckled Bird*, an underground counterculture magazine out of Atlanta, in May of 1971, "but one day, after we had moved out of the holler, they were havin' pictures made at school. People used to send us things, like relatives who had children, they'd send clothes and rags and things and mama would make quilt tops out of the rags. This particular time though, she made me a coat to have my picture made."

Modeled after the biblical coat Joseph wore—"an ornate robe" made for him by his father, igniting his siblings' jealousy—the garment was fraught for Dolly too, though via her classmates, not her siblings. Nine years old and attending the two-room Caton's Chapel School, she was among the poorer students, and her classmates mocked her coat. When she refused to take it off, they accused her of having nothing on underneath (she did not, in fact, have anything on underneath; she was too poor for more than one layer), and they locked her in a closet. That ubiquitous photo of sweet, little, short-haired Dolly in her famous coat in her school picture? She's smiling through tears. In 1977, Dolly told *Rolling Stone*'s Chet Flippo, "I didn't have a blouse on under it because I had done *well* just to have this little jacket to wear. So when the kids kept saying I didn't have a shirt on under it, I said I *did*, because I was embarrassed.... I was ashamed to even mention it, and for *years* I held it in."

"Coat of Many Colors" appears on an album of the same name and was recorded on April 16, 1971. Dolly wrote her own liner notes for the *Coat of Many Colors* album, and she writes that the title song is especially dear to her "because it holds a precious memory of my Mama, a mama that loved and raised twelve children with the help of God and a daddy with a strong hand and a gentle heart." Here Dolly recounts none of the trauma of the song and turns it into something heartwarming. That Dolly wrote her own liner notes comes as little surprise considering her genuine gift for the written word, and for self-expression in general. In a 1980 *Rolling Stone* article entitled "The Unsinkable Dolly Parton," actress Jane Fonda is quoted as saying, "I had never met her [before filming the movie *9 to 5* together], but I was really into her music. Anyone who can write 'Coat of Many Colors' and sing it like she does has got the stuff to do anything." The idea for the popular song came to Dolly when she wasn't near a note-pad or a typewriter, so she scribbled it down on the back of a dry-cleaning slip belonging to her then performing partner Porter Wagoner. Wagoner recorded two versions of the song in 1969, and it became an audience favorite well before Dolly recorded it herself. When she eventually did, and released it in fall of 1971, it rose to number four on the *Billboard* Hot Country Songs chart.

In the Dollywood gift shop, you can buy "Coat of Many Colors" Christmas ornaments, butterfly pens, and an over-whelming array of other merchandise. For all the possibilities the gift shop has to offer, though, it's Dollywood's Chasing Rainbows museum that is by far my favorite part of the theme park—which is saying a lot because Dollywood is the happiest place on earth (sorry, Disneyland). The rides are var-ied enough to please everyone, the snacks are dripping with sugar and fat, and the whole place is just so darn folksy, it is like another, easier world. You have to walk up a flight of stairs to get to the museum so it has the feel of going into someone's attic—and that section of the museum is literally called Dolly's Attic. When you first walk into the museum exhibit, a hologram of a butterfly flutters onto a ramshackle stage behind a pile of stuff—old paintings and chairs and other wooden whatnot placed carefully so as to seem care-lessly jumbled together. The butterfly soon morphs into Dolly herself. She expresses delight that, in this way, she can greet each and every visitor to her museum. "Well," she tells us, cheerfully, "we all have our own museum. I bet you have a special drawer of things that you kept to remind you of special moments or a whole wall filled with photos of family and friends. Well, it's fun to hang on to those special memories, because sometimes when you look back, it actually helps you see better."

The Dollywood website states that Dolly created the museum "to share the results of her decades of dreaming, and to inspire others to follow their own." Early on in the progression of the museum exhibit, in the section about her impoverished but spiritual, loving, music-filled childhood, is the coat of many colors. It's not *the coat*, but it's a coat remade by her mom, resembling almost exactly *the coat*. It stands right next to the lyrics of the song written on that dry-cleaning receipt, framed and donated to the museum by Wagoner. I snapped a photo of the coat. A close-up. What I failed to capture—or notice until I saw it mentioned in an article—is that behind the coat is a giant black-and-white photo backdrop of young white children pointing and laughing. You guys! Dolly did this! Instead of letting the coat stand on its own, representing love and resilience, she doesn't want us to forget the trauma of the moment, that the taunting isn't theoretical. Real people with real faces traumatize and terrorize those they perceive as different and vulnerable. I texted Cliff and Jessica to see if they had any wider shots of the coat display from our trip, and Jessica did and texted them, and there they were, the angry young faces.

I actually didn't snap a whole lot of shots of Dollywood the day I visited. The photos I took in Chasing Rainbows included the Dolly hologram, the coat, the lyrics on the ticket (my favorite part is always the lyrics), a re-creation of her childhood kitchen, a couple of photos of Dolly and Carl together, Dolly dresses, Dolly dolls, and her honorary doctorate degree from the University of Tennessee. "Dr. Dolly," the display case boasts. A lot of Chasing Rainbows is devoted to Dolly's philanthropy, specifically her Imagination Library. Dolly began the project because of her father's lifelong illiteracy. She often wonders what his life might have been like had he been able to read. But except for her mother's bible, she didn't have books in her home growing up—they barely had food and clothes. In her 1978 *Playboy* interview, Dolly says she doesn't read much. Now she frequently talks about how much she reads. She calls herself a "book a week" reader and acknowledges how reading is a comfort and an inspiration. The *New York Times* recently included her in their By the Book column, where she recommended people read science fiction writer Octavia Butler.

The Imagination Library started small, in Sevier County, Tennessee, in 1995, sending one picture book a month to kids from birth until they hit kindergarten. In the years since, the program has expanded both nationally and internationally, and in 2018 Dolly was honored at the Library of Congress for having given away one hundred million books. One hundred million books! In typical Dolly fashion, the first book kids receive is her favorite, her lodestar even: *The Little Engine That Could*. They also receive a picture book of *The Coat of Many Colors* with the lyrics in both English and Spanish. "It warms my heart to know that for many people, these words have become a lesson to try to stop bullying in school," writes Dolly in a note at the end of the book. "On that fateful day, I felt the terrible hurt when people made fun of me. It is a pain that takes a long, long time to go away. In fact, it never really went away until I sat down and wrote this song." I know this experience exactly. I'm doing it here right now with this book. Dolly goes on to share the link for a free song she recorded for kids, called "Makin' Fun Ain't Funny."

I grew up in a series of apartments overflowing with books. Like my own apartment now, there were maybe too many books, and bookcases and piles of books in every room. Weekend trips to the library to check out a huge stack were the norm as a kid, and I'd spend whole days reading those we owned or borrowed, often books I was a bit too young for. When I reread *Jane Eyre* as a college student (rather than a too-ambitious sixth grader), I was like, ohhh, okay, that's what that was about. In first grade I received an award for reading one hundred books in a year. I got to sit on the special chair (it had cushions!) usually reserved for birthdays. It was the crowning achievement of my early education. In truth, it was all those books that saved me.

In interviews and at Q and As people often ask me how I managed to survive what I have written about in my poems, and the truth is, as you can see in these pages, it was a bit of a mess and "survive" is a moveable notion, but the other truth is: I had a lot of privilege. When I stopped going to high school at fifteen, I was able to easily ace the California High School Proficiency Exam (the state equivalent of the GED) shortly after my sixteenth birthday; the education I'd received in my well-to-do public K–8 school—and all the books that surrounded me for years—prepared me and made it possible for me to show up at community college at sixteen decently ready for college-level work. And—I am white. White people get more second chances. White people get to romanticize hardship, as it is only seen as a stepping stone to the inevitable happily ever after. For white people, struggle is noble and temporary, poverty an origin story. Dolly can write songs as bleak as "Gypsy, Joe and Me" or as clear eyed as "In the Good Old Days (When Times Were Bad)" because we know the happy ending, and even more of Dolly's songs about growing up poor follow the "Coat of Many Colors" model of poor being a mindset and not a permanent reality. "Poor Folks Town" (1972) explains that people are rich if they're rich in love. "Paradise Road" (1998) similarly preaches that "paradise is a state of mind."

In a move that would be inconceivable outside of whiteness, Dolly, in the words of Graham Hoppe in his book *Gone*

Dollywood, "gently folds the issue of poverty into the theme park." Here poverty is resilience, scrappiness, and possessing the infinite hope—and proof—that rags to riches is possible. Dolly's movie based on "Coat of Many Colors" (originally airing on NBC in December of 2015) also presents being poor as a somewhat difficult yet also heartwarming series of struggles that build character and faith. There is—no surprise—no mention of the systemic truths of generational poverty, and this smoothness allows the movie to resonate as placidly as the song resonates. I don't know if this is a critique. Sometimes gentle is okay, sometimes insidious.

For people of color, our society perceives their poverty less as a temporary situation and more as a failure; they are seen as lazy, deserving of the pain. The Opportunity Agenda, a social justice communication lab, recently reported that the split in thinking about poverty and those living in poverty is, in large effect, a result of our racist thinking about who is poor: "Stereotypes about the work ethic of Black Americans have skewed assumptions about the percentage of Black Americans living in poverty and [have] greatly affected support for particular anti-poverty policies." Which is to say, racism hurts everyone. Structural change can't happen if we deny so much of that structure even exists.

On an episode of actress Reese Witherspoon's 2018 interview show, *Shine On*—in which she conducted weekly interviews with different famous women to figure out how they achieved success—an emotionally overwhelmed Witherspoon, born into a well-educated and well-off family, gets to hold Dolly's guitar that's decorated to resemble her famous coat. Suddenly it seems that poverty doesn't so much represent poverty as it does anyone's struggle to be themselves and achieve their dreams. Reese loved Dolly growing up. And now look at her, holding her special guitar. Divorced of the actual realities—Dolly and her siblings used to literally pee on each other to keep warm at night in winter, and Dolly's dad at some point told his kids that Santa couldn't find them because they lived too far back in the woods—we can overlook any larger and uglier attitudes toward the poor and just feel good about the survivability of . . . everything?

Dolly often brushes past the trauma of her own poverty in interviews and in her autobiography. She doesn't hide what she experienced—we know about the peeing and her not wearing shoes in the warmer months, about her mother making stone soup, about her younger brother Larry, who was meant to be Dolly's to help care for but who died as an infant, and how she felt, at age nine, as if "I'd lost a baby of my own." But she rarely publicly acknowledges the pain and fear and anxiety that must have accompanied all of that insecurity. We know her early difficulties drove her on to conquer the world, but in the world of Dolly, we're supposed to think that that's all it did.

In the movie *Dolly Parton's Coat of Many Colors*, the attitude is one of plucky resilience. The movie entwines the story of the song with that of the death of Dolly's baby brother to tell us something about endurance in the least intense way. Critic Melissa Maerz, in *Entertainment Weekly*, closed her review of the film with the conclusion that "Parton's story might be pure hokum. But daggum it, some of that hokum ain't bad." In one scene, young Dolly (played by the remarkably good Alyvia Alyn Lind) stands in a field crying, calling God a bully for making her family suffer (here I can at least agree that the Old Testament God is totally a bully). The movie, aimed for a Christmastime audience, is concerned with God, church, and religious awakening quite a lot more than the song (which is almost not at all), but Jennifer Nettles—the country singer who you might remember recorded "That Girl," my favorite "Jolene" response song—plays Dolly's mother with such a graceful practicality, it's hard to quarrel with the ease with which all the trauma and spirituality is spoon-fed to us and then overcome. Pam Long, the screenwriter for *Dolly Parton's*

Coat of Many Colors, spent most of her career as a writer for soap operas like *One Life to Live* and *Guiding Light*.

Dolly's songwriting, though, is different; the trauma of poverty seems to soak through so many of her songs, despite her often incongruously rosy outlook. Especially early in her career, as she told podcaster Jad Abumrad, she wrote a whole lot of "sad-ass songs" about the hardscrabble lives of the kinds of people with which, and near which, she grew up. "Gypsy, Joe and Me," from 1969's *My Blue Ridge Mountain Boy*, is the tragic story of a woman, the man she loves, his dog, and their impoverished lives together. "Down from Dover," which we'll get to a bit later, is the tragic tale of an abandoned unwed mother. "Daddy Come and Get Me," from the same album as "Down from Dover," 1970's *The Fairest of Them All*, is the tragic tale of a woman put in a mental institution for reacting badly to a broken heart. I direct you to Porter Wagoner and Dolly's duet "The Party," a tragic, Anglo-American-style ballad written by Dolly for their 1968 album, *Just the Two of Us*, which ends with parents bringing their dead children to a church service.

"Coat of Many Colors" is also a sad-ass song. The speaker's mom made her a coat out of literal rags and then she's cruelly mocked for being poor, right at the moment when she finally feels pretty and special. Sad. Ass. Song. But it's not tragic, it's triumphant, in part because the music is that of celebration. It's not quite a sad banger, it's more like a sad jingle, with soft and near-spoken verses giving way to the intensely melodic chorus. If "Coat of Many Colors" had been recorded by Joan Baez or the Weavers, we might have listened to it in my house growing up. It's a folk song. It's a folk song with the tiniest twang.

The album recording features simple guitar in the background and later a bit of organ mixing in with the backing vocals, which have a church-choir feel. When Dolly performs it live she uses mostly a guitar, or an Autoharp. At Glastonbury in 2014, she performed it with a bluegrass backing. On Ralph Emery's radio show in 1981, she tells him, "When I do it onstage, I look out in the audience and I see 'bout five or six people just a-slinging tears. . . . And sometimes when I'm singin' it I sling some of it myself!" At the Ryman Auditorium in Nashville in 2015, she surely looks like she might cry. When she sang it at Forest Hills Stadium in 2016, I was surely slinging some tears. The whole audience sang (and slung) along.

In what appears to be the late '90s—the era of *The Grass Is Blue*—Dolly wound up singing "Coat of Many Colors" at a random pub, Páidí Ó Sé's, in Ventry, Ireland, when she stopped in on vacation and a man there had a guitar and knew the music. What feels remarkable while watching the video is the kindness and joy Dolly seems to find in total strangers she knows she will never see again. What's also remarkable is the obvious joy she finds in singing this particular song, as the crowd sings with her. Maybe it's not a sad jingle. Maybe it's a giant and life-spanning fuck you to every kid who mocked her that day. When Jessica sent me the photo of the coat at Dollywood, and the black-and-white photo backdrop of the kids mocking Dolly, I texted back, "This is so maudlin and bananas." But now it does seem to me like a giant fuck you. Not content to merely create an inspiring song about overcoming the abuse of bullies, Dolly is *showing us the bullies' faces*. And how they could be so many of us.

"I still have the picture [of herself as a child in the coat]," Dolly told the *Great Speckled Bird*, in that spring 1971 interview, "and about a year and a half ago I wrote a song about it, when it didn't matter so much anymore. And if I write about things that bother me then they don't bother me anymore. That's really why I wrote it." Telling you about my fluorescent-spattered overalls that Desirée derided made me feel better. I'm also going to tell you that in ninth grade, when I was probably dressed in all black with way too much eyeliner, Desirée came up to me in our art-studio class and asked me if I knew where to get cocaine. She'd heard I knew where to get cocaine. I was fourteen, and I felt a mix of victory and scorn when she gave me her phone number. (I never called, though I did, in fact, know where to get cocaine.)

"The coat itself," writes Helen Morales in *Pilgrimage to Dollywood*, "and this is a testament to Avie Lee Parton's skills as a seamstress as well as to the ironies of fashion, looks as if it could have come from the Gap." It's artfully sewn, with a one-button closure at the top. The ironies of fashion would probably make my 1984 overalls super cool right now, maybe rolled up and paired with some fun ankle boots. And though I've been told I dress too young and flirty for my age because I still like colorful, sometimes sexy dresses, and heels (who does this sound like?), if magically gifted those overalls today, I don't know how I'd feel about wearing them. I'd certainly try them on, take a selfie for you, store the pic in a drawer to find years later as a symbol of spirited resilience, next to the pile of butterfly pens I bought at the gift shop in Dollywood.

CHAPTER EIGHT

Islands in the Stream

Greatest Hits, 1983, 4:09

THE FIRST NIGHT I WAS in rehab, in 1988, at fourteen, I had to stay in the detox room. It was basically a hospital room, with a hospital bed, and all those tubes and wires and machine hookups. It was made for patients with such serious dependencies that they'd suffer medical risks like fever or vomiting or even seizures when detoxing. I was not that—most of the other kids on my floor weren't that—but I do recall the room being used for a girl named Jennifer, who was a PCP addict and who detoxed pretty hard for a while. "Why don't you wash your hair," the nurse said to me that first night, not meanly, nor gently. Her neutrality made me realize I was, in fact, alone. I'd never gone to camp; I'd never stayed away from home without my family longer than a night at a friend's every now and then. It felt scary and weird and, though I was locked in, freeing.

The few weeks prior to arriving had been my worst. I wasn't sleeping, I was very much trying not to be sober, and things like teeth brushing and showering were not something for which I could muster the energy. I kept my energy for hiding things, like the clothes I'd change into at the bus stop, the money from the rabbi stashed in my old coin purse, my very broken heart. But I was mostly kind and polite, if moody like every teenager, coming home and hiding in my room after school. I still sat with my family for Friday night Shabbat services; I was fairly obedient. My parents knew something was wrong—they had, after all, already seen me expelled from school for alcohol use on campus—but they couldn't have known how wrong. I took the generations-long impulse to walk stoically through pain very much as a mantra. More than not wanting to get into trouble, I didn't want to trouble anyone with the fact of my *self*. I wouldn't realize until decades later that this is a classic trauma response.

The mellow, buoyant sounds of "Islands in the Stream," overheard earlier at check-in, were still in my head as I stepped under hot water that first night in rehab. I'd been putting my hair up for months while never brushing it and it took a very long time to untangle. I had to rip the knots out, the sound was a crunching. I have a lot of hair. I have big Jewish hair. Humming Dolly and Kenny Rogers because I hardly knew the words, I scrubbed my body in the shower, my skin feeling tingly, pink. I felt excited for the possibility of life. This was my detox. When my hair dried, a thick mane of brown waves, it was majestic.

"Islands in the Stream" was written by the Bee Gees— Barry, Robin, and Maurice Gibb—originally for Marvin Gaye or Diana Ross (reports conflict) but ultimately winding up with Kenny Rogers, who'd just come off of his first pop crossover hit, "Lady." In the studio with the Gibbs, Rogers almost decided to scrap the song; he'd sung it for four days and it wasn't working. "I finally said, 'Barry, I don't even like this song anymore,'" Rogers recalled to *People* in 2017, "and he said, 'You know what we need? We need Dolly Parton.'" Some kind of serendipity was happening that day because Dolly— coming off her own pop crossover hit, "9 to 5"—happened to be in the same studio. "She came marching into the room," Rogers said, "and once she came in and started singing the song was never the same. It took on a personality of its own."

The above story seems to change with each telling, but the gist is the same: Dolly rescued the recording. The song takes its title from the posthumously published Ernest Hemingway novel about fishing, and drinking, and sons. I remember staring at the spine of that book on my father's bookshelf; he's long been a fan of the whole Hemingway thing, that very midcentury, white masculinity. The *New York Review of Books* was less favorable in a review from October 1970. "There is the reducing of life to the sensation and the sensational," wrote Christopher Ricks. "And there is the problem of how much in the end someone can know about men who know so little about women. It was a disaster for Hemingway that he had no daughters; it might have been a disaster for them if he had."

A woman and a daughter myself, Hemingway was always pretty lost on me, but I did find this particular title to be a catchy one. The similarities between the song and the book end there though. The book is an "elaborate refusal to say what is wrong," Ricks wrote; the song is a laid-back, wide-eyed look at love going *right*, at the first flush of love and that moment where it starts to slide into comfortable, yet still exciting, reliability. This isn't a crush or a summer fling; this is the start of an enduring romance.

The two had met and sung together before, but the song was for sure the start of the enduring friendship between Dolly and Kenny Rogers. "Islands in the Stream" first appeared on the Rogers album *Eyes That See in the Dark* and then on about a gazillion of each of their many *Greatest Hits* releases. They'd go on to have one more huge hit together, 1985's "Real Love," from Dolly's album of the same title, as well as to record the terribly touching "You Can't Make Old Friends," from Rogers's 2013 album of the same name and Dolly's 2014 *Blue Smoke*. In a 1985 clip of Rogers at the Portland Rose Garden (now called the Moda Center), Dolly joins him onstage for his hit "Who Needs Tonight" (originally sung with Sheena Easton), and the moment Rogers hears Dolly's voice—"Deep in my heart . . . ," she sings as she enters and then walks through the arena, surrounded by bodyguards, her voice strong and unwavering, finally climbing onto the stage joyously—he drops his mic a bit and closes his eyes.

I've watched this moment dozens of times. It's at 1:03 in the YouTube video. Rogers is overwhelmed with love, in part for his friend but also in the way we're all overwhelmed when we hear Dolly's voice rise from the void: clear, reassuring, a signal of the beauty and goodness in the world. It's how I felt when I first heard her in the waiting room at rehab all those years ago. Dolly as clarion, as rainbow, as beacon. Throughout most of the recording of "Islands in the Stream," the two sing some of the verses and all of the chorus together, but when Dolly takes the lead in a later verse, firmly stating that without love, little matters, she brings her deep feeling; she does that thing where her voice wavers, to show emotion, but stays completely in control so the encounter as a listener isn't marred in worry, just filled with shared experience.

Rogers's voice is kind of straightforward. Affably gruff. "That's what magic is supposed to be," Rogers says of Dolly's work on the song. "I sang the first verse in the studio," recalls Rogers in a 2013 special on the Great American Country channel, "and I'm singing along and doing my thing, and all of a sudden here comes Dolly marching into this song." Dolly giggles demurely, but she knows. She also knows exactly what they are together. "This is a *sound*," she says, of the way their voices blend, but also the way they blend in general. Watching them together is a pleasure, the affection between them a delight. Dolly is comfortable in a way we rarely get to see, her words less measured. By the end of the interview she's leaning forward, her legs not only uncrossed but parted—unladylike, as my maternal grandmother would have said. Then she lets out a true guffaw. It's startling to see beneath the veneer of Dolly, even briefly.

"Islands in the Stream" is a groovy song, kinda hot for Lite FM but definitely a Lite FM staple. The keyboard does a lot of not-sucky work here, despite the early-'80s-ness of it all. The horn break two-thirds through is a kick, but never such a kick that we lose the mellow spell of it. Musicologist Jocelyn Neal wrote that the song "perfectly encapsulates countrypolitan as a musical style in the early 1980s, speaking to how disco, country, and pop were merging, with the song becoming popular in the easy-listening category too." Like Dolly, the song is all things to all people. Even her singing, Neal notes, uses the 1980s pop and rock style of switching from a big belty moment to a demure, breathy moment.

Released in August of 1983, it's a summertime groove, and that year I'm sure it was everywhere. By the end of 1983 it had gone platinum, and it was later nominated for a Grammy and for Country Music Association awards. It kicked Bonnie Tyler's classic of histrionic brilliance, "Total Eclipse of the Heart," out of the number one spot on the pop charts and went on to top several US charts and a handful of charts around the world. It was a capital-*H* Hit. Recorded in Los Angeles, it feels like it was recorded in Los Angeles. Dolly traveled just southeast from her apartment on Larrabee (near the famed Whisky a Go Go, and later the Viper Room) to Kenny Rogers's own studio, Lion Share, which is probably most famous as the location where "We Are the World" would be recorded a couple of years later.

I was nine years old when "Islands in the Stream" was recorded, within walking distance of my family's apartment, and nine months post-rape when it was released. If I heard it before the night of rehab check-in, I don't remember. By 1988, I knew Larrabee best for being near where a van drove us most nights from rehab on Pico to an AA meeting on Sunset Boulevard. I loved those meetings and I was scared of those meetings. I loved getting out of the hospital, into the "real world." We traveled with the adults from rehab, who were usually on a different floor. I became friendly with a man named Stanley who was a decades-long smack addict. He seemed old but he was probably in his midforties, as I am now. He had long hair and wore loose-fitting Hawaiian shirts. He'd lost his family, his job (he'd been a sound engineer on movies), and his home. He was on his third or fourth "last ditch effort," he would say. He had great stories peppered with celebrities, as if that's all it took to validate failure.

The AA meetings were intense because the adults had lost a lot more than we kids had. It was like staring into the future. The other teens would get so impatient and squirmy, but I always felt I had to be respectful, like how I'd always felt in shul with my family. My brother, Cliff, would squirm and get reprimanded but I would sit still and zone out. At fourteen, I was a wreck, had already been kicked out of ninth grade twice, but it wasn't rebellion that I felt; I still went to shul with my family many Saturdays, swallowing the prayer rhythms that would later re-form inside my poems, watching the slow body signals between elderly couples in nearby pews, listening to the prattle of the rabbi's sermon. I still felt those people, and the people at the AA meetings, had something to teach me.

The adults in rehab all had great stories of the before times, the times when they could get high up and down Sunset in the late '60s, the '70s, even through the early '80s, and it was fun, they said, and trippy, and sometimes you felt like shit but everyone did and you'd just get up the next day and make music, or build a building, or whatever you did and feel that Southern California sun going through your skin. I get it. It's a kind of aliveness I've never felt anywhere else. Those rays wash out consequences. It's like you can't see the gum stains and pools of spit anywhere on the sidewalk. There's a term for it: air light, "light scattered or diffused in the air by dust, haze, etc., especially as it limits the visibility of distant, dark objects by causing them to blend with the background sky."

Even still, the glossy Hollywood of the early '80s had, by 1988, let in those dark objects and given way to a seriously spent and run-down Hollywood. Grit was glamorized. Hair-metal guys abounded at the AA meetings, guys from bands like L.A. Guns or Poison, or guys who just styled themselves after hair-metal musicians. They seemed very old and sophisticated, but they were in their early twenties and shockingly misogynistic, though I didn't realize what that was at the time. Poison's song "I Want Action"—which peaked on the charts at number fifty in July of 1987—is straight up about rape. If he can't have her, Bret Michaels sings in his wan but kicky way, "I'll take her and make her."

I messaged my friend Jess recently: "A lot of adults would be there, musicians, and I always felt like this tiny nerd person, just a total shit show, and all the older people at these meetings seemed so fully formed and together." I was certainly not one of those teens whom the rockers would call "jailbait" because they looked over eighteen. I looked eleven, but with big boobs, and was an otherwise small, dorky mess, with tape keeping my pink plastic eyeglasses together. Jess wrote back, "My first instinct is that your view of self was WAY screwed." And then she added, "I'm not sure that your fucked-up perspective was YOU, but rather, how much credit you tossed to everyone else." I think I still assume everyone else has it much more together and might be much more important.

One night, when I needed to go to the bathroom in the basement of the church on Sunset, where the Glen Recovery Center van would drive many evenings, Stanley offered to go with me. He could see the younger men leering at me—although I didn't know why they would be, given the older, sexier, more interesting women in the room—and I took Stanley up on the company because I was nervous about even finding where the bathroom was and I had to pee from all the free coffee with too many creamers I'd drunk from little Styrofoam cups. The building was so mazelike, and everywhere in the basement were discarded pews, and also there was a statue of Saint Christopher, the patron saint of travelers but also of bachelors. Stanley was leaning against the wall between the ladies' room and men's room when I came out of the former. He pulled me to him. "I'm so lonely," he said. I didn't know what to say. I knew about loneliness, but not the particular loneliness of a washed-up, middle-aged, white man with long, thinning hair. I wasn't compassionless, just confused. For a girl who'd already experienced things many adults never will, I was kind of innocent.

Stanley, easily over six feet, with wide shoulders and huge hands, pulled me, fully grown at just over five feet one, into a stall in the men's room. I didn't understand about rape culture—although the normalization of sexual violence, harassment, coercion, and misconduct were the drugs we were all on—or toxic masculinity or the toxic celebrity culture of Los Angeles, where worth was measured in proximity to celebrity or else the curves of your body, but I did know what it meant when a grown man pulls you away from the group. You pleasure him. So I did, like I had pleasured the rabbi all those weeks, only this time I was paid with Stanley crying to me about his lost family and me feeling so grown-up and helpful, telling him this time he would get better, this time it would stick. He ran his fingers through all my newly spectacular hair.

We rejoined the meeting as it was ending. All the cookies were gone but a lanky young man with a leather jacket and a scarf tied across his forehead let me smoke a few of his cigarettes. I'd only started smoking in rehab. The counselors freely handed out cigarettes, which seems absurd to me as I type this, the parent of a fourteen-year-old. Still, when I think of Sunset Boulevard, I think of those cigarettes studding the steps of that church near the Strip, of all the butts lighting up the night like string lights at the end of the world.

Hollywood's grit of the late '80s would turn back around, if not strictly to glamour, as in its heyday, to some kind of prepackaged notion of fun and entertainment and glamour. I moved to New York City in the summer of 1994 just as it was being ruined, many New Yorkers would say, by that very turn back around from grit. Times Square got rid of overt sex workers and porn theaters, Bryant Park was swept for drug dealers and on its way to being a hipster lunchtime haven, with a carousel and free ping-pong. I grew up visiting the New York City of the '80s and I was thrilled to finally get there, so in 1994 I didn't care what was going on in Midtown and I'm pretty unsure that grit is great; I've met grit. Up in my apartment on 112th Street, I felt like I was finally home. My grandparents were out in Queens but I had no friends in the city, so my first week there, with no work yet and no school, I rode the subway each day to a different part of town, watched a movie in air-conditioning, and felt such a thrill with all of it. I had packed so quickly in California that I had very little with me. I bought a small radio with a cassette tape player at a Love's drugstore on Broadway and at a Duane Reade I found a bunch of cassettes in a bin, including a collection of Dolly's hits, which I wore out, like the several I'd had before.

That fall, to some people's surprise (including my own), I started graduate school at Columbia University. I had "Islands in the Stream" in my head constantly, up through to my first-ever snowfall, the day before Thanksgiving. I was walking down my block, wondering at the grandeur of real weather, really hitting Dolly's part hard—"No more will you cry!"—thinking I was singing quietly on a street emptied by damp chill, when a man walked by and said, "You really sound like her!" He was generous, of course, but I could hear his enthusiasm in my ears for years. I've long lamented that in a karaoke situation I'm much better suited to the Kenny Rogers part. I can keep a tune, but I have no range and I am not a soprano. I will take this opportunity, however, to say yes to anyone who would like to be the Kenny to my Dolly. Please join me. "That's the beauty of that song," Rogers has said. "Once you hear it, you want to sing it." Many people have covered it: Olivia Newton-John with Barry Gibb, Miley Cyrus and Shawn Mendes, Feist and Constantines do a sluggish interpretation. Pras reworked the lyrics for Ol' Dirty Bastard and Mýa to sing in 1998 on "Ghetto Supastar (That Is What You Are)." Of course, none can come close to singing the genuine affection that Dolly and Kenny Rogers possess.

I never stopped believing in that kind of love and affection, the hope Dolly's voice always possesses. Those soothing countrypolitan sounds got me through 2018, through a friendless summer in 1994, through rehab. The day I checked out of rehab, the lead counselor thanked me. "You made everyone here happier," he said. "You lifted all of our moods." Yesterday—a gloomy, frustratingly chilly late April day—I sat in the living room with Ada and Stella and I played every live version of "Islands in the Stream" I could find on YouTube. Scholar Leigh H. Edwards writes, "The cultural reception of their duets was gendered, with audiences interpreting them as a romantic couple onstage." On a 1986 TV special with Kenny Rogers and Willie Nelson, Nelson says, "I'm gonna go away and let you two lovebirds sing." When the two clasp hands, the audience cheers, and then cheers some more when they put their arms around each other. In a 2005 CMT special celebrating the best country duets of all time, "Islands in the Stream" took the top spot, and the two singers seemed to enjoy each other live as much as ever. "Had to do my bluegrass licks!" Dolly exclaims when she ends with a flourish. "I love you," says Rogers. "I love you too!" says Dolly.

Their final performance together, during a Rogers tribute show in 2017, is of course the most touching. He's clearly unwell and has lost some of his oomph; Dolly has to carry the song and the performance of it, but their affection is palpable, as always. He reaches for her and she playfully swats his hand away. She gives him a moment to rest on a stool while she struts around the stage. They put their arms around each other at the end and Dolly leans into him. "People really sense what we really feel," Dolly said in 2013, sharing a couch with Rogers. "We are soul partners," he says. "A good friend will kill for you," Dolly jokes, "but a true, old friend will help you hide the body." Rogers laughs back in mock resignation. "I'll help you. . . . I'll help you hide the body." I like to think Jess, my truest, oldest friend, would help me hide the body. "We'd so be hiding ALL the bodies," Jess wrote to me this morning, and I'm grateful for that.

Kenny Rogers died on March 20, 2020, at age eighty-one, about a month before I'm first writing this. That morning, Dolly woke up, put on leopard-print hot pants, a black turtleneck, and high-heeled slingbacks, and filmed herself at home. "I loved Kenny with all my heart and my heart's broken. And a big ol' chunk of it has gone with him today." She holds up a framed photo of the two of them and her voice cracks for a moment—Dolly crying is an almost unbearable thing, like watching a parent cry, or the first time an infant cries with actual tears—and then she recovers and says, "God bless you, Kenny. Fly high."

CHAPTER NINE

Do I Ever Cross Your Mind

Heartbreak Express, 1982, 4:02

I WAS CHATTING WITH MY friend and former coworker Paul yesterday—a drummer, in mostly rock bands—and because of me (and specifically a question I asked him last spring about the construction of the song "Jolene"), he's been doing a lot of reevaluating of Dolly and her musicianship and talent. Like me and so many Gen X kids growing up in blue states (his was New Jersey), he was mostly exposed to Dolly as the kind of cartoon she made herself out to be on late-night shows, because we weren't listening to a lot of country radio. It occurred to me while chatting with him that in the 1980s many of Dolly's biggest hits, like "Islands in the Stream" and "Why'd You Come in Here Lookin' Like That," were written by other people, and while they're magical, they didn't showcase to the world all that Dolly can do. In 1982, Dolly released the song "Do I Ever Cross Your Mind," from her album *Heartbreak Express* (featuring a wistful and old-timey Western-tinged Dolly on the cover, looking out a train window). The album was recorded in both Nashville and Los Angeles, but songs from the album didn't place on the pop charts—they were a little bit too country. "Do I Ever Cross Your Mind" peaked at number one on the US country charts in August of 1982.

If I, or Paul, or any of us country-averse kids had listened to country radio in 1982, we might have found "Do I Ever Cross Your Mind"—an up-tempo yet wistful song that wonders, in a burst of nostalgia, if a beloved ever thinks of the singer as much as she thinks of the beloved—to be pretty thrilling, certainly more so than the number one pop song throughout that August, Survivor's "Eye of the Tiger." My brother, Cliff, liked the latter song, though, in large part because it featured in the boxing movie *Rocky III*. I was particularly drawn to Survivor's "The Search Is Over" a few years later. I swooned over the idea that the love of one's life could be there the whole time without you realizing it; I was, as a kid (and now), prone to big feelings and thought the song's scenario the most romantic thing that could ever happen to a person. Yet hold up anything against Dolly's complex song construction on the classic sad banging of "Do I Ever Cross Your Mind," and these overblown pop songs wither into embarrassing oblivion.

"Do I Ever Cross Your Mind" was packaged in 1982 as a double A side with the previously released (on the 1974 album *Jolene*) "I Will Always Love You." It's the latter song that made Dolly one of the few artists to earn a number one twice with the same song—and then later a *third* time, as a writer, when Whitney Houston's version took over the world a decade later. Throughout her very long career, Dolly has had the tendency to record songs multiple times. She's recently stated she's written thousands of songs: "I am a lucky person. I've got hundreds, hundreds, even thousands of songs and a big part of them have never even been records, there's enough stuff to go on forever with my music." Dolly certainly doesn't have to double-dip. Still, I can imagine why she'd want to explore all the angles of some of her best compositions. I've wondered what it would be like to revise my published books sometimes; a reprise, a rerecording, a different take on the same poem.

"Do I Ever Cross Your Mind" was copyrighted in 1973 but not recorded until Chet Atkins wanted it for his album *The Best of Chet Atkins & Friends*, in 1976. Country music legend Atkins—ranked twenty-first by *Rolling Stone* in 2015 on their list of "100 Greatest Guitarists"—grew up an hour from where Dolly grew up in Tennessee, and they recorded the song together in Nashville. It's a merry recording. In one moment, the two find themselves singing different parts of the song at the same time and they both laugh at the error and keep going. Two brilliances at work, laughing at themselves and delighted by the music, despite the forlorn lyrics.

I don't have all that many past romantic relationships I look back on fondly, except for my teenage love, Jason, and he does cross my mind. He played jazz piano, and I think sometimes of how his fingers would play, without him realizing it, on tables, his thigh, my back. The first time he saw me he just stood there staring at me, smiling. He thought I was beautiful long before I could even look at myself without cringing. I think about lying on top of him for hours, just kissing. I think about how on my sixteenth birthday, when neither of us had money, he stood in a mostly unfurnished living room in his boxers and lip-synced all of Ladysmith Black Mambazo's "Hello My Baby" to me and I smiled and pretended it was the best gift ever, but really I was frustrated because I wanted us to have enough money to have a birthday. Now I wish I'd basked in the huge and absolute love of that moment. I haven't seen him since not long after that birthday and I wonder sometimes if and where he is, and if he ever thinks of me. I'm easy to find (there aren't a lot of Lynn Melnicks) and very googleable, so I'm just going to have to assume I don't cross his mind. Given what a post-traumatic mess I was through that relationship— subject to fits of terrified hysteria and panic—maybe that's for the best.

In August 2011, I did get a message on Facebook from an old friend, though: "Omg no way! Hi Lynn! You have to remember me! Lisa! Holy crap it's been 23 years!!!!" I wrote back the next day: "OMG right back!! 23 years. . . . That was such a messed up time in my life—what a trip to be reconnecting with people from those years! How are you? What are you up to? You look beautiful (as always) in your profile pic! I'm a writer now, living in Brooklyn with my husband and our two daughters. I'm so touched that you remembered me!" The good thing about social media is that it keeps us connected, right? As I said, I'm easy to find. Slowly, over the years I've been on social media, I've reconnected with a lot of people I didn't really remember but who wanted to marvel at my general aliveness and okayness. I'll admit a bit of pride in going from Most Likely to End Up Dead in Las Vegas to posting my books in my profile. Sometimes someone will friend-request me and I'll have to ask my BFF, Jess—she who has been the keeper of my secrets since about 1986—who they are because my memory of those years is so shot. Hers is too, but she kept her journals.

My most enduring memory of Lisa is sitting around her building's courtyard pool, a pool swampy with leaves and other neglect, drinking her mom's booze straight from the bottle, ranking our crushes in order of depth, and talking about what we imagined life as an adult would be like. She wanted to be a lawyer, though she ended up a hair stylist, which makes so much sense because she was always skilled with hair. She once straightened mine with an actual iron and it looked goyish and *good* (and then she teased it up again because it was the '80s). "May I ask??? (ONLY because I so care!)," continued Lisa in our chat. "Did you get sober? Or did it subside or get worse??? You seem to be well now for me not knowing anything whatsoever about you now! You have 2 daughters and a husband so you must have!! ??? I hope you were able to get through that ok. I remember the issues you had. And you know MINE at that time too. So, no secrets NOR judgements!!! PLEASE trust me that I am NOT judging you ok?? I have a very genuine concern that is ALL. I'm assuming you are sober now or it was just something you went through and it's over now . . .?? Oh how cool that you are a writer!!" It occurred to me then that she'd reached out not in the hope that I'd gotten my shit together but with nosy curiosity about just what further chaos my life might have unfolded into. It stopped feeling like a heartwarming reunion and I soon dropped my end of the conversation.

In 2015, Lisa died of an accidental overdose after suffering for years in pain with injuries from a car accident. Immediately, a Facebook Messenger chat was started by those of us who knew her as young teens. "Simpler times," said one of the women, referring to when we'd been an in-person friend group in the late '80s, which seemed like an absurd thing to say, when we'd probably been suffering then more than at most other times in our lives. Even Lisa had mentioned in our chat that her teen years were the hardest time of her life, and that was including the physical pain after her accident. After Lisa died, we kept up the group chat for all of six days and then haven't really spoken since, except me and Jess, who chat pretty much every day. Nostalgia is a funny thing. The deep inexplicable pull of it makes you feel tenderly toward those with whom you'd never otherwise be friendly. I guess we will reconvene when the next one of us dies. Stephen King has that last line in his novella *The Body*, made into the movie *Stand by Me*, which was released the summer I was twelve: "I never had any friends later on like the ones I had when I was twelve. Jesus, did you?"

Dolly's best friend from elementary school is Judy Ogle. Aside from a stint in the armed forces, it seems that Judy's career has mostly been as Dolly's right-hand woman. Portrayed in the two "Coat of Many Colors" movies as the beta to Dolly's obvious alpha, the glimpses we get of the real person through Dolly's interviews and books are of a very competent, fun woman who, like Dolly's husband, Carl, likes to stay out of the spotlight. For a star like Dolly, having an assistant she trusts must be everything. Their friendship is a delight to read about; it humanizes Dolly in a very particular way. In the 2006 documentary about Dolly's most ardent fans, *For the Love of Dolly*, we see two women in a used-car lot taking a test drive of a car they somehow know was once Judy's. They totally freak out when they find some blond hair in the passenger seat. In another scene, a married couple bid on the opportunity to meet Dolly as part of a fundraiser for the Dollywood Foundation, and during the meet and greet, the men are very happily surprised when Judy shows up as well. It seems like the biggest possible peek into Dolly's private world, just short of what meeting Carl himself might be like. For years there have been rumors about Dolly and Judy being more than friends, the way there have always been rumors about talk show host Oprah Winfrey and her best friend, Gayle King.

On an episode of *Nightline* in 2012, Dolly tells Juju Chang that she and Winfrey chat about the rumors. "I love [Judy Ogle] as much as I love anybody in the whole world, but we're not romantically involved." In a 2006 interview in *Q-Notes*, an LGBTQ magazine out of North Carolina, Dolly once again shoots down the lesbian rumors. "We are very close and together all the time," she says, but "it's not like I'm carrying around this lover to accommodate me. We work our asses off!" In *Out* magazine in 1997, Frank DeCaro writes, "Some of her gay fans—and probably some of her detractors—cling to the belief that there's a bull dyke with a crew cut under all the gussy." This was indeed the rumor in the 1990s. I might have heard this rumor every time I stepped into the Clit Club, a former lesbian space originating in the Meatpacking District of New York City; I swear everyone there had a friend who had a friend who saw Dolly at a lesbian bar in Nashville, butch haircut freed from under her wigs, and tattoos (ribbons and bows and butterflies, as Dolly describes them: "tasteful") from under her trademark long-sleeved tops. "People just think you can't be that close to somebody," Dolly told Chang.

I think about Timothy and Lucie and that deep love. People still ask me if I think they were ever romantically involved. I wonder, have you ever loved a friend as much as a lover? I have. I don't know what I'd do without my friends.

In the mid-1970s, somewhere in the hills above Hollywood, before my family even arrived in a Datsun to our sea-level dingbat in 1978, singer-songwriter Emmylou Harris had her friend Dolly over to what I imagine was a very fab house. Dolly describes it as kind of a hippie house, musicians everywhere, freewheeling. Linda Ronstadt, who in the 1970s was filling arenas as the biggest female act in rock, remembers that "Emmy called me up and said, 'Dolly Parton's at my house [and] you have to come over.'" The three sang the classic country song—first recorded in 1927 by the Carter Family—"Bury Me Beneath the Willow." "It was just chilling, chilling, chilling," Dolly remembers of the way the women's harmonies melded together. "When we heard our voices it was like injecting some kind of serum into your veins, it was a high like you've never felt." Harris adds, "It was like the sound of sisters, musical sisters." For years the three tried to find the time to record a whole album together, and eventually it happened, culminating in the release of 1987's *Trio*.

Making the album seems to have been an all-around wonderful experience for the women. "The only big disagreements would be are we going to use autoharp or dulcimer on this song," Ronstadt recalls. By this point, Ronstadt was on the other side of her uncharted (for a female rock and roller), stadium-filling success but still enjoying regular hits. "Crossover is certain," *Billboard* predicted for the album, "and will most likely be instantaneous, fueled by Ronstadt's current ride atop the Hot 100—in a duet with James Ingram—with 'Somewhere Out There.'" Dolly was on the other side of her major crossover success, but she hadn't gone back to country; she was soon to release *Rainbow*, her most insipid pop album. Cultural critic Ken Tucker points out that with *Trio*, "it was significant that at precisely the moment when Parton had probably transcended the country artist label, she chose to remind the public of it." *Trio* was an all-around success. It peaked at number one on the country charts, where it stayed for many weeks, and it hit number six on the *Billboard* 200 chart. It was nominated for the Grammys' Album of the Year (it lost to U2's *The Joshua Tree*), and the women won for Best Country Performance by a Duo or Group with Vocal.

Almost as soon as the *Trio* album came out, people were already talking about whether there would be a follow-up. "I've never liked sequels," Dolly told William Stadiem in *Interview* magazine, "and I've often said I don't like to chew my tobacco more than once. . . . Could we ever find the time again? Should we?" In 1994, the three women finally did. While the first time around the three had bickered over little more than the choice of instruments, the recording of *Trio II* was kind of a disaster. Scheduling issues stalled the production. Dolly felt frustrated with Ronstadt's endless perfectionism in the studio, telling *Ladies' Home Journal* in 1995 that Ronstadt "loves to live in the studio and works so slow, it drives me nuts. I wanted to get a cattle prod and say, 'Wake up, bitch, I got stuff to do.'"

Dolly was clearly frustrated if she was letting her guard down like that in public. Like how Dolly finds the pace of moviemaking unbearable, Ronstadt's slow studio pace proved constitutionally painful for Dolly. Further, she felt irked that the two other women wouldn't wait to release the album until she could clear her schedule and find the time to help promote it. Instead, Ronstadt and Harris abandoned the project and decided to erase Dolly's vocals and put the songs out on their own albums. "They pitched a fit and dumped the greatest project ever," Dolly recounted. "It was a sin and a shame—and a stupid decision—to give that album an abortion. It got into a power play. I was made to feel hurt, insulted, burdened with guilt. I would have lived up to my word, but my word wasn't good enough for them. Finally I just said, 'The hell with it, sue me.'"

"I think friends can literally save your life," Dolly told *Ladies' Home Journal*, and I agree. In his book *Nothing Personal*, James Baldwin writes, "I have always felt that a human being could only be saved by another human being. I am aware that we do not save each other very often. But I am also aware that we save each other some of the time." That saving doesn't have to be sexual. There's a particular sadness in thinking—as wonderful as sex is—that it's the only kind of love that can save us. During the worst of the many wounds of 2018, if I hadn't had my friends messaging me throughout the day and night, I would have folded. I can assure you I never fucked any of them, but the intensity of my love is not less than if I had. "You can't make old friends," Dolly and Kenny Rogers sang to each other in their 2013 duet. In so many ways I think of my friend Jess as a life partner, and she is just about the straightest woman I've ever met. Maybe sex is easier for people to understand than love. It's more straightforward. Love is complicated and easy prey for nostalgia, which itself is not nearly as simple as it seems.

These days we think of nostalgia as a harmless walk down memory lane, but the term was actually coined in the eighteenth century to describe a unique kind of depression experienced by sailors away from home. It was seen as an actual ailment, and that seems correct. Think of the whole "Make America Great Again" thing (and get ready for Dolly's Dixie Stampede in a later chapter); think of people's yearning for things to be as they were, when life was "simple." A lot of forgetting is involved in this. In an episode of her 1970s talk show, Dolly visits noted monster, and former president, Andrew Jackson's house wearing an antebellum dress and holding a parasol. She sings—and one can't cringe enough—that de facto Confederate anthem "Dixie." Later in the same show, she has musician Freddy Fender on to talk about Chicano music, and they sing "Before the Next Teardrop Falls" in Spanish. I wonder how much she stopped to think about any of that, because it's not like she's not a thinker.

Dolly herself, in her 1969 song "In the Good Old Days (When Times Were Bad)," ultimately rejects the notion of the past as preferable, although her songs are very often steeped in nostalgia, whether rosy or wistful. Still, the song states that you couldn't pay her enough to go back and live like she did in her youth. This is pretty unequivocal! Yet when my grandmother lost most of her memories, what she retained were mostly those from her foundational years into young adulthood. Maybe we're hardwired for nostalgia. I'll admit that the last time I was in Los Angeles, riding down Fairfax or La Brea or La Cienega and seeing the dingbat apartment buildings with their tiny windows, my throat choked up, not because I miss being inside of them but because my body felt so far from it and yet those sights and sounds and all of it are actually inside of my body, somewhere, waiting to be reactivated.

"Is nostalgia even an emotion?" poet Becca Klaver wonders in a 2017 essay about the subject. "Maybe it's a drive, like hunger or lust. It's in the body." She notes that "the past seems so easy to lose." Remembering, then, is urgent work.

For the 1982 release of "Do I Ever Cross Your Mind," Dolly added a bridge, which ponders whether a love object might ever find himself awake at night, missing her. The lyrics of the bridge—intended, as bridges are, to shift us from one section of the song to the next—are more intense and the music itself becomes more smooth, less bouncy, more mournful. The bridge, in a more poppy ¼ time while the rest of the song is in ¾ time, tips the song close to losing its sad-banger status as the more melodically bland interlude dips into that early-'80s pop song territory. While I never thought of the bridge as anything but country, it's a kind of Lite FM country, like Shania Twain's "You're Still the One" or Faith Hill's "Breathe." I have a perverse fondness for Lite FM hits because the cheese and the mush are laid so bare, and while this goofy temperament of mine first fell for Dolly's song with the bridge, the more bridgeless live-performance recordings I've watched of "Do I Ever Cross Your Mind" prove the power of the sad lyrics with the peppy music setup. The original version finds Dolly singing absolutely joyously, authentically herself and happy, like when she's performing the original version of "The Seeker," rather than the one from the 1995 *Something Special* album. In that joy we hear the longing.

One of my favorite takes on the song is the 1990 version that Dolly recorded with Randy Travis for his album of duets called *Heroes & Friends*. It's very aggressively country, as there's really no way to de-twang Randy Travis. It's a particularly fast version, and the light chatter that bookends the song—"Pretty dang good!" we hear Travis say at the end—reminds me of the banter between Dolly and Chet Atkins fourteen years prior, and Atkins lends backing guitar and vocals on the 1990 version as well. "Thank you," Atkins says at the end of their 1976 version, and Dolly giggles and says, "I love you," dragging out the key vowel in "love" just the smallest bit. In *Chet Atkins: The Greatest Songs of Mister Guitar*, Mark S. Reinhart writes, "'Do I Ever Cross Your Mind' was a sweet, simple, country ballad that sounded for all the world as if it could have been a traditional folk song that had been around for generations." If it had been, I would likely have heard it growing up; my dad might have played it on his guitar, along with "Blowin' in the Wind" and "If I Had a Hammer." It's the guitar that makes this duet so remarkable. Playing a classical guitar custom built for him by a Kentucky luthier named Hascal Haile (and featuring ornate inlay work, because country), Atkins shows off on the recording why he's a legend. "All that good part ain't all Chet," Dolly teases as they pick at their guitars toward the end of their recording. "But all that bad is me," she adds, laughing. Atkins is an absolute legend of a guitar player, but Dolly more than holds her own.

After all the fighting and the threatened lawsuits and Harris and Ronstadt rearranging the songs to put on their own albums and Harris and Dolly both leaving their long-time record companies, the group reconciled and *Trio II* was released to radio in February of 1999. "I realize now that we're just a bunch of crotchy, cranky women, set in our ways and getting up there around 50 and going through change-of-life mood swings," Dolly eventually decided about all the bickering. In her autobiography, Dolly goes so far as to apologize for holding up the release of the album. A review of *Trio II* in *Billboard*, not far from a hits chart featuring Dave Matthews Band and Britney Spears on top, says, "Dolly Parton's pop-ish 'Do I Ever Cross Your Mind' is rendered forever country by Emmylou Harris' trilling lead vocal." It's a funny distinction, of course, because Dolly's first recording of it was with Chet Atkins and her most recent recording of it at that point was in 1990 with Randy Travis, and both were done in the country style without the bridge that makes it more pop. Harris's version includes the bridge and does very little to make the song more countrified, except play up the mandolin. The review seems lazy and based on assumptions and stereotypes of Dolly as a persona and not an artist.

"Sometimes we'd disagree on who would sing lead because Emmy and I always wanted Dolly to sing lead on everything," Ronstadt recalled quite recently. When discussing their first album together, Harris commented, "Linda and I are in mutual admiration of Dolly as our favorite singer. Dolly's voice is almost the focal point of this record, in a way." Ronstadt added, "No one can copy Dolly, but you try to go into her consciousness and sing the way she does from the heart. You get to ride along and feel the way she does." This nails the experience of listening to Dolly; no matter what she is singing, scores of disparate people stop and feel it in a way that gets cellular.

In 1977, Dolly, in a giant bouffant wig and sparkly salmon-pink muumuu, appeared on *Der Musikladen* (The Music Shop), a West German TV show that ran from 1972 to 1984. She sings a number of songs, including "Do I Ever Cross Your Mind," and before she performs the song she instructs her backing band that only she will play guitar on it. "People often ask me how I play the guitar with long nails," she tells the audience. "Well, I play pretty good." Midsong she asks, "Ain't that hot?" and it is, spry and dexterous. The fact is, Dolly wouldn't be where she is today as a singer and song-writer if she wasn't also a gifted musician. She can play numer-ous instruments, despite the long acrylic nails. At the end of her performance, she tells the audience to imagine the song as a 45 rpm single played at 78 rpm speed. As kids we did this, played a record on the wrong speed, just for kicks. Perhaps you did too. Dolly starts to play the song very quickly, her fingers on the guitar are astoundingly deft, and she sings it in a super high-pitched voice. It's a gimmick—one she'll repeat in many concerts over the years—but it's an impressive one. Remember how "Slow Ass Jolene" played "Jolene" at 33 rpm and the internet was floored by Dolly's passion and artistry when her voice was deep? Well, here it's basically a chipmunk and I can't help but be in awe of her genius anyway.

In 1979, Dolly returned to her alma mater, Sevier County High School in Sevierville, Tennessee, to perform a concert the evening after the Dolly Parton Parkway was dedicated. Introducing her sped-up "Do I Ever Cross Your Mind" gim-mick, she makes a joke about slowing it down (!) to sound like her once singing partner Porter Wagoner and then she and her band launch into the high-pitched fun. Throughout the show, Dolly complains (lightly) that it's too warm in the auditorium. Her wig seems a poor fit on her head. She seems wrong in that milieu, on a stage too small to contain her. She seems more guarded than usual, like how you feel at dinner with your family at Thanksgiving, like they will never, and really shouldn't ever, know the real you. She introduces "My

Tennessee Mountain Home" by saying, "I'm so proud to be from this part of the country and I know you are." She closes while holding a bouquet of flowers, singing, "I Will Always Love You."

I guess the thing is you can go home again, but home is different. Nostalgia, then, is longing for what doesn't still exist, if it ever existed. I can group chat with a bunch of women I knew at fourteen but nothing is as heightened as at fourteen (just ask Ada, smack in the middle of fourteen as I write this) and nothing is simple. Those weren't simpler times. Maybe I'm projecting onto Dolly that she has her guard up, performing at her old high school, because I have my guard up with everyone from my adolescence except for Jess. I'm afraid to feel all those big feelings again, to be that freaked out and out of control. I'd be lying, though, if I said Jason's beautiful and smitten face doesn't ever flash through my head. I'd be lying if I said that those girls I knew back in 1980s Los Angeles, in their baggy metal-band T-shirts, acrylic nails, and walls of teased-up hair, those girls sneaking into bars, smoking on the beach, naked in the hot tub of one of their parents' condos—I'd be lying if I said those girls don't often cross my mind.

CHAPTER TEN

Will He Be Waiting for Me

The Grass Is Blue, 1999, 3:26

LIKE "DO I EVER CROSS Your Mind," Dolly's "Will He Be Waiting for Me" is a song of wistful longings and nostalgia; here, the speaker regrets her decision to leave her old life and love behind. The song opens as she recounts the moment she left her man, the stretch of open road so seductive and yet so lonely.

First recorded (as "Will He Be Waiting") for her *Touch Your Woman* album in 1972, like "Do I Ever Cross Your Mind" and so many of Dolly's other songs, "Will He Be Waiting for Me" found its way to another album, my cherished *The Grass Is Blue*. Leigh H. Edwards, in *Dolly Parton, Gender, and Country Music*, notes that although the album cover for *Touch Your Woman*—Dolly sitting on a bed, surrounded by pillows, ready for that touch—suggests intimacy, "Will He Be Waiting for Me" contains less critical realism and more positive nostalgia, both in how Dolly describes the relationship and in how she projects this positive nostalgia onto the homeland to which she's returning. This move of idealizing the rural landscape is a hallmark of a lot of country music, from "Seven Bridges Road" to John Denver's "Take Me Home, Country Roads" to the Chicks' "Wide Open Spaces." I love how humans can love their patch of earth so fiercely.

My grandmother Evelyn Melnick, née Rosenberg, born and raised in the Bronx and living in Queens from 1966 until almost the end of her life, idealized her urban landscape, which would come to be my urban landscape, New York City, which I sure love fiercely. Most every summer of my childhood we'd fly from Los Angeles to visit, and the feeling I'd get when the plane landed at JFK was one of urgency, and joy, and belonging. My grandfather Lester would pick us up in his minivan, and the drive from the airport to Bayside, almost at the Long Island border, felt like a miracle to me, all the big brick housing complexes and loud, bustling streets so different from the midcentury apartment buildings with tiny windows that spotted my much less frenetic cityscape at home. The light is different in New York, more austere; it won't glow out the city's harsh realities, but it holds promise. It's when the sun goes down in the city that possibility seems endless. Lying in my aunt Barbara's old bedroom at night, looking out onto other brick buildings with their stacks of balconies, listening to the city noises, I knew it was where I had to be. "Los Angeles is very beige," I remember my grandmother commenting. "I think you would survive in New York City."

My grandmother died in May of 2018, two months after Lucie's death, in the midst of Ada's very difficult year, and days after my father-in-law had to have emergency open-heart surgery. He texted me from his hospital bed in Rhode Island to offer me condolences, because he's that kind of person. Evy was ninety-three when she died, mostly gone from dementia for several years prior. As sad as it was—she was an icon, really, a woman who could never die—she'd been saying for years, since my grandfather died, that she was ready. I struggled with what to say about her at her funeral. Even in her prime, something about her was always unknowable, the way Dolly always seems ultimately unknowable. Dolly may be full of cornball sentiment, but it's impossible to know what she really thinks about anything because her manner is so

conciliatory and there's a Dolly for everybody. My grandmother was a chameleon like that too, and, like Dolly, a teller
of stories. At the end of her life, Evy's dementia was such
that she told stories in a loop, like a drunk person might, forgetting she had just finished telling it. When we'd visit, only
Timothy had a magic gift for reacting as if he'd never heard
each story before, whether the first time or the fifth time. My
eyes would glaze over. My kids would ask to get up from the
table so they could play.

Evy told stories of courting my grandfather, of early motherhood, of middle age—"I'd give anything to be fifty again,"
she told me when she turned ninety. Yet by the very end of
her life, her stories were only about her childhood. She told
stories of her mother keeping her home from kindergarten
so they could shop on Fourteenth Street and visit her favorite
nut store. She spoke about her father angrily confronting her
anti-Semitic teacher. She talked a lot about having wanted to
be an actress—she was uncommonly beautiful her entire life.
She recounted her lead role in the musical comedy operetta
Pickles, or, In Old Vienna when she was in eighth grade. She
kept the costume from that production in her closet until the
end, until we had to clean out her Queens apartment to sell
toward assisted-living costs. In her closet, we also found an
early Schick electric razor, a bottle of penicillin from 1968
with a handwritten label, and a first edition of *Our Bodies,
Ourselves*, the landmark book of women's health and sexuality.

In the risky-at-the-time title song from her album *Touch
Your Woman*, Dolly sings of a lover who knows exactly how to
please her. When demurring about whether she's a feminist,
Dolly often jokes that she was the original bra burner and it
took the fire department three days to put out the fire (she's
got big boobs!). But Dolly becoming a superstar through sheer
determination to transcend society's expectations for her suggests feminism. Dolly writing and recording about whatever
the fuck she wants suggests feminism. My grandmother didn't

follow her career dreams. Sometimes in dementia she would admit she had been too scared, sometimes she would say marriage and her five kids and eleven grandkids got in the way. When I was a girl, my grandmother seemed like the worldliest person I could ever know, which baffles me now, because she was so often on the outside of the world, looking in.

I emailed my aunt Barbara about my grandmother (her mother) and regrets because I email her every time I'm trying to untangle our family and its heritage. "In her old age, Grandma talked a lot about not having the courage to have pursued other things," she wrote back to me. "And mothering and housekeeping was largely a good choice given that, but I think this 'lack of courage' kept her from pursuing other things beyond mothering when the time was available. I think she struggled with risk, I think she struggled with having unreasonable expectations of other people, and I think she struggled against any inclination she might have had to be part of a larger world. I think that's what she later articulated as a lack of courage."

Introducing the song "Little Sparrow" to an audience at the Ryman Auditorium several years ago, Dolly, speaking of her mom, says, "She loved my daddy more than she loved any other dream." In her 1976 song "To Daddy," Dolly sings that if the mother had ambitions beyond marriage and motherhood, she kept them to herself. While my grandmother never outright said to me that she regretted any of her life decisions, she did tell me from the time I was small not to marry young, to go to college, to have a career, to be out in the world. She was as feminist and hip as could be then, ruling the roost of a three-bedroom co-op in Queens. I think even she would say if she'd been braver, if the path of women of that generation had been easier, she might have ruled the world too.

I used to seriously fear regrets. As a young woman, already with a lot to regret, I would actively tell myself that I would never end up like the adults I experienced at the group-therapy sessions in rehab: men who'd lost jobs and lovers, women who'd birthed babies the state immediately took from them, users whose brains had changed so much from so many years of drug dependency that they were largely made up of a neon sign that read, "Get Drugs Get Drugs Get Drugs." I am not like that, I told myself in that hospital meeting room. I will live my life authentically, I told myself, pushing away any dark disappointments. I had things I cringed over, of course, usually involving hurting people's feelings or bad outfits, but I didn't have all-caps REGRETS.

When asked about regrets in 1994, Dolly says, "I have learned something from everything that has happened in my life. I am who I am because of my past experiences, good and bad." This is what I have always told myself, and so it wasn't until I became a mother that I experienced the full anguish of regrets. They arrived almost with the placenta. They arrived when I was so depleted from preeclampsia and blood loss that I couldn't hold Ada in the minutes after she was born—I was too weak to hold a six-pound, two-ounce baby—and I thought we'd never have a bond because of this. They arrived like dominos: no sooner did a day happen than by evening I'd regret how I'd handled all of it. I regret how distracted and impatient I am on a daily basis. I have checked Twitter when I should have been watching Stella do cartwheels, I've raised my voice over how long it takes her to tie shoes, I've hoped that Ada's angst was just adolescent angst and not illness, and when we first suspected ADHD and anxiety, I wish we'd fought harder for doctors and teachers to see through her disarming charm and help her sooner. Will I regret putting my children in these pages?

But there's another side to this. The first thing Ada taught me, when I was finally able to hold her tiny swaddled body several hours after she was born, was how to forgive myself. I had to, or I could not have endured even a moment of being anyone's mom. Stella, in her plastic bassinet in the hospital almost four years later, just calmly stared at me. I felt, as I once put in a poem, "flown by her forgiveness," as if she already knew what was ahead, and she was cool with it. Shit happens, Mom.

Writing this feels bad in my body. My stomach hurts. I feel dread. I feel . . . regret. Our society expects mothers to prioritize their families or else suffer deserved repercussions, and whenever I have allowed myself to be the priority, and it hasn't gone well, I have felt it as a consequence. So I have had to figure out a way to live with myself, a way to survive: aggressive self-forgiveness, and reminding myself that for every fuckup my kids will turn over for decades, there have been moments of grace, wisdom, solidarity. Ada admires my activism, my sense of style, she knows she can come to me with anything—even if she doesn't always do that—not just because I'm hard to shock but because my love for her is limitless. I might rush us out of the house with an increasingly agitated tone, but my walks to and from school with Stella are something I think we'll both always hold on to. Plus, she gets my taste in music! She'll gleefully sing Carly Simon's "Let the River Run" with me. She'll appreciate both the Prince and the Cyndi Lauper versions of "When You Were Mine." Most importantly, she'll listen to—and think about—Dolly quite a bit. Yesterday, after I played several versions of "Will He Be Waiting for Me" on and off all day long, she asked, "Do you ever wonder if he'll be waiting for her?"

I honestly hadn't. I'd never registered it as a real question. Not because it's a given that he will or he won't be waiting for her, but because, to me, it's a given that she did what she had to do by leaving and whatever happens next is what was meant to happen. I can't live with myself if I think I've fucked up my life irrevocably, and I can't deal with Dolly having done that either. *Cashbox* noted in a 1972 review of *Touch Your Woman* that Dolly "shows a very progressive attitude" toward the lyrics on many of the album's songs, including "Will He Be Waiting for Me." Yet it's not the meaning of the words, but the way Dolly bounces them off each other, that most strongly resonates. "Will he be waiting for me / He will be, won't he?" is so sonically tight and deceptively simple that it feels good to hear it hit again and again. It's a poem, the way the words are elevated by their sounds and placement. The question is a bit of a mantra, willing the right answer into being.

Canadian singer-songwriter Sarah Harmer recorded a version of the song for her 2005 album, *I'm a Mountain*. Hers is straight folk—though the line between genres, as ever, is mostly a sociological one. Growing up in a workaday Catholic neighborhood, Timothy always understood folk music to be the hallmark of PBS-watching, academic families (checks out with my own upbringing). I often think of journalist Sarah Smarsh answering the question of whether she ever gets frustrated with Dolly for not proclaiming herself a feminist. "Only the part of me that went to college," Smarsh answers. Harmer's version has a bit of fiddle, a bit of guitar picking, but it's mostly guitar strumming. In her original version, Dolly's singing has the final remnants of that kind of grand, stylized sound that older country vocals have—think Patsy Cline's "I Fall to Pieces"—and she sings the harmonies herself. The song starts off very poignant and them almost becomes too much, but at that moment where it is becoming too much, it ends.

The backing instruments are very classic country, and the bass rules here more than in Dolly's later bluegrass version. "It's walking around a bit more," my friend Paul noted when I sent him the two versions. The version I keep on my playlist is her bluegrass recording—I think because it's the less mournful and yet the most poignant throughout. It suggests a lack of regret. It suggests a longing, but one steeped in the knowledge of having done what she had to do. The harmonies—here with singers Claire Lynch and Keith Little—like all the harmonies on *The Grass Is Blue*, are intricate, calibrated toward perfection. With a similarly insistent rhythm guitar, this version is also backed by the whole slew of bluegrass instruments running at a faster tempo, urgently insisting that whether he is or isn't waiting for the singer, there is still, in this often difficult world, a hope launched from beauty.

My grandmother always talked about writing poems to help her process the world, but it seems she disposed of them at some point, and Barbara only found two among her papers, written in her last years, both about her star turn in the eighth-grade operetta. In the first, her eighth-grade performance "Was lauded / The audience all applauded." Barbara also found my grandmother's script from *Pickles*, with her lines checked off. She played Ilona, the ingenue role, a role, in a way, she'd lean on her whole life. Of course, she was never naive, quite the opposite; she was scared of not being several steps ahead. In the second poem she left behind, she writes,

> She found a new play
> Like no other.
> It goes by the title of
> "Mother."
> What better role could
> She play
> Up on her stage every
> Day.

In her poem "Prayer," Jorie Graham writes,

> This is the force of faith. Nobody gets
> what they want. Never again are you the same. The
>   longing
> is to be pure. What you get is to be changed.

I think of these lines whenever I rely too hard on my own expectations for outcomes.

In a March 1972 *Billboard* review of *Touch Your Woman*, the reviewer praises several of the songs penned by Dolly but also dishes out a good bit of condescension. "Miss Parton is currently enjoying a highly successful career and this LP will take her higher up the ladder as both a fine stylist and a superb songwriter. Produced by Bob Ferguson, this terrific package is a showcase for the beautiful voice and writing talent of the lovely country girl." The thing is, like my grandmother, I think Dolly wouldn't mind so much. They love and loved to be adored. Unlike my grandmother's, though, Dolly's attitude has always been, well, let me show you what a lovely country girl can do. "I've certainly had to put up with a lot of BS," she told *Elle* in 2019. "I was always strong enough to walk away from it and not to have to fall under it."

There's a moment in Reese Witherspoon's interview program, *Shine On*, that I've watched probably one hundred times (I'm actually not exaggerating here!). From Tennessee herself, it's little surprise that Witherspoon would choose Dolly to be her first interviewee, and the two women chat easily and warmly at the kitchen table of Dolly's home in Nashville. In the scene I'm obsessed with, Dolly invites a visibly excited Witherspoon to take a peek into her closet and then—Gasp! WHAT?—Dolly asks the perky actress what she'd like to try on. When Witherspoon, sort of dazed and still holding her cup of tea from earlier, moves to touch one of the dresses, Dolly puts the brakes on and says, "First you have to put your tea down." I mean, sure, good move. But it's not what she says, which on its own is definitely what your grandma might say to you if you're coming toward her best fashion with a cup of dark liquid. It's the look she gives Witherspoon, which is a look my grandma would definitely give to any of her kids or grandkids (or even her great-grandkids, as my girls could tell you about the time they jumped onto her couch). In our family, we call it the Evy Look. Although many of us—including me, my dad, Barbara, Ada—can employ it quite handily, no one could wield it better than my grandmother. The eyes sharpen. The jaw stiffens. She loves you so much, she expected better from you.

"I could watch Dolly make that face on a perpetual loop," Barbara messaged me after I posted the clip. "It's basically all I do now," I wrote back. Dolly's definitely throwing the Evy Look, a face that says, "I might still love you but you are very disappointing with your bad decision-making." I've got probably a hundred more viewings of that clip in me. There's a strength and surety there that feels victorious, despite any regrets. In 2019, when once again asked about regrets, Dolly said, "It's almost like everything I've ever done, good or bad, seemed to be the thing to do at the time, and to change one thing could change the whole thing, so I don't think you can live your life like that, to regret. I might, I mean, I regret it if I hurt anybody else on my journey, I regret maybe getting caught a time or two, there are some things I might shouldn't have been doing, but I'm not saying I wouldn't do it again." And then, when the interviewer logically follows up for juicy details on what Dolly might have gotten caught doing, she throws him the voice equivalent of the Evy Look and says, slowly, "You can't know everything, can you?"

CHAPTER ELEVEN

Down from Dover

The Fairest of Them All, 1970, 3:45

I HAVE SPENT NOT A moment of regret over the two abortions I had as a young teenager. One thing I instinctively knew was that abortion should be my choice and my choice only. The first time, my friend Jess's mom found me a clinic near the airport, two bus transfers away, no ID required. I'm not sure if I knew in 1988 that you needed parental consent for abortion if you were a minor, but I definitely knew I wasn't going to tell my own parents. In the 1980s in my school, in a liberal part of a liberal state, "sex ed" was all about how to use sanitary napkins and not about birth control and not about consent and not about how sex is supposed to be enjoyable and certainly not about where to find an abortion in Los Angeles. The only time either of my parents ever talked to me about sex was to tell me not to have it until I was married. This was after I'd already had the two abortions. While I didn't regret the abortions, I for sure felt anguish over the situations that made them necessary. Still, I didn't know how lucky I was. How many states in 1988 (and still now) had easy access to abortion clinics, had one on a bus route, had one on a street so bright I had to stand in the joke of shade under a palm tree to read the building numbers? My guess is there were a lot of unwanted babies born in the United States in 1988 and 1989. But not mine.

Dolly and her husband, Carl, never had children, and over the years Dolly has described the reasons in various ways. In her 1994 autobiography she says, "Carl and I had never really wanted to have kids. I love kids. I'm crazy about them, as long as they're somebody else's. People had often asked me about having children, and I always felt guilty and selfish if I said I didn't want them. So sometimes I would just say I couldn't have them, and that lie made me feel even more guilty." In a 2008 interview she blames her period of depression not on, as earlier stated, her emotional affair, her body size, or phoned-in death threats, but on her endometriosis and . . . her inability to have children. In a late 2019 piece in *Cosmopolitan*, Dolly says, "Early on, when my husband and I were dating, and then when we got married, we just assumed we would have kids. We weren't doing anything to stop it. In fact, we thought maybe we would. We even had names if we did, but it didn't turn out that way." Sometimes it's hard to know where Dolly's truth lies. Maybe all these things can be true at once. We have different ways of telling our own stories, of accepting our own reality, of surviving.

Clearly pregnancy is something Dolly has long thought about. Especially early on, she has a lot of songs about unwed mothers and the choices they must make, no doubt influenced by the struggles faced by many young women in her home-town. "The Bridge," on 1968's *Just Because I'm a Woman*, finds a pregnant young woman committing suicide by jumping off the same bridge where she fell in love with the man who would knock her up and then leave her. "Love Isn't Free," from 1972's *Touch Your Woman*, is about the tragic life of a girl abandoned to an orphanage by her unwed mother, who had to leave school because of the shame she'd brought upon her family. Writing recently, sociologist Tressie McMillan Cottom noted, "Dolly circumvents the sentimental version of country music's white motherhood and replaces it with a gothic version that is as complicated and painful as actual motherhood can be."

It's not hard to see why these songs were so resonant in country music at the time. The year 1965 saw the birth control pill finally available to women in all states, but not available to unmarried women in all states until 1972. Since heat-of-the-moment intercourse is a time-honored tradition, and unplanned pregnancies are bound to happen even with the best sex education available—arousal is a drug, and drugs don't care about the future—these kinds of stories Dolly sings were not uncommon. On a podcast recently, when her sad-ass songs came up, Dolly said, "All of those things you were talking about in those songs were things that were unfolding in my family."

Probably Dolly's most popular song in the unwed-mother genre is 1970's "Down from Dover." Synopsis: a woman can't refuse her boyfriend "when he needed me," so they fuck, she gets pregnant, he skips town, she is steadfast in thinking he'll be back, but come on, in the back of her mind she knows he won't, she gives birth, the baby is stillborn, the woman thinks, well, I guess that's a sign my man isn't coming back. It's impossible to overstate the absolute mawkishness of this song. It's kind of painful to get through. Sometimes when I reach this point in my playlist, I'm like, hmm, no, not in the mood, and I skip it. And yet often I do listen to it and I did put it on my playlist. Why? Why is it one of Dolly's most popular and enduring songs? Why is this one that she so often performs in concert?

"Down from Dover" opens with a serious bass line and a lighter guitar on top of it, which immediately grabs us with an eerily ominous . . . hope. The strophic construction—there is no chorus, all verses are sung to the same melody, like in the folk song "Michael, Row Your Boat Ashore" or the hymn "Amazing Grace"—means that every line rises with hope, then falls with disappointment. Like with most of Dolly's songs, it's her voice that imbues the lines with so much feeling. Reviewing the album *My Blue Ridge Mountain Boy* (but which could equally apply to *The Fairest of Them All*, on which "Down from Dover" first appears), Gene Guerrero says, "[Dolly] has a distinctive delivery, placing her emphasis on surprising syllables, cutting off short on one word and allowing her voice to drop off gradually on another. In the finest country tradition she conveys intense emotion without using her voice as an emotional gimmick."

Dolly recorded another version of "Down from Dover," for 2001's *Little Sparrow*, and, to my own surprise, I prefer the 1970 version. The updated "Down from Dover" is less intense, less determined, more willing to give in to the inherent maudlinism, including with Dolly's voice breaking sometimes, whispering others. The hardscrabble resilience of the earlier version, and so many of those sad-ass songs, is gone. She's less inside of it and more looking in from the outside. The low whistle that opens the more hushed arrangement paradoxically doesn't help the over-the-top feel.

The *Little Sparrow* version of the song adds a verse back in that Dolly had previously taken out. Her former singing partner, the often-controlling Porter Wagoner, found it to be too graphic, apparently, this verse about a lady on a farm who takes in the pregnant narrator. This lady, Miss Grover, never asks the young woman about her growing body one way or another. I puzzled over this for a while and then emailed the lyrics to Timothy to see what he thought; I know no one better at reading poems.

"The only explanation I can come up with," he emailed back from the bedroom, "which I think is legit but also sort of finer than I would have expected, is that the lyrics can be read not just sympathetically, but as a cautionary tale, one in which she is punished for everything she has done, except for that verse. Miss Grover doesn't seem to judge her and accepts her as is, and takes her in. I think that suggests that others might have to, or should have, but failed to. I'm pretty sure that's it." I'm pretty sure that's it too. Dolly's also good at poetry; while for sure prone to big moments, her moments of searing subtlety are enviable.

In 2020, a so-called heartbeat bill, intended to ban abortion once a "fetal heartbeat" can be detected—which is most likely before a woman even knows she's pregnant—made its way through the Tennessee General Assembly and to the governor's desk. As I type this, its implementation has been held up in legal challenges by the Center for Reproductive Rights, Planned Parenthood, and the American Civil Liberties Union. I looked up abortion providers in Sevier County, Tennessee, and was largely directed to women's health centers with web pages on abortion that are meant to steer you away from abortion. "The Women's Care Center," for example, "established in 1990, is a Christian organization that exists to engage in the life of our community by empowering individuals and families to make healthy, life-affirming choices regarding pregnancy and reproductive health." The page on abortion information is titled "Abortion: The Costs and Dangers." In Knoxville, about thirty miles away, several pro-choice women's healthcare centers exist, and I'm not exaggerating when I say that reading their kind and compassionate websites following the propaganda of the anti-choice sites made me tear up with gratitude for the work these organizations do, controversial well into the twenty-first century.

In 1970, "Down from Dover" was clearly too controversial to become a radio release from its album. In a February 1970 review of *The Fairest of Them All* (which peaked at number thirteen on the Top Country Albums chart), *Billboard* says, "The 'Dover' tune is very beautiful and well produced, but the theme is perhaps a little too strong for airplay, even in this day of enlightenment."

Several years later, Loretta Lynn's 1975 song "The Pill"—

about a married woman announcing that she is finally *done* having children—proved too risqué for many radio stations. Introducing "Down from Dover" in 1979 at her high school show, Dolly says, "It never did get much play on the radio back then [when it was first released] because it was a little bit touchy because it talks about a girl who got in trouble." Later she adds, "I never know when to hush." For her 1983 *Dolly in Concert* television special, filmed in London, Dolly introduces it as "a song that I wrote when I was about eighteen. . . . It's just a story about a girl having a baby, nothing too unnatural about that, you think? . . . But it seemed to be too heavy at the time so I only put it out on an album. I do get quite a bit of [performance] requests for it from the album." In 2020, on *The Late Show with Stephen Colbert*, Dolly says, "Back at the time when I put it on a record they wouldn't play it on the radio. Lord, now you can have a baby right on television!"

Introducing the "Down from Dover" episode of the *Dolly Parton's Heartstrings* television series in 2019, Dolly says, "Back when I first recorded it, it caused a lot of fuss because it was such a controversial subject back then, but it was an important message for me to share." The episode spins the song into a commentary on love and acceptance and loss. "If you have hope, you can survive anything," Dolly continues. My first book of poems was called *If I Should Say I Have Hope*, and I believe firmly in its possibilities. "Down from Dover," though, despite its sliver of hope, is a pitiful, sad-ass song. So sad-ass, in fact, that on Nancy Sinatra's 1972 seriously overwrought duet of it with the absurdly baritone Lee Hazlewood (as the dastardly impregnator!), her voice actually breaks at the end. So sad-ass, in fact, that no less than bad-news buffet Marianne Faithfull herself covered it—with a funky orchestral and electric guitar backing—on her 2008 album, *Easy Come, Easy Go*, her North London accent mixed with a sheen of hard living especially strong on the lyric where her mama calls her a fool.

In 1988, I was lied to. I paid my $200 money order (a

fortune, an absolute fortune at the time, paid for with the hand-job money from the rabbi who gave me *When Bad Things Happen to Good People*). I eyed the other girls and women warily as I waited in what felt like an assembly line to turn in my paperwork, to have my blood drawn, to get in a gown. Eventually a comradery unfolded, all of us on gurneys in a row in a pretty big room, like the comradery that happens in the security line at the airport or in a stuck elevator because you're suffering together and it feels close, even though you'll never see each other again. The nurse remarked on how tiny I was and I felt special, how I felt when I was the youngest person in rehab, everyone looking out for me because I was small. What fuckery went into that logic; no one was looking out for me. "You are so young," the doctor said to me before I went under, "my guess is you will have too much scarring to ever carry a child to term." I woke from the anesthesia crying.

Before discharge the doctor told me to keep my legs shut from now on, and then I went out into the sun and bled all over some concrete steps, waiting for my ride to show. When he didn't, and another man slowed and asked me if he could take me somewhere, I got in. He offered me a cigarette. He wasn't a bad man, he dropped me off on the corner of La Brea and Pico. I wrote my very first poem about the blood on those concrete steps. I spent the next decades thinking—although multiple ob-gyns told me otherwise—that I would be unable to ever have babies. In so many ways, my girls, whom I hear downstairs singing and giggling right now, are a miracle.

In *When Bad Things Happen to Good People*, Harold Kushner writes, "People who pray for miracles usually don't get miracles, any more than children who pray for bicycles, good grades, or good boyfriends get them as a result of praying. But people who pray for courage, for strength to bear the unbearable, for the grace to remember what they have left instead of what they have lost, very often find their prayer answered." After years of gynecological problems, Dolly, in Los Angeles without her husband, got her tubes tide. "In my mind," she writes in her autobiography, "it was almost as if I had had an abortion, having my tubes tied and not even consulting Carl about it." When I told this anecdote to my friend Ashley, my partner in all things Dolly (it is she who went to the concert in Queens with me), she let out a southern holler (she's a Tennessee gal) and said, slowly, "She is such a badass."

Dolly, being Dolly, prayed to God after that surgery, and God imbued her with the understanding that her work in this world was to use her gifts to help others. Maybe this is why she performs "Down from Dover" so frequently and why it stays on my playlist. This is why I read my poems about abortion to possibly hostile audiences who think I'm a baby killer. A handful of people walked out of a reading I gave in a very red state when I read a poem about abortion, but I also had people come up to me after that same reading, breathlessly thanking me for speaking truth about the subject. This is why I'm telling you my story even though I never expected to write my story in this way. I'll have nothing to do with shame and I'm done with silence. Now I never know when to hush.

CHAPTER TWELVE

Silver Dagger

The Grass Is Blue, 1999, 4:55

BORN THE FIRST YEAR OF the baby boom, like Dolly, and coming of age in a Jewish household in conservative, working-class Seaford, Long Island, my mother was twenty and a year married already by the time the so-called Summer of Love rolled around in 1967. She was going to dental-assistant school because she thought she might be a dental assistant, and living in Queens with my dad, who was going to dental school because he thought he might be a dentist (neither stuck). "I smoked a cigarette once," she told me of her rebellious youth. She is an extremely gentle, kind woman. In their passion for literacy and mentoring young children, my mom and Dolly have a lot in common. My mom went back to school when I started kindergarten, and she slowly worked her way through undergrad and grad school and became a teacher when I was a teenager; she only recently retired after having taught second grade for twenty-five years.

The happiest moments of my childhood were lazy summer days going to the library with my mom, or running errands with her, or helping her do housework. I loved dusting. I loved dusting a music box with figurines of a boy and a girl (me and Cliff, I always thought) that played "Raindrops Keep Fallin' on My Head" when you wound them up and let them spin. My mother worried, a lot, and about the wrong things. She had an outsize worry—as, to be fair, so many did in the 1980s—about her kids being kidnapped. If I was late walking home from the elementary school only a handful or so blocks away, I'd inevitably see her walking toward me in a mild panic and I could see her relief in seeing me even a block away as she stood there panting. Her severe asthma was a constant presence in my childhood, my own source of worry, similar to how Avie Lee Parton's ill health overshadowed all of Dolly's younger years.

Of course, having children of my own now, I understand that particularly mind-reeling feeling of wondering where your kid is and why she's late. Being good at imagining the worst is a genetic trait at which I shine. I more than understand why one would head out to find her daughter even when one can't breathe; it is singularly terrible to worry about your children being vanished. There were other worries too. My mom and my dad were obsessed, in a very midcentury Jewish way carried over from their own childhoods, with my intelligence, my grades, my musical ability (my flute teacher said I had "perfect pitch"). I'd learned to hide all things about myself that didn't fit the narrative of the dutiful Jewish daughter. I hid bad grades, I hid music or clothes my parents thought were trashy, friends they didn't like, my rape, all the drugs I tried, and all the sex I was having before my mother even thought to tell me, post-rehab, not to have it until marriage. At the time, hiding my chaotic life seemed like the only possible approach. I never wanted to upset anyone.

The fraught relationship between mother and daughter is what defines Dolly's version of "Silver Dagger," on 1999's *The Grass Is Blue.* Though the song has so many Dolly-style sad-ass themes to it—love, family, betrayal, mental illness, tragedy, loneliness, death—Dolly didn't compose "Silver Dagger"; it's a traditional American folk ballad perhaps best known by way of Joan Baez's forceful 1960 recording, to which Dolly's version closely adheres. *American Songwriter's* Rick Moore reports, "The origins of 'Silver Dagger' stretch back to the nineteenth-century British Isles, to such songs as 'Drowsy Sleeper' and 'Who Is At My Bedroom Window?' It came out of various stories of love lost that featured a dagger as either a suicide weapon for desperate lovers or an intimidating tool to keep suitors away. . . . Melodies were learned from performer to performer until they ended up becoming tradition."

The basic sung melody behind the two lingering versions of the ballad—"Katy Dear" and "Silver Dagger"—remains essentially the same. Like "Down from Dover," the music is a strophic construction. In the "Katy Dear" version, to sum up, a man urges his sweetheart to ask her parents if they may marry. If they say no, he suggests, let's just run away. Seems classic. He's trying to do the right thing. But his beloved can't ask her mom, because her mom is sleeping. Next to a silver dagger. The dad too, except his dagger is golden: "Oh, Willie dear, there's no need in asking / He's in his room a takin' rest / And by his side is a golden dagger / To slay the one that I love best." Basically, Katy's brought Willie to a murder house.

With these two noes, you'd think Willie would go ahead with his backup plan and run away with Katy. But no! Willie (who has somehow also gotten ahold of a golden dagger at this point) stabs himself through his "troubled heart," followed closely behind by Katy, who, wanting to die with her true love, picks up the bloody dagger and does what she must do. I mean, this is some William Shakespeare overreaction here! This did not have to turn out this way!

The other lingering version of the song falls into the intimidation-by-dagger camp, which is where Dolly comes in. Jim Mills's banjo on 1999's "Silver Dagger" rivals only his banjo on 2001's "Seven Bridges Road," from *Little Sparrow*. The banjo starts off insistently with a repeated six-note lick that immediately pulls the listener into the song. It is only at the eighth go-round that Dolly comes in with her iconic voice and the direct admonishment: "Don't sing love songs / You'll wake my mother." Then the banjo gets playful a little in that running bluegrass way until the start of the next verse: "My daddy is a handsome devil." This unrelenting, almost ominous consistency matches the spookiness of the song, and although the other instruments do completely kicky work throughout, the banjo is the sinister through line. Jerry Douglas, Dolly's frequent backup musician, who here plays dobro, says that "Dolly's performance brought this cream of the crop band leaping to its feet." Mandolin, fiddle, guitar, and bass round out the band, as well as Dolly, doing her own backing vocals on the song.

"The banjo and dobro are as hard as spear-tips," David Honigmann wrote in the "Life of a Song" series in the *Financial Times*, "and the bluegrass fiddle dances through an ornamented cadenza." All the same characters as in "Katy Dear" appear in the action of the song. The melody is the same, as is the weapon, but the lyrics are jumbled around like a redone mosaic. The song was handed down through oral tradition for decades, and each performer likely added their own spin and nuance, while keeping the music and, it would seem, the major players intact. It's impossible to imagine that the two versions didn't originate from the same song.

In "Silver Dagger," the female protagonist—Katy in the other version but not named here—brings home a man and instructs him not to wake her mother, who sleeps with a silver dagger by her side, which is just her way of saying, yeah, you're not marrying this guy or any guy. "All men are false," the mother has told her daughter. Which leads us to the important information that, in this version, the father is nowhere to be found.

My daddy is a handsome devil
He's got a chain five miles long
And on every link a heart does dangle
Of another maid he's loved and wronged

So we see now what the problem is. Does the woman choose love, despite her family's history and her mother's drastic assertion? Does she, or does her beloved, choose suicide? In "Katy Dear," I get why they ended up back at the house, because there was that brief time where they might run off together. In "Silver Dagger," it's almost like she invites him over to assess the state of things, almost like, *Look, love, do you see why this is never gonna happen?* The protagonist sings, "For I've been warned, and I've decided / To sleep alone all of my life," but not before she selflessly encourages her man to court another, more well-adjusted, and presumably less maternally surveilled, person. We don't know how things end for the man in this, although I like to assume he gets out alive.

My aunt Barbara sent me a recent *New York Times* article by Maggie Master called "Navigating the Wilds of Maternal Love," and it tells the story of this woman's mother, who was so overprotective that when, at twenty-three, Master took a trip across the country, her mom instructed her—in the age before cell phones!—to call *every six hours*, and then her mom actually called the park rangers at Yosemite when Master failed to call one day. Master, now a mother, writes that she understands the feeling of wanting to keep her kids "in a bunker" because "that bunker isn't for my children. It's for me. Because, if something terrible happened to them, I wouldn't survive. . . . That's the fear that comes with loving someone almost to the point of irrationality." The problem is, there's no way to ever know for certain what the danger is.

As a parent now, I have also focused on the wrong things at times and wish I hadn't, even as I know that keeping my kids in a controlled bubble isn't practical, helpful, or even possible. I think that's the pain you willingly or unknowingly accept the moment your first child arrives in the world. How little I've been able, and will be able, to protect my own children. How much have they or will they hide from me? "Deny thy father and refuse thy name," says Juliet, in Shakespeare's play *Romeo and Juliet*. In "Silver Dagger," though, the singer decides to listen to her overprotective (dagger alert!) mother, and to accept a lonely life without love rather than open her heart up to the wounds of heartbreak. Is the choice always loneliness versus pain?

In 2018, a month or so after we returned from Dollywood, we adopted kittens. I'd resisted getting cats or any pets for years because I knew I'd be the one to do the thankless practical tasks (this premonition was, of course, correct) but more so because of my heart. I didn't think it could hold more love or worry. I even thought maybe if I was allergic it would be an easy no. My mother, who has a gazillion allergies, told us for years she was allergic, but she's actually not allergic to cats, they just creep her out. I tested negative for a cat allergy and we adopted brothers, one we named Elliot (gray) and the other Anubis (black), and the first days they were home with us I was frenzied. I couldn't eat or sleep. I was afraid for them. It was like having babies again. It was miserable. I couldn't tell what they were trying to communicate but I knew they were in distress. They'd been rescued off the street, they'd suffered terrible ringworm and giardia, Elliot's tail had been injured, and they were skittish and scared. I felt in love and in a panic and I knew my heart might burst from that love, and from the inevitable pain that comes with it. I love those boys so much, there are cat-shaped spaces in my heart now, which, pre-August 2018, I would have never believed.

Why would I add more possibilities for heartbreak during a heartbreaking year? I'm not entirely sure. Except that the heart is all there is. When I was a kid, the radio in our kitchen was always tuned to either the news or the classical music station. My mother loved that music, and especially opera, and I used to ask her the stories behind the operas, and she eventually bought me a record of operas packaged for kids, which I wore out. I loved the music too, which, at its best, is overwhelmingly beautiful in so many directions, the impossible voices like from another planet, but I also loved the absurd, overwrought stories: a couple falls in wild love during a five-minute aria (*La bohème*), two men make a bet that they can bag each other's girlfriends (*Così fan tutte*), a princess agrees to marry a man only if he can first solve her three riddles (*Turandot*). I guess I'm a sucker for romantic overreactions. "Silver Dagger" is exactly that. "Songs get rearranged and changed," Rick Moore muses, "but some live on for decades, even centuries, simply because they tell great universal stories."

There have been other notable versions of "Silver Dagger." Like with "Seven Bridges Road," the Eagles use "Silver Dagger" to warm up before or at the start of their shows. Fleet Foxes' Robin Pecknold sings a touching version with a bouncy guitar. UK folk/punk band the Men They Couldn't Hang released it as a B side and sing it with that Pogues-style throat rattle that suggests a drunken, hardscrabble evening; their fiddle is beautiful. Bluegrass artist Justin Hiltner's 2021 version highlights the banjo and serves as "a good analog for my own experience coming out of the closet and the ways my parents tried to keep me sheltered and sequestered from queerness and my identity," Hiltner told *Country Queer*. The UK's indie dance pop band Saint Etienne released a song in 1994 called "Like a Motorway" that uses the "Silver Dagger" melody over a synth beat to tell the story of a love who mysteriously vanishes. That same year they performed it at Glastonbury, twenty years before Dolly would headline there, but they can't seem to capture the crowd the way Dolly does. The gap between the stage and the audience seems cold and unbridgeable.

What I love about the way Dolly performs "Silver Dagger," and just about anything else, is the exultation that comes through her act of singing. Here it is made haunting and mysterious, less like she's willing it into being and more like she's sinking to it. She's also singing in D-sharp minor, a key German composer Christian Schubart, in 1806, declared creates

"feelings of the anxiety of the soul's deepest distress, of brood-
ing despair, of blackest depression, of the most gloomy condition of the soul. Every fear, every hesitation of the shuddering
heart, breathes out of horrible D-sharp minor. If ghosts could
speak, their speech would approximate this key." Dolly's "Silver Dagger," as music critic David Honigmann notes, is "sung
with an intensity that sounds almost possessed."

Dolly's own backing vocals add to the poignancy—you can
feel the heft of her lifelong familiarity with the haunting melody and harmonies—and when she sings, "I've been warned,"
followed by an astonishingly plaintive, "So I've decided," we
know that her decision "to sleep alone, all of my life," is far
more complex than this drastic lyric would have you think.
She almost whispers those lines, and yet there's a book of pain
in her voice. No good options. "If love be rough with you, be
rough with love," Romeo's buddy Mercutio says in *Romeo and
Juliet*. "Prick love for pricking, and you beat love down." All
love is entrapment, "Silver Dagger" seems to believe, and to
love is to entrap, and yet we knowingly walk into it anyway. I
can't tell if this is hope or surrender. Maybe both.

The version of "Silver Dagger" on *The Grass Is Blue*
includes a kind of musical addendum I haven't heard in any
of the many other versions I've listened to. Why does art matter? Because it bores a tunnel between our hearts and minds
and still refuses to solve any of life's riddles, just leaving a tender pathway. After almost four minutes of song, the insistent
strings slow until there is complete silence for about four seconds before a lone guitar reappears with a minute left in the
song, then joined by Jerry Douglas's dobro. I wish I could ask
them what this coda is meant to say. It's not completely sad,
it doesn't point to tragedy. It points to beauty, maybe, beauty
amid pain, the resiliency of art, its persistence through the
centuries. It is unhurried, and feels kind of dangerous.

CHAPTER THIRTEEN

Don't Think Twice

Blue Smoke, 2014, 3:21

WHEN I WAS A LITTLE kid, my dad invented a silly game to play with my brother, Cliff, and me. It was called Land of the Mean, and it basically involved a blanket with which he threatened to cover us and which would then send us, through some kind of bad magic, to the aforementioned terrible land. Of course we knew it was just pretend, but also of course we got all worked up anyway, squealing and running away. At that age, things are so starkly binary that there could exist such a land, and by contrast, we were supposed to think of the land we were in as the Land of the Nice. The running joke in the family became that once caught, Cliff would say, "No! Send Lynn to the Land of the Mean!" easily sacrificing his younger sister for the sake of safety. Under the big blanket I'd go, knowing, of course, that I was just under a blanket. It was like an important secret my dad and I shared: the Land of the Mean didn't exist except in the anticipation of it.

My father might be the most complicated person I've ever known. He's a scientist, ferociously methodical about everything, who believes in a very spiritual kind of relationship with God even though I don't get the sense that he believes in God. He finds outrageous stories of Hemingway and the Beats to be compelling, but he himself never gave in to the kind of regular hard drinking or partying or womanizing that derails a life. He keeps himself up at night trying to solve everyone's problems, to figure out how we can always have smooth sailing. Yet his moods are so dire and his rage sometimes so unchecked that I occasionally have nightmares where he's yelling at me. The moments where he is unguardedly happy are rare, and they flood my body with ease. He often thought maybe he could be an artist, a poet, something creative, and the truth is, he could have. He's been talented at everything he's tried, but he came to realize he's a scientist, a problem solver, an uncoverer of the world's mysteries.

When I was small, he often sang folks songs and played his guitar. Like Dolly, folk songs are what I was born listening to. When I was a baby and then a toddler and then old enough to remember, my father was still in school and would work in his lab until it was almost my bedtime, but then he'd sing me to sleep. He has a beautiful tenor voice and doesn't miss notes. It was a pleasurable thing, a comforting thing, listening to him sing. In the set for her 2016 concert in Forest Hills— just blocks from the first-floor studio apartment where my parents lived as newlyweds in 1966—I spilled over with joy when Dolly did a medley of folk songs, including "If I Had a Hammer" and "Blowin' in the Wind," two songs I remember in frequent rotation during my childhood. When my father would sing, "The answer is blowin' in the wind," I pictured that old-fashioned image of wind, a sort of cloudlike male face often seen on schoolroom maps. I didn't think the answer to the world's problems was around here somewhere and we'd find it. No! Instead I thought of this figure, who I'd come to learn later was the Greek god Aeolus, known to be a "keeper of the winds," who held the harsh forces contained on his island, only for them to be released by the most powerful gods when they wanted to bring havoc upon the world.

Maybe this is a metaphor for my dad—keeping the harsh forces away until he blows—but I'm afraid it would be a metaphor for me as well. My rage is also often unchecked, it's just that I can usually form it into words I then empty onto my laptop. Written in 1962, the year my dad graduated high school on Long Island and began to commute into Manhattan to go to New York University on a scholarship received from my grandfather's electricians' union, and released the following year, "Blowin' in the Wind" was the A side to the B side of one of my all-time favorites of Bob Dylan's songs, "Don't Think Twice, It's All Right."

In the latter song, a lover is leaving what seems to be at best an exhausting relationship, and he is, I think, kind of passive-aggressively telling his lover not to worry about it, he's fine, he's not any worse without her than he was with her. He gave her his heart, the singer tells us, but "she wanted my soul." It's either hyperbole and he's trying to make her feel shitty, or she's a real shit. In the liner notes to the original album, political commentator Nat Hentoff writes that the song is "a statement that maybe you can say to make yourself feel better . . . as if you were talking to yourself." In any case, the song is beautiful. Dylan's version never allows vulnerability in, really, although we can wonder about it under the surface. The song has been covered so many times that the layers of the song get to shine in their turn.

The Peter, Paul and Mary version maybe comes closest to living on that line between anger and sadness, possibly because the three voices get to do different work. When Joan Baez—conspicuously and cruelly dumped by Dylan as his fame began to eclipse hers—sings her version, she brings their history into it. José Feliciano recorded a very tender version. Willie Nelson and Merle Haggard recorded a version not long before the latter's death, and it has a kind of forthright *knowing* to it that I imagine comes with age. Elvis Presley recorded it rockabilly cool with a lot of spirited guitar picking and a choppy vocal featuring his lower registers. Jackie DeShannon does a version. Randy Travis. James Taylor.

Shelby Lynne. Eric Clapton. Frankie Valli and the Four Seasons recorded a bananas falsetto version of it in 1965, which, although recorded as a joke after they just couldn't get it right, and released under the band name the Wonder Who, nevertheless peaked at number twelve on the charts. That's the power of the song.

The song itself, while written by Dylan, wasn't exactly written by Dylan. It was cribbed from a song called "Who's Gonna Buy You Ribbons (When I'm Gone)" by the folk singer Paul Clayton. "[Dylan] not only ignored his debt to Clayton's composition," Bob Spitz wrote in *Dylan: A Biography*, "he copyrighted the tune in his own name without acknowledging its origins or, as was custom, listing the melody as 'traditional.'" Dolly listed the writing credit as "traditional" on "Silver Dagger."

Clayton was a mentor to Dylan in the Greenwich Village folk music scene—a scene where my dad was likely often in the audience with my mother, who was still in high school at the time—and even after their record companies sued each other over the possible plagiarism of "Don't Think Twice, It's All Right," the two remained friends until Clayton committed suicide at thirty-six. Years later, Dylan did publicly acknowledge the similarities in the songs. Clayton has an elegant voice, more suited to Billy Eckstine–style jazz crooning, perhaps, than folk singing. It's certainly the polar opposite of Dylan's testy scratchiness, and an exquisite listening experience. The echoes of the song "Who's Gonna Buy You Ribbons" ultimately bounce back onto the song now, and vice versa, which is part of what makes it enjoyable, sort of like how echoes of earlier incarnations of "Come All Ye Fair and Tender Ladies" return to Dolly's "Little Sparrow" when I listen to it now. There is something comforting about venerable melodies, which is perhaps why going to shul is so comforting to my dad and, I'll admit, why sometimes those old Jewish prayers pop into my head at the most necessary times. I always recite the Sh'ma prayer on airplanes, even though I don't believe a word of it. One night when Ada was struggling, in 2018, I found myself sitting on the floor near her bed, watching her sleep because I couldn't, and singing the hymn "Adon Olam"—ironically, a bedtime prayer— quietly to myself. It is a song about giving oneself over to God, releasing fear to God, and, in that moment, the words and melody soothed.

"Who's Gonna Buy You Ribbons" is itself borrowed, or stolen, from an older melody. "Who Gon' Bring You Chickens" was collected in a book called *Old Negro Songs* published in 1923. I couldn't find a recording of the song, only the sheet music, so I asked my friend Alicia Jo Rabins—a writer, musician, and Torah teacher—if she could record herself singing it, and she did, from inside the RV in which she was traveling with her family, somewhere in the United States. Her full and mournfully beautiful voice filled my Brooklyn apartment and confirmed the similarities to later incarnations of the song. The lyrics to "Who Gon' Bring You Chickens" are darker than either the Dylan or the Clayton versions; here, the singer is off to jail for six months and wondering who will take care of his beloved.

After its peak in the early '60s, protest folk music fell out of fashion for many years until singer Tracy Chapman released her self-titled debut the spring I went into drug rehab. Its breakout song, "Fast Car"—about love and hope amid poverty and desperation—rose into the top ten on the charts, having gotten a lot of exposure at Nelson Mandela's seventieth birthday party and a heavy rotation on MTV. I got the album when I got out of rehab and I listened to it so much that it seems like the guy who sometimes sings a cover of Chapman's "Baby Can I Hold You" in the cars of the A Train is singing to me only, because I remember. I listened so much that when Ed Sheeran went on *Saturday Night Live* in 2017 to debut his song "Shape of You," I instantly said to Timothy,

"That's 'Mountains o' Things"—a *Tracy Chapman* album deep cut—because the melody is so similar.

After obsessing over the album for weeks after I first got it, I did a thing I never did: I brought it out of my bedroom and showed it to my dad. I told him he would like it. I told him "Talkin' 'bout a Revolution" reminded me of "The Times They Are A-Changin'," which he used to play for me on his guitar. My father, probably like a lot of white academics of his generation, had long since gone cynical, or maybe just bored, about revolutions and times changing, but we sat there and listened to all of *Tracy Chapman* on vinyl and then all of Dylan's *Greatest Hits* on vinyl, and it was one of those moments where the future felt wide open with promise. It remains one of the defining moments of my teen years.

"My dad was a very hard worker," Dolly told Gloria Hunniford in 2001, shortly after her father had passed away from a stroke. "I got my talent and my personality mostly from my mom and my mom's people, because they were all very musical. And I lost my dad. . . . I never realized what a Daddy girl I was until Daddy passed." When I was small and my father would have to travel for work, he would bring back gold foil from the cigars he mysteriously smoked while traveling (at home he only ever smoked a pipe) and he would ball them up into little nuggets and tell us he'd been prospecting for gold. I wanted to believe it, because imagining what my dad's actual life could be like without us was maybe even more absurd.

Dolly's dad was a sharecropper and then a farmer on his own land. He was illiterate. He didn't allow his kids to bring books home from school or the library because he knew he couldn't afford to replace them if they were ruined or lost. "The bible was the only book we had in the house each and every day," Dolly said. "I have such fond memories of sitting on Mama's lap, huddled near the warmth of the fire. The stories from the Old Testament were wild, vivid stories of good and bad that scared and excited me. It made me want to know more. It made me want to read more."

Sitting every Saturday with my father, learning Talmud, I didn't quite have the same experience, except in the end to think of the Old Testament God as a raging, vindictive, toxic asshole—the best example being when God tried to get Abraham to kill his son Isaac to prove his loyalty to him. Still, I know those stories as well as I know my own. And I know the fortune I've had in my life, to have had so many stories and books at home and school, so that when I flunked high school I still had the formative, good-school-district education to end up in community college and get straight As; so that when I almost quit my first real office job, at an ad agency, because my PTSD was so bad I was flashing back at work when I should have been typing up envelope labels, I somehow held on; so that when I kept anger as big as the ache in my ribs from where a bookcase's shelves once struck, knocked, thudded onto my body, I instead try to hold gratitude for my life and gratitude for the books. I believe books are spiritual things, regardless if they are old, new, or any testament.

In her dedication for *Dream More: Celebrate the Dreamer in You*, Dolly writes, "This book is for my daddy, who never learned to read and write, and paid a dear price for that, and inspired me to not let that happen to others." When she received the 2014 Library of Congress "Best Practices" literacy award for her Imagination Library program, upon donating the one hundred millionth book to children, Dolly said, "In the bible it says honor thy father and mother. I don't think that means just not disobey, but to bring honor to their name." These days, my dad sends me articles on Dolly—of which there are lately so many—including one from the Jewish newspaper the *Forward*, titled "The Secret Jewish History of Dolly Parton." It's all coming together.

In 2009, *American Songwriter* ranked the thirty best Bob Dylan songs, and in an extraordinary catalog, "Don't Think

Twice, It's All Right" ranked fourth with its "elements of a classic: the plaintive vocal, sweet and doleful finger-picking, cathartic, hillbilly harmonica, and a melody that builds momentum like a freight train." It was always kind of ripe for Dolly to cover. Dolly and Dylan came up at roughly the same time, and Dylan's songs would likely have been around on the radio when she was in high school and first in Nashville, although it's unlikely much Dolly Parton found its way to Dylan's ears for a while. Dylan won the Nobel Prize for literature for his songs—and it's true he's written my favorite song lyric of all time, "I wasn't born to lose you," from the song "I Want You"—but Dolly is only now being recognized for the immense songwriter she is. The opening lines of her song "Wildflowers"—"The hills were alive with wildflowers / and I was as wild, even wilder than they"—are a triumph of pacing and rhythm and internal rhyme. The poet, and the poetry teacher, in me thrills every time I hear them sung. After watching a documentary on Dolly recently, my former Cullman Center colleague Melinda texted me, "I thought about how Bob Dylan always has respect but [Dolly] is constantly re-earning it. I mean, Bob Dylan won the Nobel and didn't show up. Dolly always shows up, in heels."

Dolly's songwriting catalog makes up about a third of her estimated $350 million fortune, and retaining the rights to her own work has proven both lucrative and important to her personally. "I'm a songwriter first," Dolly said recently to Bobby Bones on his radio program. "I've always been grateful I'm a writer," she told the editor of *Time* magazine in 2020. On the radio program *Mountain Folk Vault*, she told David Kline, "Almost every day I come up with something. I'll either write a title, or a chorus, or a few verses." She goes on to share that she finally realizes what a good writer she is— she was sixty-eight when she gave this interview—and she talks about taking off two to three weeks a year just to write. She travels to a cabin or her lake house, takes off the nails and wig, and gets to work. She fasts for a few days. "I don't want to be bothered with nothing, or nobody," she says. That kind of sounds like what I hear writing residencies are like, besides the fasting (people seem to eat well at those things). Between work and kids, I have had to schedule writing on my to-do list or it doesn't get done.

I'm writing this on a Friday and when I'm finished I can cross it off my list for the day and move on to laundry and dyeing Ada's hair black. Sometimes, especially before books and book tours and teaching, it was easy to forget I was a writer unless I steadfastly reminded myself. I think people often forget Dolly is a songwriter because she's also outrageous, and folksy, and beautiful. I think people often forget Dolly is a songwriter because she interprets other people's songs so well. Not always, of course. Her cover of Johnny Cash's "I Walk the Line" is a boring disappointment, and her version of the 1980s one-off "Walking on Sunshine," performed first by Katrina and the Waves, is next to unlistenable. Her cover of the Beatles' "Help!," though, takes that song to emotional places it was unlikely to ever have gone without her. Her cover of Joni Mitchell's "Both Sides Now" has a depth that brings in warmer, but still similarly sad, colors. I love both versions. I'm glad Dolly went for all of it.

Dolly's version of "Don't Think Twice, It's All Right," shortened to "Don't Think Twice," appears on her 2014 album, *Blue Smoke*. Dolly didn't have to stretch wide to make this one her own. Jim Hoke plays harmonica on the album track, but in concert footage I've seen from the album's tour, Dolly is playing her own harmonica, subtly wiping the lipstick smudges from the corner of her mouth after she's done. Like with "Seven Bridges Road," the fiddle—here again played by Stuart Duncan—is doing a lot of ecstatic work, and it's what moves the meter from folk to Americana on Dolly's version. Dolly has sung Dylan before, most notably on "Blowin' in the Wind," which she recorded for her *Those Were the Days* album.

Unlike others whose songs she covered on that project—Yusuf/Cat Stevens, Kris Kristofferson, Tommy James—Dylan never got back to her about appearing on the album.

In a 2005 interview with Jon Stewart on *The Daily Show*, Dolly says, "To be fair to him [Bob Dylan], he wrote the song, and that's all he needed to do." But I agree with Jon Stewart in thinking that it was kind of douchey for Dylan not to get back to her personally. "I was gonna do a whole album of his," Dolly tells Stewart, "and I was gonna call it *Dolly Does Dylan*," at which point Stewart looks at the camera, points to Bob Dylan out there somewhere, and says, "Now you really blew it!" Coming twenty-eight years after Dolly's first *Tonight Show* appearance, this comment makes it clear that Dolly can still charm talk show hosts to the bone.

That same charm helps Dolly sing feeling into songs like no one else, which is what she does on her remake of "Don't Think Twice." "I'm from poor people," she told David Kline on his radio program. "Way back in the mountains, music was one of the ways people said what they felt and you just really felt what they were singing about." It's the singing on Dolly's "Don't Think Twice" that brings it from a good cover of a great song to a boundless cover. What Dolly can do that Dylan cannot, that Willie Nelson and Joan Baez and Elvis Presley can reach toward but cannot quite achieve, is sing deep complexity into every word. The way Dolly hits just the word "hear" in "Don't Think Twice," in the lyric "I can't hear you anymore," triggers my brain at its peak. It's immensely pleasurable, and addictive. Dolly's voice is clear, and firm, and also heartbroken. It's mournful and remorseful. It's celebratory, even. It's everything. Just that one note from that one voice; it has a hundred more stories to tell.

CHAPTER FOURTEEN

I Don't Believe You've Met My Baby

Always, Always, 1969, 2:11

IN 1996, WHEN I WAS hired at Bennett Book Advertising to answer phones for $27K a year, it seemed to me I'd be rolling in riches. In 2017, when I heard I'd been awarded a Cullman Fellowship from the New York Public Library and would receive $70K the coming academic year just to sit on my ass and write, it felt—and was, for sure—like a once-in-a-lifetime opportunity. When Dolly was summoned to entertainer Porter Wagoner's office in 1967, she thought she was being asked to provide him and his then sidekick, "Pretty Miss Norma Jean," with some songs; at the time, Dolly was better known in Nashville for her writing than her performing. She had watched Wagoner on TV back in Pigeon Forge as a teenager. His variety show was huge and syndicated, and he was about as big a celebrity as you could find there and then, always decked out in colorful, sparkly suits. Featuring country and gospel songs performed by regulars and special guests, as well as comedic interludes in between, *The Porter Wagoner Show*, filmed in Nashville, reached about one hundred markets at its peak. Norma Jean had decided to go back to Oklahoma to get married, Wagoner told Dolly in his office that day. He needed a new "girl singer." He offered Dolly $60K a year to be that. She "tried to act cool," she recounts, but she was stunned by the amount. "When I got to be the girl singer, that really just shot me right into the top," she recalled decades later in an interview with Canada's CBC. She wasn't just financially comfortable for the first time in her life; she was now in front of the public regularly, becoming a star.

At first she was booed by Wagoner's audiences; they missed Norma Jean. The show was such a bro fest that watching it now I get the same out-of-place feeling as any other time I have found myself the only woman in an all-male space. In her first appearance on the show, Dolly looks overwhelmed. Her style is demure and her body language is timid, but when she belts out "Dumb Blonde" and "Something Fishy," she's all confidence. It's hard to resist Dolly for long; soon enough she was beloved by audiences. Still, Wagoner was the boss and never let anyone forget it. He constantly put his arm around Dolly like he owned her. He called her "little" in many an intro ("pretty little," "little gal").

When Wagoner and Dolly won and accepted awards for their work together, he was the one who spoke at the podium. "You didn't do that as a woman and you didn't do that as a professional person, and it was his show, not mine," she told NPR decades later. "He'd had this show for years, he didn't need me to have his hit show. He wasn't expecting me to be all that I was either. When he hired me, as a singer, he was just hiring what he thought was a right pretty little girl. But I was a serious writer. He didn't know that. I was a serious entertainer, he didn't know that, he didn't know how many dreams I had."

Throughout the late 1960s, none of Dolly's solo efforts charted as high as those with Wagoner. Her albums were ignored at awards shows, while her collaborations with Wagoner would win the duo a 1968 CMA Award for Vocal Group of the Year, the same year that Dolly's phenomenal "Just

Because I'm a Woman" was only a moderate hit at number seventeen on the charts. In June of 1969, Dolly and Wagoner released their third album, *Always, Always*, which would go on to peak at number five. Two weeks later *Billboard* wrote, "In the tradition of the country duet, you would have to see far to find another as polished and professional as Porter Wagoner and Dolly Parton—and few of those would be as successful. Here's their hit 'Always, Always,' and the impactful 'Yours Love.' Also recommended: 'I Don't Believe You've Met My Baby.'"

I would recommend that last one too. It first came to my attention on 2001's *Little Sparrow*, Jim Mills's banjo and Stuart Duncan's fiddle as inspiriting as ever, Keith Little and Clare Lynch crystalline on harmony vocals. "I Don't Believe You've Met My Baby" is a short song, 2:11 on the original album, 3:02 on the bluegrass. The genders are reversed in Dolly's solo version, but either way, the song tells the story of an evening walk where the protagonist runs into a beloved who has an arm around another, who (phew!) turns out to be a sibling. It reminds me of the misunderstanding, then quick turnaround in fortune, in the Rays' 1957 doo-wop classic "Silhouettes," also a relationship crisis resolved in around three minutes, but not before the protagonist, in a jealous frenzy, threatens to beat down the door of the woman he thinks is cheating on him.

In *The Possession*, Annie Ernaux writes of her jealousy toward her former lover's current lover: "I caught glimpses of all the acts I would have been capable of if society hadn't constrained my impulses. . . . Suddenly I understood the leniency of the courts toward so-called crimes of passion." It's true I don't quite understand romantic jealousy, but I for sure understand grudge holding. "Forgiveness? Forgiveness is all there is," Dolly said in 2019, and my Old Testament–raised soul arches an eyebrow. "I see somebody I love in every face I see," Dolly told the audience at a concert in London, and I do admire that, but I also wonder how that plays out in the end.

Most of my life, I've given people a pass, men a pass, for the ways in which they've tried to control me, or my body, or have physically harmed it. I've let it go so I can move on, not get stalled in a place of anger or frustration or resentment, but I don't know if I'd call that forgiveness. Picking my battles maybe. Life in patriarchy maybe. But does some good old-fashioned Torah-style smiting of my enemies live somewhere in the back of my mind? I'm afraid it does. Harold Kushner writes, "Forgiveness is not a matter of exonerating people who have hurt you. They may not deserve exoneration. Forgiveness means cleansing your soul of the bitterness of 'what might have been,' 'what should have been,' and 'what didn't have to happen.' I've seen forgiveness defined as 'giving up all hope of having had a better past.'" Fortunately, as in "Silhouettes," the protagonist of "I Don't Believe You've Met My Baby" only has to deal with the residual heft of an almost-been.

"I Don't Believe You've Met My Baby" was written by country and rockabilly musician Autry Inman and recorded by the Louvin Brothers (their only chart-topper), becoming a number-one hit on *Billboard*'s country charts in 1956—a year before "Silhouettes" would hit number three on *Billboard*'s R&B and Hot 100 charts. Ira and Charlie Louvin were an odd couple, brothers separated by about a foot in height and yards in temperament, but their voices melded beautifully together. Though normally straight-country artists, in 1959 they released an album of country gospel tunes called *Satan Is Real* featuring an album cover I could try to describe fully here—the brothers dressed in white suits and black ties, expressions of a ta-da kind of amusement on their faces as they stand in front of an inferno that looks like a pile of burning rocks, with a crudely drawn but very tall Satan looming behind them—but words fail, even my training as a poet fails me now, and you should probably just google it. The cover was designed by Ira Louvin, the taller of the two brothers, the more volatile. Charlie broke up the group when he could no longer deal with his brother's hot-tempered alcoholism. Ira was a violent man. His wife, Faye, shot him six times after he tried to strangle her with a telephone cord; he somehow managed to live.

"Strangulation is a significant predictor for future lethal violence," warns the National Domestic Violence Hotline. "If your partner has strangled you in the past, your risk of being killed by them is 10 times higher." It leaves marks, or it doesn't. Years later you might forget the words for simple things. You might experience changes in mood or sleep habits. You might wonder why choking is such a thing in porn, but then you remember rape culture. Satan is real. You might have to leave this part of the story incomplete. Does it matter why he threw the bookcase on me? Is there even an answer to the why? I'll tell you about the bookcase. I think it was oak, some kind of solid, old hardwood, not particleboard like the shelves in my childhood bedroom. It stood over six feet tall and was crammed with books, books laid horizontal on top of the vertical books, more books perched on top of it, squeezing out the cactus I'd bought on a whim at the grocery store and that—out of my sight line—I'd mostly forgotten about. It felt like an important centerpiece to my bedroom, to me more important than the bed. It was a statement. We found it on the side of the road somewhere on California's Route 1, the part where it goes inland a bit. The man who would later throw it down on top of me hauled it into the bedroom. *Look at all he's done for me.*

"I didn't hit you on purpose," Gary Busey's abusive character tells Dolly Parton's country-singer character in the singularly terrible 1991 made-for-TV movie *Wild Texas Wind.* Later, having been battered and her face bruised, Dolly's character shoots her abuser and winds up in jail; no one believed her about the abuse because she never reported it. I had to fast-forward through much of that movie.

On the podcast *Dolly Parton's America*, writer Sarah Smarsh observes that Dolly's relationship with Wagoner "sounds very much like an abusive relationship." Indeed, it starts that way. When I first met the man who threw the bookcase on me, he would listen to my voice on his answering machine over and over until he could recite my messages back to me, with the same cadence. He gave me power; he said my voice was so sexy to him, he was almost afraid to call me back. When I fell on a hike in the Santa Monica Mountains and skinned my knee, he cleaned the cut so tenderly, you would think I would have otherwise turned into the dust of the landscape. "He had seen 'something magical' in me," Dolly remembers of her first meeting with Wagoner. "He makes casual jokes about hurting her," Sarah Smarsh observes. On several of their songs, he insults her. In "Fight and Scratch" he calls her "all mouth and no brains" and declares he could whip her with his hands tied behind his back. "I oughta box you in the jaw," Wagoner jokes on one show. "Oh you'd hit your mama before you'd hit me," Dolly drawls back, but this is the drawl of a woman who is no stranger to violence.

"Denver [Dolly's older brother] needed no special occasion to harass and needle me," Dolly recalls in her autobiography, published the year I moved to New York City. "He was always beating the tar out of me, and I couldn't do much about it because he was older and stronger than I was." Dolly, who we've seen is averse to declaring herself a feminist, calls herself "a sort of early Appalachian feminist guerilla" in her attempts to stop Denver's violence. Once, when she fought back against Denver and landed a hard right, he "gave me a beating twice as bad as the one that inspired my sneak attack. I took the blows, but I still had that sting in my right hand that told me I had struck at least one blow for womanhood."

Throughout interviews and her autobiography, Dolly talks about beatings and whippings from her dad and brothers in an offhand way, as if it were normal—as if it was just what happened to girls—or even as if she'd deserved it. Of course, I can't help but wonder how this violence—and the violence she witnessed all around her growing up—shaped her. Her relentless eye on her dreams, her relentless rainbows, her "urge to do," as therapist and rabbi Tirzah Firestone puts it. I recognize that way to survive.

Once pop culture began to prove Dolly lasting in a way Wagoner was not, Wagoner seemed to reframe what went down. To Ralph Emery, on Emery's radio show, Wagoner said, "The duets we did were great for both of us. At that particular time, I signed the checks, so at that time I was boss." "He was the boss, but he didn't have all the creativity but he had the control, let's put it that way," Dolly told Ralph Emery on a later show. "I didn't come to Nashville to be a girl singer in somebody's group," she said. When a woman starts to see her own worth, or to act on the worth she knows has been there all along, that's when things can get particularly dangerous. When I won an award for my writing in college, the man who threw the bookcase on me wouldn't attend the ceremony, but he did stand outside the building during the reception, seething as I put a bit of fruit on my plate at the buffet.

Platonic friendships suffer too under that weight of power and change. Given that Wagoner was a star and Dolly was young, seemingly accommodating, and beautiful, rumors always swirled that they were romantically involved. Sometimes they'd lean into the rumors a bit, but mostly they'd insist the relationship was never romantic. Still, the fallout from it was like that of any other intense relationship, sexual or not. By the end of their time together, Dolly recalls, "I couldn't think, I couldn't sleep, I couldn't eat . . . and he wasn't happy either." Dolly famously claims that she wrote her iconic song "I Will Always Love You" as a way to say goodbye to Wagoner when he wouldn't entertain the possibility of her leaving his show. Singing it on *The Porter Wagoner Show* on March 25,

1974, she is very genuinely emotional in the performance. Now, of course, the song tends to represent all kinds of loves and goodbyes—Elvis Presley apparently sang it to Lisa Marie on the courthouse steps after their divorce was finalized; it's played at funerals; it's the song Dolly has long used to close out her television and live shows as a message to her fans— but at the time it seems to have been a weapon in the fight against control and emotional abuse. Words have always been Dolly's best, and often most subtle, weapon, and she wields them expertly. When she sings that both parties know she's not what he needs, it's a kind of checkmate.

After she wrote "I Will Always Love You," but before she left the partnership, Dolly released an album of all-Wagoner cover songs, called *My Favorite Songwriter, Porter Wagoner*. I mean, I have some questions. She's clearly the more accomplished songwriter, a "natural born hook writer," singer Mac Davis has called her. So, was it a peace offering? A master stroke of passive-aggression? A way to cover things over and be done with it, a clean slate? *Cashbox*'s review glowed: "Dolly Parton—which is more beautiful, her voice or her looks? Whatever the answer, the combination of the two is simply devastating! Dolly radiates her inner soul through both her looks and her voice, and has shown time and time again that purity of feeling wins out over flashy singing tricks—her talent stands the test of time. . . . A superlative album."

At first after they parted, things were amicable, until Dolly's career started taking off and Wagoner sued her for a million dollars, claiming he was entitled to a percentage of her earnings. The National Network to End Domestic Violence reports that "financial abuse—along with emotional, physical, and sexual abuse—includes behaviors to intentionally manipulate, intimidate, and threaten the victim in order to entrap that person in the relationship. In some cases, financial abuse is present throughout the relationship and in other cases financial abuse becomes present when the survivor is attempting to leave or has left the relationship." In an interview from around the time of the lawsuit, Wagoner tells a morning show host, "To me, Dolly Parton is the kind of person I would never trust with anything of mine. I mean, her family, her own blood, she would turn her back on to help herself. I'm not that kind of person." He then goes on to claim that he's not bitter. Dolly, meanwhile, is always careful about how she talks about Wagoner. "I don't feel like we're enemies," she told Ralph Emery, and she describes their time together as "seven of the best and worst years of my life." She continues, "There's a lot to be said about Porter, both ways, but I'm sure there's a lot to be said about me."

It's hard to tell if she's choosing diplomacy, forgiveness, gratitude . . . or care toward her career. Of course, it's likely all of these at once, and more. We can't know everything, but what she goes on to do next might bring things into focus: she settles his lawsuit out of court and pays the million to Wagoner. In 1988 she has him on her talk show and he stands onstage with her as she closes the show with "I Will Always Love You." He sings backup on the title song of Dolly's 2005 *Those Were the Days* album. When he later spendthrifts the lawsuit money away and winds up in massive debt to the IRS, Dolly buys his entire back catalog—and then gives it right back to him so his kids can inherit it. When he dies, Dolly is one of the last people to visit him in hospice. She holds his hand. "We had a special bond and . . . I was happy that I was there," she remembers. Forgiveness is all there is. I love that idea. I don't know if I can believe it, but I love it.

When I listen to Dolly and Wagoner's duet version of "I Don't Believe You've Met My Baby," I hear lightness, delight in their own voices, adjacent and together. Dolly's style is still firmly in the more formal '60s than in the folkier '70s country. Think Lynn Anderson or Tammy Wynette or Patsy Cline. Less emotion gets in. It's not dissimilar to what the Louvin Brothers do in their version. It's as if the beautiful sounds are all that's necessary, and maybe they are, and certainly Dolly's and Wagoner's voices do allow one to forget anything but beauty.

Jerry Douglas, on his 1992 album, *Slide Rule*, released a version of the song with Alison Krauss doing vocals, and aside from Douglas's bluegrassy dobro interlude, it's mostly scrubbed clean of anything but early-'90s easy-listening vibes. Douglas appears on Dolly's 2001 version of the song, playing resophonic guitar, and this version hits all the right bluegrass notes (thanks quite a bit to Stuart Duncan's fiddle too), and Dolly's voice here is stripped down and then filled up with all the roller coaster of the song—infatuation, jealousy, worry, relief, joy. I think it's probably the best version I've heard, and yet on my playlist I keep the duet with Wagoner. I guess sometimes straight-up beauty is what I need. I guess sometimes I can forget backstory, or I guess sometimes I want to remember where and how Dolly started—the replacement, the "girl singer"—and how far she's come since then.

"It was his show, not mine," Dolly remembers, "'til I went out on my own, 'til I claimed and owned myself." Dolly understood the importance of owning one's power. All those years she bided her time, but it was there, ready to come out. On her drive home after she quit *The Porter Wagoner Show*, Dolly began to compose "Light of a Clear Blue Morning," a song about dawn and new beginnings. She just kept going. Sometimes, when I was still with the man who threw the bookcase on me, I'd lie awake at night and imagine scenarios for my wished-for life in New York. Then I started to plan. Like Dolly has said: "If you're gonna make a dream come true, you gotta work it. You can't just sit around. That's a wish. That's not a dream."

CHAPTER FIFTEEN

Little Sparrow

Little Sparrow, 2001, 4:14

LIKE "SILVER DAGGER," "COME ALL Ye Fair and Tender Ladies" is an Appalachian folk song of unknown origin. Some version of it dates back to Scotland in the eighteenth century and likely even before that. It keeps the same melody as another American folk song of unknown origin, "The Wayfaring Stranger," sung most famously in versions by Johnny Cash and Emmylou Harris and in the 2019 movie *1917*. "Come All Ye Fair and Tender Ladies" was also recorded by Emmylou Harris, as well as the Carter Family, Pete Seeger, the Kingston Trio, Joan Baez, Odetta, Bob Dylan, Peter, Paul and Mary, and many more. It was featured in the 2010 movie *Winter's Bone*, in which it was sung by Marideth Sisco, and a 2016 episode of the teen mystery drama *Pretty Little Liars*. It does that thing—as one can see from the lineup of those who've covered it—that smudges the line between country and folk and Americana. The title of the song changes from recording to recording; before the 1960s, it was more often known as "Tiny Sparrow" or "Little Sparrow," which is where Dolly's version brings it back to on her 2001 album of the same name, the anticipated follow-up to *The Grass Is Blue*, which was the most well-reviewed album of her career thus far.

Like its predecessor, *Little Sparrow* features bluegrass sounds, but it also adds mountain music and a bit of traditional Irish folk as well. The album concept came to Dolly in a few days when she was in Los Angeles, far from the milieu of the album, which is a setup I truly understand, since I've been writing about Los Angeles since the moment I left it in the 1990s. Steve Buckingham, Dolly's longtime producer, was nervous. Coming off the high of *The Grass Is Blue*, he felt "there was nowhere to go but down." Yet Dolly is Dolly, and Dolly was confident. "I believe this album has more depth, breadth, and soul than all of the other albums I have ever done." I agree; it is my favorite Dolly album, one I've played start to finish more than any other, and the one that got me through some of the lowest lows of my twenties.

In 1996, having just completed my coursework for an MFA in poetry at Columbia University, I went looking for a salaried job. I hadn't had too many straight jobs at that point; I'd been an office assistant at a phone-sex line, an artist's model, a clerk at a porn video store. Later, I worked at a frozen yogurt counter and a health food store. I work-studied. I temped. When I applied to be the receptionist at Bennett Book Advertising, an ad agency that represented only book publishers, I didn't have much I could respectably put on my résumé. Lucky for me, the owner of the company had once been an aspiring poet, and it was my good luck that she liked poets and hired me after two interviews and offered me, as I mentioned in the last chapter, buckets more money than I'd ever had before. I spent the first few months there cold-quitting Zoloft because I didn't yet have health insurance. I was dizzy around the clock. I'm not actually sure how I managed to stay upright all those weeks. I kept to myself, mostly. I was shy. I showed up on my second day of work wearing five-inch, royal blue, vinyl heels because that's what I had in my closet. I knew I didn't quite fit in.

The idea of leaving behind my old self, my traumatized

self, my sultry self, my self who thinks she's telling a funny story from her youth until she realizes everyone is looking at her with alarm . . . the idea of trading in that person for a calm, sexless, small-talking other was actually very appealing (although ultimately impossible). Sometimes I think about how when I was at the New York Public Library, I brought a bag of McDonald's to the lunch table one day and the head administrator of the Cullman Center actually gasped. I'll admit I kind of brought those fries to the communal lunch table because I knew it would get a reaction, an eye roll maybe, a side-eye, but a gasp was something truly special. The McDonald's bag was my vinyl shoes at the ad office, but back then I wanted so badly to fit in as an upstanding adult that I learned to keep my wild to myself, began reading *People*, and bought more sensible (but still high-heeled) shoes.

Bennett Book Advertising was on the fourth floor of what was then known as the Lincoln Building—across from Grand Central Station—and over the nine years that I was there, I memorized a section of Lincoln's second inaugural address from the plaque outside the building's entrance during my very frequent smoke breaks. "With malice toward none; with charity for all; with firmness in the right, as God gives us to see the right, let us strive on . . ." In the lobby was a small statue of the sixteenth president. It was before 9/11, so there was little security in the building.

Almost a year in—I'd just been promoted to media buyer, but I wasn't to start until we found my replacement—the front door to the office opened and the man who threw the bookcase on me was standing right there in a brown hoodie. He'd bulked up a bit, gotten a lip piercing, but looked otherwise the same. I knew in my body before I knew in my head that I needed to walk out of the office, to get him out of there ASAP before anyone else noticed. The rest of the staff had convened for a birthday party in the conference room, so thankfully no one saw me slip out into the hallway. I was wearing a khaki linen dress from the Gap and my hair was pulled back into a low ponytail.

I don't know how he found me—this was way before the internet made that easy—but he stood there awkwardly, like he'd been neutered by the dull efficiency of the office building environment. He told me he'd find me the next day too, and the next, and we could have lunch together. Then he just kind of stared at me for a while, mumbled something about missing me, and headed back to the elevator. I headed to the birthday party shaking from the inside out. I held on to the doorframe like it was a rescuer's hand because I thought I might faint. The next day he found me again, near the public library steps, as I mentioned to you earlier, remember? He mansplained to me about pigeons? It was weeks later that he came to my apartment building miles away from work. I lived by myself in a rent-controlled studio on 102nd Street. I hid behind the mailboxes in the building's small lobby until he gave up waiting for me. Then, fortunately, and somewhat bafflingly, he went away for a while.

"Come all ye fair and tender ladies," goes the Joan Baez version, "Be careful how you court young men." Pete Seeger sings, "Come all ye fair and tender ladies / Take warning how you court your men." Dolly's "Little Sparrow" takes a different approach. "All ye maidens heed my warning / Never trust the hearts of men." There's a world of difference between "Be careful how you court young men" and "Never trust the hearts of men."

On the *Little Sparrow* album, the title song has full bluegrass backing—including mandolin, banjo, fiddle—and background vocals sung by Alison Krauss and Dan Tyminski (the same voices that backed "The Grass Is Blue") as well as Dolly herself singing harmonies. Dolly has said that she didn't tour for *Little Sparrow* or *The Grass Is Blue* in some part because her backing band were such hot commodities in the bluegrass world that they had many other touring commitments already. In concerts since those years, Dolly usually sings "Little Sparrow" slower, and a cappella. When she sang it at the Ryman in 2015, she combined it with her song "If I Had Wings," from her *Blue Smoke* album. The songs have a similar melody, both springing from "Come All Ye Fair and Tender Ladies," a song, Dolly notes, that her mother used to sing to her when she was small.

"If I Had Wings," though, has a different message than "Little Sparrow," one not about the evils that men do but about making your own path, about creating your own, more secure future. The AA book *Twelve Steps and Twelve Traditions* says, "An honest regret for harms done, a genuine gratitude for blessings received, and a willingness to try for better things tomorrow will be the permanent assets we shall seek." I haven't been a part of that for decades, but it makes sense to me. When Dolly sings "Little Sparrow" (and sometimes "If I Had Wings"), as she did at the Forest Hills Stadium when I saw her on the Pure & Simple Tour in 2016, her voice is so clear, so strong, so damn fraught, that her insistence on moving through each line slowly almost makes it medicine, makes it holy, and maybe makes it a little unpleasant.

I prefer the album version of "Little Sparrow," and love it maybe more than any other Dolly song. I love all the classic bluegrass instruments melding into this transcendent, next-level thing. I played the *Little Sparrow* album incessantly when it came out in 2001. By that year, I'd been promoted to media director, in charge of all the ad plans at the agency and finding myself frequently having to lunch with businessy advertising sales reps from print media who were trying to win my favor and our clients' dollars. It was fairly absurd since I'm introverted and I don't like chitchat and I don't watch enough television to chitchat even if I did like it, but it paid well and I can't not give my all to things—because I'm certain that people will easily see under the surface to what I really am, which is a flunky, a druggie, a small body on a shag rug—and so I did rather well at it. I was only twenty-six.

After I'd had the job for a while, Paul became my media buyer—Paul whom I've mentioned in earlier chapters and who is a drummer and who answers my questions about music. It was a relief to work with him, someone for whom the office was not a career but a job, someone whose passions were in creating. Our chemistry was undeniable, the way Timothy and Lucie's always was. I had—and still have—many friends from that office whom I cherish deeply, but the culture there was rough for me, and I began to forget who I was, going to luncheons where the promoting of books was celebrated and yet not the writing of them. I, by that point, was barely writing at all, although, in fairness, my mental health and all those years of untreated trauma were probably just as much at fault as having to coo over Celine Dion's new baby photos in *People* (her son was born two days after *Little Sparrow* came out in January 2001) in some bustling Midtown bistro. Paul was still well entrenched in the music world and I got to see him play sometimes and it was a reminder that I, too, could continue to be an artist.

Once, coming back from an ad-rep lunch not far from the office, Paul and I ran into the man who threw the bookcase on me. "Hey, Lynn," my ex said, and it was like he'd again grabbed me so hard in anger that I was afraid to move—even though on the sidewalk he stood a bit away from us. I hadn't seen him in a couple of years—I had sort of assumed he'd left the city and gone back to California, or wherever—and yet there he was, frozen while the rest of New York City bustled around us. Paul could tell I was scared but of course didn't know why exactly. I could sense Paul's body moving to put a kind of protection between me and my ex, but I still felt pinned in place, and the square of concrete where I stood, the corner, I believe, of Forty-First and Madison, was in such sharp relief, like if someone had to commemorate the spot where my earlier life met the new life I was trying to build. What might bloom and wilt next was anyone's guess. I have little memory of what words were spoken there on the corner. Paul asked him if we had a problem here, and maybe that was enough to scare him away, because he eventually walked away and I asked Paul to walk around with me for a bit because I was again shaking from well inside, like a deep, cellular rumbling, an adrenaline-spiked mix of scared and embarrassed, and I couldn't go back to the office yet. Once we did, I tried to play it down but my body was in full panic mode for the rest of the day and everything out of my mouth about work-related matters came from a completely dissociated place. I overheard Paul telling our coworker about the run-in. "He was a scary dude," he said. I physically could not get myself to talk about it with anyone at the office or even Timothy at home studying for his PhD. I vomited in the fourth-floor bathroom. That was the second to last time I ever saw my ex.

Paul and I sat within feet of each other in the office and he had to listen to me play the *Little Sparrow* album that day and every day. I played other things too—Joni Mitchell's *Blue*, Prince's *Dirty Mind*, Fleetwood Mac's *Rumours*, Mozart's Symphony no. 25 in G Minor—but *Little Sparrow* most of all. I'd come in every morning with a large coffee with soy milk, always early because lateness makes me panicky, and the office would be quiet and I'd press play on *Little Sparrow* and I'd listen to the title song over and over again so that even after Paul got there he'd still have to hear that song a few times before I continued on to the rest of the album.

Dozens of musicians play on *Little Sparrow*, five on "Little Sparrow," but it is Stuart Duncan's two fiddle notes at 2:58 and 2:59 that were (and are still) like a drug to me, soothing me and exciting me at the same time. They arrive at the crest of the song that has built to just that moment, and then

they fall so quickly after the singer realizes she's not a little sparrow, she's just the human victim of a real capital-*A*
Asshole. Despite my relentless and clearly obsessive playing
of the song, Paul never complained, and that still means the
world to me. He was the first person I emailed with a music
question when I began writing this book. "What is the name
for the thing singers do with their voice where it gets gravelly temporarily," I said, "kind of as emphasis, but when it
isn't normally gravelly (like, not Tom Waits). I'm writing this
morning about the Dolly Parton song 'Why'd You Come in
Here Lookin' Like That' and at 2:01 she says the word 'why'd'
like that and it seems important. But I can't seem to get to
it on google and thought you might know." He wrote back
with earnest enthusiasm—and through our conversation I
eventually landed on "throat rattle"—and we later went out
to lunch and talked Dolly, office gossip, life stuff. I told him
that my outed love for *Little Sparrow* was the first time, probably, I felt fully in the world as a Dolly Parton obsessive. She
had seemed to be a goofy caricature in the '80s, and then, at
the turn of the century—in her fifties, wearing a black turtleneck on the *Little Sparrow* album cover, a wistful look in her
eyes—she seemed an anomaly in the detached, focus-grouped
age of Britney, NSYNC, and Creed.

And then 9/11 happened. That impossibly mild, sunny
day of sudden horror. I walked several miles home from Forty-Second Street in open-toed slingback heels that ruined my
feet for months. "One of the lesser tragedies of the day," I
could joke to my friends years later, when we were able to
joke again. That morning, early for work as usual, I'd gotten
off the train just after the first World Trade Center tower had
been hit by terrorists who commandeered commercial air-
liners to use as missiles, and I could see the smoke rising all
the way downtown. Walking home hours later, I ran into a
woman who had overslept and missed a meeting in one of
the towers. She was turning around in circles, unable to stop

saying the sentence "I missed a meeting in one of the towers," and I, who does not touch strangers, took her hand to still her from turning. By the time I reached my block on 106th Street in Upper Manhattan (I was by then sharing a different studio apartment with Timothy), both towers were gone and any familiar world was kind of gone too.

I stocked up on cigarettes at our local bodega and Timothy and I smoked our way through all of them while unable to turn off the televised images coming from several miles south. I went back to work on 9/13 amid a gruesome slew of missing-person posters. I began having flashbacks again and I began drinking more than I ever had before or have since in my adult life. I said yes to the dreadful cocktail parties Paul and I were always being invited to. Everyone declared irony dead, as if human nature was done detaching, but the shock had in fact called me back. If I had before then lost myself in that gray, humming ad agency office, 9/11 was the slow call I needed to find myself again, though it would be several years before I could break free of office life, make a go of freelancing, write a poem again. I found a therapist who specialized in PTSD. I listened and listened to that spell of Stuart Duncan's fiddle and I thought, maybe art and beauty do get us through. Recently, my younger daughter, Stella, described "Little Sparrow" as having "an epic fiddle solo" and she is not wrong.

The 2:58 and 2:59 fiddle notes (and all fiddle notes) are missing from Dolly's live versions, and while the slow a cappella versions are haunting, her voice emboldened with firm sorrow and the clearly more personally meaningful way she's chosen to perform—"a cappella" translates to "in chapel"—I miss those two notes terribly in the live versions. In an article on Jimmy Webb's song "Wichita Lineman," Dylan Jones writes, "Some neuroscientists believe that our brains go through two stages when we listen to a piece of music that we like: the caudate nucleus in the brain anticipates the build-up of our favorite part of the song as we listen, while the nucleus accumbens is triggered by the peak, thus causing the release of endorphins." I feel this when Bob Dylan sings, "I wasn't born to lose you," in "I Want You." I feel this when Prince shrieks that there's no particular sign he's more compatible with on "Kiss." And I for sure feel it for those two notes in "Little Sparrow," listened to over and over in an industrial gray cubicle ("cubes," we called them) and listened to now in my sunny living room.

In Dolly's 2019 TV series *Heartstrings*, one of the episodes is based on the song "If I Had Wings." As in all the episodes, Dolly introduces the short film. "Dreams don't just come true by themselves," she tells us from the Showstreet Palace Theater in Dollywood, dressed in white with silver accents and holding a guitar that matches her outfit. "You've got to put wings on them and see where they take you." Birds and their wings are a recurring theme for Dolly, and sparrows especially hold her. "I must just relate to the idea of soaring," she's said. "I like things with wings. If I ain't writing about angels, I'm writing about eagles and butterflies. I just love things that move and get on out of here."

In his 2009 song "Boots and Sand," Yusuf (Cat Stevens) refers to Dolly as the "Bird of Nashville." Cas Walker, who gave Dolly her start on his radio show, *Farm and Home Hour*, when she was ten in 1956, called her the "Smoky Mountain Nightingale." In the unfortunately named "Crippled Bird," on her 1995 *Something Special* album, Dolly sings of a bird too sad to leave the ground. On her 1969 album *In the Good Old Days (When Times Were Bad)*, she sings to the "Little Bird" to please take her with it and leave her in a happier place. "Light of a Clear Blue Morning," off her 1977 *New Harvest . . . First Gathering* album, finds Dolly musing that she's like an eagle in her quest for flight. On the 1991 album *Eagle When She Flies*, in the title song—written for but not used in *Steel Magnolias*—Dolly ponders that while a woman can be a sparrow in her weaker moments, she's got some soaring eagle in her too.

Dolly loves eagles. She started a sanctuary for eagles at Dollywood, where they take in injured eagles and care for them until they can be returned to the wild, and she remains the biggest benefactor to the American Eagle Foundation. Between 1992 and 2018, the foundation released 166 young bald eagles and 11 golden eagles into the Great Smoky Mountains foothills. In a 2001 interview for the British talk show *Open House with Gloria Hunniford*, Dolly speaks about constructing the Dollywood Splash Country water park in the Smokies but trying to work around all the trees. Eagles build their nests in trees, so they kept as many as they could. "I relate to eagles," Dolly says. "Eagles are the strong ones, flying the hardest, the fastest, the highest."

But here's where the complexity of Dolly comes into play. For all the grand showiness of the eagle, it's the sparrow with whom she has most often identified over the years—that tiny, fragile bird with no bright plumage or particularly spectacular song, which nonetheless, and unlike the singer of "Little Sparrow," isn't mired in broken dreams. I think that's what the *Little Sparrow* album did: it unmired me, it returned me to myself. And I think that's what those two notes at 2:58 and 2:59 did for me: they gave me courage to return to myself, and to soar, despite my fragility. Dolly canceled all her public events the week after 9/11. "I'm a very patriotic person," she told the *Knoxville News Sentinel*, "but I also know that when things are at their worst I need to be at my best. . . . Everybody deals with this differently. I deal with it internally. . . . It's very strange and deep places where I am going." Those strange and deep places that keep (and keep) going toward the light, those are the sparrow's wings.

CHAPTER SIXTEEN

9 to 5

9 to 5 and Odd Jobs, 1980, 2:46

IN THE FALL OF 2017, I landed back in an office for my Cullman Center Fellowship, where in the morning I'd climb the library steps past the lions, near where the man who threw the bookcase on me once grabbed my arm while explaining pigeons. The offices inside were beautiful and well appointed, with wooden chairs and golden nameplates on each office door. The lighting, though, was the same gruesome fluorescent that glowed from the ceilings at my ad agency job, so eventually I asked a custodial worker from the library to remove the bulbs and I bought myself desk lamps with warmer light. It had been over a decade since a daily commute, the morning hellos in the kitchen area, the small talk. I'd forgotten how coworkers become a kind of important that proximity allows.

The lunch table at the Cullman Center was more fraught than you might imagine, and maybe more fraught for me than others, maybe only in my head, with a circle full of scholars and writers and their overpriced salads and sushi, or the food they'd made in their Instant Pots (all the rage that year) the night before. There was a daily crossword puzzle, which was fun to solve all together. There were a lot of people with better pedigrees explaining things to me, a lot of people with lesser or the same pedigrees assuming my ignorance, perhaps because I came there to work on the book after the one so explicit that Amazon actually filed it (for a while, until an outcry) under "Adult Content." Sexual violence and its aftermath are as much chronic to the human condition as poetry-stalwart subjects like love and death and moody landscapes. It took my publisher and me weeks to get the behemoth store to reshelve my poetry under just plain poetry.

Among the Cullman crowd, I felt not infrequently like frenzied monster drummer Animal from the Muppets, while most of the rest of the women and men were more like those two old guys in suits who sit in the balcony. That entire academic year, we were in the thick of the post–Harvey Weinstein #MeToo moment, and every day was a trigger. I had to get up more than once from the lunch table while the women and men sitting next to me decried the fate of certain literary men who were being called out for toxic behavior. One of those literary men had once grabbed my ass at a bar and told me I was giving him a vibe; now he was newly fired from his very prestigious editorial job, and many in the office were shocked or even felt sorry for him.

One morning I was sitting in my office when someone called from the New School, investigating a male professor. They'd heard, through the grapevine, that I'd been sexually assaulted by one of their creative writing faculty back in the 1990s. I said, "My goodness, it only took you twenty-two years to call!" I told the voice on the other end of the phone about being at a dive bar and this professor sitting next to me and then grabbing my vulva under the table. But he hadn't been *my* professor, just *a* professor, so it was unclear if telling my story mattered. I texted my office neighbor and friend Melinda, asking her to come into my office so I could bemoan the nonjustice justice I finally got.

One of the oft-repeated stories that my grandmother Evelyn told when she was in her dementia was how her boss at her first job out of high school asked for a kiss before he would give her a paycheck. She was like, uh, no way. My aunt Barbara filled me in on more: "She also talked about being sent on a job interview by an employment agency and the boss somehow suggested, in action, word, or just general creepiness, that he would expect more than bookkeeping. She went back to the agency and told them why she wouldn't take the job and they said, 'You're not the first one.'" Which is to say, this is a tale as old as women in the workforce. At the Emmys in fall of 2017, Dolly reunited with her *9 to 5* costars Jane Fonda and Lily Tomlin to present the award for Outstanding Supporting Actor in a Miniseries or Movie. This was just before #MeToo broke, and much of the country was still in shock from the first months of the Trump presidency. No strangers to politics, Fonda and Tomlin used the language from their beloved movie to describe the current president. "In that movie, we refused to be controlled by a sexist, ego-tistical, lying, hypocritical bigot," Fonda says, and then Tomlin continues, "And in 2017, we still refuse to be controlled by a sexist, egotistical, lying, hypocritical bigot."

This put the usually neutral Dolly in a tough spot, so she broke the tension with a boob joke and then added, "I'm just here to have a good time tonight." Her right-wing fans were . . . furious. On her Facebook page she got comments like "I'm saddened that you would stand with these idiots and bash our POTUS" and "You just threw so many of your fans under the bus" and "You stood up there while those two ran their mouths. You are just as bad." In a moment like the Trump era, it's hard to stay neutral, but, damn, she tries. Dolly is in the eye of the beholder, as ever. "I wanted to say let's pray for him, the president," she told podcaster Jad Abumrad, with a weariness in her voice. "I wanted to say that, but I thought, no, keep your damn mouth shut, that won't work either, so . . . tit joke." When all else fails, she knows she can objectify herself. "Do I get mad when men whistle at me?" Dolly asked on a 1987 episode of her talk show. "Lord no, I tip 'em!"

When asked by the *Guardian* in 2019 if she's ever experienced workplace sexual harassment, Dolly replied, "I have, but I have always been able to maneuver because I come from a family of six brothers, so I understand men and I've known more good men than bad men." Dolly hedging her bets again. Throw it back to a 1981 interview with Lawrence Grobel in *Playgirl* and she says, "I was never harassed where I didn't have control of it, really. . . . I guess all women are harassed to a degree, but a lot of people bring it on themselves and then want something to bitch about." Oh, but it gets worse! After Grobel asks her if she understands the depth of the problem, she replies, "I know that it puts you in a hard spot. You can't just walk off, you can't just say to hell with it, because you've got to consider everything. But I also know that there are a lot of business women who are sexually aggressive towards people too. I'm seein' both sides."

In a handful of interviews I've watched recently, when asked if she's a feminist, Dolly replies, "I'm feminine!" She places deep emphasis on that last syllable, lest we mishear. In her interview with *Bust* magazine in 2014, she says, "I consider myself a female. I think of myself as somebody who's just as smart as any man I know. I don't think anybody should ever be judged by whether they're male or female, black, white, blue, or green. I think people should be allowed to be themselves and to show the gifts they have, and be able to be acknowledged for that and to be paid accordingly. You know, I love men, but I love women too and I'm proud to be a woman. I just really try to encourage women to be all that they can be and I try to encourage men to let us be that."

It's worth noting here that Dolly's backing musicians tend to be almost exclusively male. Often by her own decisions or design, Dolly has been the only woman in the room. Whether this is a result of an industry that discourages women from taking up instruments that have long been the provenance of men, or whether it's a failure of those in charge to hire women, this is a conversation that happens similarly in literature as well. When I worked with the feminist literary organization VIDA, we were constantly told that female-identifying writers didn't appear in top journals as often because they didn't submit as frequently as men. To which I would reply, wearily, to whatever well-meaning stranger or outright troll on Twitter, that it's possible to seek out women writers if they don't merely appear at your doorstep. Just as it is possible to seek out women musicians. That said, "I just really try to encourage women to be all that they can be and I try to encourage men to let us be that" is a profoundly feminist thought process.

Dolly's first movie, *9 to 5*, sparked possibly the first mainstream, widespread conversation around sexual harassment and inequality in the workplace. It tells the story of three women who enact revenge on their boss for his chauvinist-pig ways. Dolly has said that her character's efforts to deal with an aggressively sexually harassing and otherwise sexist boss, played by Dabney Coleman, reminded her of the attitude she had to take with Porter Wagoner. The movie is fun and funny, holds up decades later—I just rewatched it and felt a joyful "Fuck yeah!" throughout—and it was a huge hit the year it came out, 1980, second only to the *Star Wars* sequel *The Empire Strikes Back*. The movie is also serious as hell. In her book *She Come By It Natural: Dolly Parton and the Women Who Lived Her Songs*, Sarah Smarsh writes, "I recently attended a screening of *9 to 5* in an Austin, Texas, theater full of women shouting at the screen. . . . Women in the audience cheered when the lead characters fantasize about murder and laugh when they stuff what they think is their boss's dead body into the trunk of a car. I realized it is one of the darkest movies ever made about the female experience." I think this reading of darkness stems from the absurdity. While few of us have kidnapped our bosses, so many women have gone through experiences like those of the women in the movie;

the movie-enhanced antics don't seem all that far-fetched. Things really are that dire.

Interviewed on NPR about his *Dolly Parton's America* podcast, and discussing Dolly's political neutrality and relative silence on #MeToo (as also criticized by her sister Stella, you might recall), Abumrad says, "Dolly is an intensely political being. And yet she has been so skilled at drawing power from that political movement but never being defined by it. Like, she'll—anytime she's asked to take a political stand, she declines. She won't let people use that song for their campaign songs. . . . And, you know, Elizabeth Warren is a huge supporter of organized labor. So you would think she should be able to use the song ["9 to 5," for her political campaign]. . . . But Dolly says no. So I was really interested in her ability to be intensely political in her actions but never in her speech." In a moment like ours, between the relentless and polarizing crises and the churning hot takes on social media, staying neutral as a public figure might finally prove impossible; stay quiet and trouble finds you.

In 2021, for a Super Bowl ad for the website developer Squarespace, Dolly rerecorded her hit song as "5 to 9," an homage to the "side gig," with new lyrics about working toward your passion project after you're done with your regular workday. This did not go over well with people who have seen job stability ripped away by the gig economy and who feel like they are working more and more for less and less. The general reaction was frustration with Dolly for selling out. "Whose side was she on?" wondered Kim Kelly, writing for NBC News. "It's not 'fun' or 'empowering' to juggle multiple jobs; it's an indictment of a system in which people aren't paid fairly and workers are squeezed down to the last drop of energy." I had mixed feelings, chief of which was that the rewrite just seemed dashed off, devoid of Dolly's usual care, and that's what seemed like selling out to me. On the other hand, if the idea is to not be exploited by your boss, why wouldn't you want to work for yourself? Of course, that's not usually how it pans out for people in the gig economy. I've been freelancing since I left my ad agency job, and most every day is a question mark as to the next gig. I wonder how well Dolly understands what working life is like now, or how much she still thinks of a side hustle as how she once performed it, taking her songs around Nashville while working random day jobs.

"She is careful not to appear to choose sides in our culture wars," Brooke Jarvis reminds us in the *New York Times*, "and that circumspection creates a space for us to project, ardently, our own politics onto her choices. Perhaps she was surprised to learn how many people found an ad about hustling after your dream job—the real story of her own hardscrabble-to-superstardom life—to be political." Despite Dolly's seeming resistance to overt politics, it is not an overstatement to say that the original "9 to 5" is one of the most lasting and successful political-protest songs in US history. Dolly asserts that she said yes to making the movie—her first—with the promise that she could write the title song. The movie and song titles both take their names from the 9to5 organization. Founded in 1973, the year I was born, 9to5 aims to put working women's issues—such as fair pay, equal treatment, and family leave—at the forefront of the national agenda.

Karen Nussbaum, who founded the 9to5 organization, says of the namesake tune, "I think the song is brilliant. It starts with pride: 'Pour myself a cup of ambition.' It goes to grievances: 'Barely getting by.' It then goes to class conflict . . . And then it ends with collective power . . . So in the space of this wildly popular song with a great beat, Dolly Parton just puts it all together by herself." In the movie, when the women kidnap their boss and take over running the company in his absence, they institute reforms such as equal pay for equal work, job sharing and part-time options, childcare, and flexible schedules. These are distinctly feminist demands—and the film spurred many such actions at the time—and are part of the conversation we are still having (which is likely why Warren wanted to use the song for her campaign).

Leigh H. Edwards writes of the movie, "While the slapstick fantasy sequences and violence are not offered as viable solutions, the workplace reforms are. Again, it is notable that the film prompted actual workplace reforms along those lines." Flexible work schedules slowly grew in acceptability throughout the '80s and '90s to where they are increasingly a norm in twenty-first-century office culture. This is crucial to keeping parents, most especially mothers, competitive in the workforce. Assistance with childcare options is another issue addressed in the film, and it has become more and more common as a workplace benefit. Recently, Dollywood announced subsidized childcare for the park's employees. Still, we have a long way to go.

Karen Nussbaum knew Jane Fonda from their activism around the Vietnam War. At the time the film was made, a huge number of people across the country flat-out despised "Hanoi Jane" as a traitor. Bringing Dolly into the fold was an inspired move. Dolly told Phil Donahue on his talk show in the 1980s that Fonda brought her in because "she thought I would get the South." That is probably true. Of course, decades later, Dolly claims in an interview that it was not strategic in any way. So, who knows. Years later, the two actresses continue to be extremely admiring of each other. Interviewed for a 2020 A&E *Biography* special on Dolly, Fonda says, tearing up, "It's like through her songs she opens her arms wide and embraces such a broad swath of people that don't always feel seen, and it's why people love her. And it's why when we've been in public with her, her fans will drive for hours to be where she is. I've been with a lot of big movie stars. I've never seen the devotion that her fans have for her in anyone else. It's quite extraordinary."

For her part, Dolly has always said she supports Fonda's frequent political actions. On the television show *The View*, Dolly recently said, "She's always been out protesting something all of her life. I wouldn't get out in the streets but I kinda contribute in my own way. I'm an entertainer and I do it a little different. Everyone's got their own way of making their points. I try to do it my own way and they do it theirs." To this end, another of Dolly's longtime friends, Yusuf Islam (formerly Cat Stevens), whose songs "Peace Train" and "Where Do the Children Play?" have been covered by Dolly, has received her resounding support, despite views that would likely enrage both her liberal and her conservative fan bases. Dolly even sang on, and appears in the video for, Islam's "Boots and Sand," which is based on an incident where he was denied entry into the United States because of US security officials' "concerns of ties he may have to potential terrorist-related activities." He had been traveling to the United States at the time to record with Dolly. No big deal was made of her appearance in the song and video, but her mere act of doing it was a political act. Her own way, as she would say.

Fonda and Dolly experienced very different upbringings—daughter of an iconic movie star versus daughter of an illiterate father of twelve—and yet neither has worked much nine to five. Dolly only ever held one traditional nine-to-five job, briefly answering phones at an outdoor sign company when she first arrived in Nashville. Fonda, of course, was well familiar with movie sets, while *9 to 5* was Dolly's first movie; Dolly memorized the entire script because she thought that was required! Although she'd go on to make several more films—for the most part, like in *9 to 5*, playing working-class women striving for more—she has often said she finds the process kind of dull, much less exciting than being on the road and onstage. "You open a door one week, and three weeks later you walk through it," she's joked. Dolly likes to keep moving. "It would be hard for me to work at a sit-down job, so to speak," she told Phil Donahue, "and I admire the people that can do it."

Dolly wrote the song "9 to 5" during her considerable downtime between scenes on set and, rather famously, used her acrylic nails as percussion to emulate the sound of a typewriter. In the recorded song, we can hear a slight ding, as if the typist got to the end of the line—a type of ding that my generation might be the last to really remember. "I was writing it on set," Dolly recalled to Lawrence Grobel, "just clicking the rhythm with my nails. I had my guitar there. I figured it out in my head. It all came at once. The rhythm is like the sound of typewriters, when the little bell rings and the telephone's ringing." The nails are still in the song; on the liner notes Dolly is credited as "vocals, nails." The backing vocals are sung by the women who worked on the *9 to 5* movie in less glamorous tasks than acting, and Dolly has said she felt it was important to honor these working women in this way. Music scholar Lydia Hamessley writes of the group sing that "the power of communal singing to raise consciousness and inspire action should not be underestimated, particularly when the song's lyrics dramatize injustice."

That pulsing rhythm of "9 to 5"—iconically insistent and instantly recognizable, the way the opening licks of "Jolene" are—feels exactly like a rushed and rote morning, and Dolly's supple voice feels defiant on top of it. It is one of Dolly's most successful and enduring songs, and it's also one of her best. The opening lines are so recognizable that there are coffee mugs with "cup of ambition" printed on them (Timothy recently bought me one). "Yay!" Dolly has said of the moment she hit on those words, where originally she'd just written the lyrics "cup of coffee." The song reached number one on the country, pop, and adult contemporary charts, won Grammys for Best Country Vocal Performance and Best Country Song, and was nominated for an Academy Award (it lost to "Fame").

The same year Dolly's "9 to 5" went to number one, so did another song called "9 to 5." In "9 to 5 (Morning Train)," Sheena Easton sings about a beloved who works all day to make money to play with the singer on the weekends. With lyrics that find the singer waiting at home all day for her man to return from work, it's like the counterpoint to Dolly's song about working-class women's drive and resilience. The woman in Easton's song doesn't seem to work, and her main job appears to be waiting on a man. It's a catchy song though. I used to sing it to Timothy back when he worked ten to six at a poetry nonprofit while I worked nine to five at the ad agency. "He works from ten to six and then . . . ," I would sing as he walked in the door. Of course, now with both of us sort of working all the time, as the twenty-first century often dictates—"working, working, working," as Dolly's recent revamp sings—it all seems rather cute. In 2019, cultural critic Maris Kreizman tweeted, "Every time I hear the song '9 to 5' I think 'YES!' and then I think 'Damn, those are some pretty sensible hours.'" Someone replied, "I'm still a little bitter about this song—listening to it growing up gave me very unrealistic work expectations."

Still, the song's statement and sheer exuberance have made it last—so much so that in 2009, *9 to 5: The Musical* opened on Broadway. I felt baffled that I had no memory of this happening, much less of trying to get tickets, which is of course something I would do. Then I realized it opened about a month before I gave birth to Stella and I was on bed rest with a pregnancy that was very difficult. The musical closed while Stella was still an infant; it was not a success. Watching it now via someone's crappy YouTube recording, I can see why. It's missing some of the heart of the movie and the album; it seems like it was written at working people rather than sprung from them. It is exciting to hear the title song, of course (with lyrics added to get the audience up to speed on what's about to go down, as opening numbers in musicals often do), and Megan Hilty, playing Dolly's character Doralee, sings an enjoyable version of "Backwoods Barbie," from Dolly's 2008 album of the same title. But I guess what the musical needed was more of the icon herself.

Released about a month before the movie, Dolly's album *9 to 5 and Odd Jobs*, which went to number one on the country chart and stayed for eleven weeks, was perhaps more political than the movie (and definitely the musical). It hit number eleven on the pop chart, likely thanks to its notched-up sound—the heavier drums, electric bass and guitar, and keyboards. The album itself (which is separate from the mostly instrumental *9 to 5* soundtrack album) is about work and people who work. It includes a cover of "The House of the Rising Sun," and even though the version is less than stellar, to include sex work on an album of work is notable. Dolly also covers the Woody Guthrie tune "Deportee (Plane Wreck at Los Gatos)," about undocumented farmworkers; and a song written by her sister Freida called "Sing for the Common Man," with lines that remind us that working people "build what others plan." For a woman whom historian Jessica Wilkerson, in a *Longreads* article, criticized for not acknowledging Dollywood as a site of physical and emotional labor, this is pretty clearly a progressive, labor-minded set of songs.

"In my songwriting," Dolly recently wrote in her book *Songteller*, "I've never shied away from what's going on in the world. I don't voice issues publicly, myself. But in my songs, I can write about whatever I feel." Dolly's songs are her actions. And her actions are her actions too: Dolly's philanthropy is vast and ongoing, and we only know a bit of it because she doesn't make a show of her generosity. She's given money to combat high dropout rates among high schoolers in her home county; she's donated money to open a women's healthcare center in the area; she gave $1 million to the Vanderbilt Children's Hospital. She is intent on spreading the wealth.

Of "9 to 5," cultural historian Joanna Scutts once tweeted,

"Listened to that song over the weekend and it is a pretty good primer on basic Marxist theory." Marxist theory and the nature of work dominated many lunchtime discussions at the very cushy Cullman Center at the New York Public Library. One of the other fellows was writing a book on the world's dirty work (think slaughterhouses and such), another on Mikhail Baryshnikov and his move from the bleak Soviet world to the United States. Once the #MeToo movement broke wide open, people wanted to talk about workplace harassment every day. My cohort wanted to discuss stories of rape; many of the cohort wanted to discount them. One of the fellows recounted a family member's rape and how she didn't go to the police, she just dealt with it herself. I knew that was a kind of "suck it up" anecdote, a kind of "stop metooing all over the place and just deal like my genera-tion did." I stood up and said something rushed that I don't remember exactly, but I know that it made mention in passing of the fact that I've been raped, so that my other colleagues at the table could remember that rape isn't abstract, it happens to people they know, people sitting in front of them. I went back to my office, sat on the floor, and stared at my laptop.

About ten minutes later, one of the center's administra-tors—an upbeat, awkward, ambitious man around my age—appeared in my office doorway. Earlier in the year, when I'd been sick for weeks with whooping cough, he'd made home-made chicken soup and carted a heavy amount of it to me. A thoughtful person, now he said he wanted to apologize. "What for?" I asked. It turns out he felt he should have said something to me after I mentioned being raped and he wor-ried he'd handled it wrong. He stepped into my office a bit and I quickly stood up because his looming made me feel anxious. He was blocking my exit. He wanted to know if I was okay. Did I need anything? It was a long time ago, I said. I'm okay, I said. You handled it fine, I said, leaning against my desk to try to get as far from him as I could. I felt trapped by a man demanding I make him feel better about my having been raped. And that's what I did, I made him feel okay about it. All this progress, right? And it's still about the dude's needs and feelings. How woefully inept we can be. But how else could we be in this culture? I wasn't upset with him. Just tired.

After he finally left, I texted Melinda to come into my office, where I sat back down and tried to unpack what had just happened. It was May of 2018, the end of the fellowship year. My grandmother was dead, the #MeToo movement wasn't the force we'd hoped it might be, I had to go down to Ada's middle school again about the dress code. Melinda handed me a tissue when my eyes welled up. I felt as grateful for true friendship as I felt really, really done with patriarchy and office life. Dolly's iconic *Here You Come Again* album-cover poster hanging above me, I felt fed up with Dolly hemming and hawing about being feminine and not feminist. I wondered if progress is actually even possible.

A couple of weeks ago, I turned on a video interview that the editor in chief of *Time* recorded with Dolly as part of the magazine's 2020 series on the most influential people of 2019. When Dolly was asked again if she considers herself a feminist, I visibly winced, and Stella, sitting next to me on the couch, asked me why. I said, "Oh, she always gives the same answer." But then, at age seventy-four . . . she didn't. "I suppose I am a feminist if I believe that women should be able to do anything they want to," she said. She went on to say that she's not the kind of feminist who carries signs, but "I'm not ashamed of that title. There's just a group of people that fit into that category more than me." Listening to "9 to 5," and any number of the badass feminist songs she's written, I'm not sure if there is.

CHAPTER SEVENTEEN

Two Doors Down

Here You Come Again, 1977, 3:02

ONE NIGHT WHILE I WAS on some kind of liquid-protein diet made from bone marrow, or something equally appetizing, I was with a group of friends at a Howard Johnson's and some of them were having fried clams. I'll never forget sitting there with all of that glorious fried fat filling my nostrils and feeling completely left out. I went home and wrote one of my biggest hits, "Two Doors Down." I also went off my diet and had some fried clams.

DOLLY PARTON

I've been waiting chapters and chapters to share this story with you. It's one of my favorite Dolly stories. "Two Doors Down" is one of my favorite Dolly songs. Hooky, upbeat, and sex positive, it tells the story of a woman who, sulking in her apartment, hears a party down the hall and eventually gets over her sadness and joins in the fun—but I like it even more knowing its secret history. When I first told Timothy, from Rhode Island, this story, he was like, "Fried clams!? How does a person from Tennessee wind up loving fried clams? Did she get them at Howard Johnson's?" Well, she did. She even wrote the first draft of the "Two Doors Down" lyrics on HoJo stationery! Apparently Howard Johnson's clam strips are a thing. I grew up kosher and can't digest seafood, so I had no idea.

In a 1979 article in *Cosmopolitan*, the reporter follows Dolly to her husband's surprise party at a Howard Johnson's, where the fried clams (strips!) are being passed around in a plastic cowboy hat. "You've never had fried clams until you've et 'em from a hat," Dolly is quoted as saying, the accent spelled out as I've spelled it out. Dolly, this time, did not eat the fried clams; she was on some kind of diet where she could only have an "itty-bitty steak." Dolly, for much of her life, was always on a diet.

"I tried every diet in the book. I tried some that weren't in the book. I tried eating the book. It tasted better than most of the diets," Dolly jokes. In a Christmas episode of her 1980s talk show, Dolly sings a song about Mrs. Claus going on a diet. It drives me bananas, Dolly's obsession with weight. She's accomplished more than most of us can dream of, she's generous and talented, she's funny. And she walks around hating her body, constantly fighting against its nature.

"You can't be surprised by this," Timothy—who is always surprised at what I'm surprised by—says to me. She's had so much plastic surgery, he points out. Obviously she is at odds with her body. I really shouldn't be surprised, given how weight and diets and body image consume us all. My maternal grandmother, Shirley, had a lifelong struggle with disordered eating and died at about seventy pounds; she used to scold me for not eating enough as a child and then warn me I'd get fat when I actually did eat enough. My paternal grandmother, Evy, whom you met earlier, didn't have a healthy relationship with food either; it wasn't until her dementia worsened at around ninety that she felt more at ease with enjoying food, because she couldn't remember to think of it as a danger, she couldn't remember to care, "she couldn't remember she wasn't *supposed* to eat," said my aunt Barbara.

In a 2018 essay, poet Samantha Zighelboim writes, "The language of self-denial is the first I ever learned . . . the foundations of my identity. I come from a long line of dieters and disordered eaters, a lineage of people who spent their lives trying to halve their body size. They practiced rituals and followed rules religiously, as if it might lead to the salvation of being thin." I see so much of my grandmothers, and of Dolly, in this. My grandfather, Evy's husband, Lester, traumatized by the Great Depression, was always trying to get us to eat everything on our plates and then to take more, to enjoy the abundance! If the girls and women weren't eating, he assumed we must be on a diet. Dolly's father, well familiar with poverty and still mired in its aftereffects even years after his daughter could easily support him, felt similarly concerned that she wasn't eating enough. For most people who grow up hungry, hunger isn't something they would ever choose, much less celebrate.

In clips of Dolly on various talk shows in the late 1980s to early 1990s, Donahue, Oprah, Letterman, everyone is obsessed with Dolly's having lost weight. We hear how much she weighed and weighs, we hear her say over and over that she was a "hog" and that she still is, she just controls it better. Everyone fawns all over her for her tiny eighteen-inch waist and how good she looks. There was a kind of universal jubilation going on that she had gotten her body to behave. I started to wonder if I should be exposing my kids to all the body hate and fat-shaming to which I was relentlessly listening in the living room. My aunt Barbara wrote of her mother (my paternal grandmother, Evy) that in her last years she "forgot she was the enemy, her body was the enemy, desire and appetite were the enemy."

I can for sure say that Dolly sees appetite as the enemy in regard to food, but desire, though—sexual desire—is something Dolly welcomed from the beginning. Her autobiography, *Dolly: My Life and Other Unfinished Business*, is just about the horniest memoir I've ever read. There's a whole bit about her sexual and musical awakening in the abandoned church near her house that I mentioned earlier. "If you're gonna screw, you're gonna screw," she says about sexual tension with friends. She recommends keeping a journal to record your sexual fantasies. "Nobody else is going to see this," she says, "and sex is a much bigger part of what we want than most of us will admit."

In 1996, I wrote a sexy, sad little poem called "If I Should Say I Have Hope," which became the title poem to my first book, which took me fifteen years to complete because of work, and mental health, and kids. It's a love poem.

I scratched
your street into my arm and there
was only blood and no way
to find you

I was writing about a stuffed penguin who went missing after the man who threw the bookcase on me stormed his way into my apartment on 112th Street. My roommate and her (male) friend were there, so my ex left, because he was always also a coward, but he took my cherished item with him, and there went my heart. People sometimes ask for this poem in particular at readings because, I think, of how frequently love goes missing. I thrill that art can do this! It can make a small trauma a universal one, it can change the narrative or the backdrop. I wrote a love poem to a worn carnival prize, as Dolly wrote a lust song for HoJo's fried clams, and most of the time when these words have been consumed, they've been consumed with a more universal feeling in mind.

Dolly wasn't the first to record "Two Doors Down." Country singer and former *Hee Haw* show regular Zella Lehr recorded and released the song in 1977, and it charted at number seven. She sings it with a disco twinge to her voice but it is otherwise pure country. Meanwhile, Dolly was trying to cross over to pop at that moment; she was in *Playboy*, she had just released "Here You Come Again," her poppiest single to date. "Two Doors Down" would become one of her rare pop hits that she herself composed, the song musically decountrified quite a bit when she recorded it. It's got the country inflection and the gospel background singers, but it's also got an electric bass line, a wah-wah pedal guitar, and a synthesizer. Although the first pressings of the *Here You Come Again* album feature "Two Doors Down" in the same version that Zella Lehr recorded, every other pressing includes the song you probably know. Dolly does sing the original version in a December 1977 performance on *The Tonight Show*, but in appearances after that, the first, sad-sack verse, about lying alone in bed, gets excised and the song just cuts right to the speaker drying her tears and heading down the hall. That *keeping going* is a very Dolly move. (It's a very Melnick family move too.)

Reviewing the *Here You Come Again* album, *Cashbox* writes, "With this album, Dolly takes a giant step into the pop mainstream with a spicy repertoire that features only an occasional banjo or pedal steel lick. But even those who have seen her perform will have to be at least mildly surprised at how naturally proficient Dolly is at jumping into a completely new bag." It's her countrypolitan thing. "The song kicks off with twin fuzz-edge electric guitars," writes Nancy Cardwell in *The Words and Music of Dolly Parton*, "that seem to be having a party with a saxophone—the kind of groove *Saturday Night Live*'s Blues Brothers would have enjoyed." It is delightfully of its era. The first pressing of *Here You Come Again* became a collector's item, and the edition with Dolly's familiar "Two Doors Down" went on to enter the pop charts and peak there at number nineteen, while still becoming a number-one hit on country radio.

That same year, jazz flautist Joe Thomas released a supremely groovy funk/soul version of the song, which I'm bopping to as I write this. It gets at the joy and possibility and connection maybe even better than Dolly's versions do. In 2003, singer-songwriter and rapper Meshell Ndegeocello recorded a version for the *Just Because I'm a Woman* album of Dolly covers. It's also groovy, but more quietly so. Her tone is slower, more thoughtful, and also firmer. It's very insistent and quite sexy. For the 2018 made-for-Netflix movie *Dumplin'*, Dolly rerecorded the song with R&B singer Macy Gray and the alternative rock band Dorothy in the background. It's a funky version with lots of horns, preceded by Dolly singing the original, cut, first verse in a quiet a cappella.

Dumplin' is based on the 2015 young adult novel of the same name by Julie Murphy, and it tells the story of a young woman who, despite not fitting the pageant-world standard of beauty (she is, by pageant and magazine standards, overweight) and despite being at odds with her former-beauty-queen mother, enters a beauty contest with the help of some drag queens she meets along the way. Dolly is the young woman's idol, and Dolly's music appears throughout. A number of the drag queens from the film got together to make a dance-mix video of "Jolene" to promote the movie. Dolly is often quoted as saying some version of "If I hadn't been a woman, I'd be a drag queen for sure." "Drag queen, drag queen, drag queen, drag queeeen," she sometimes sings to the "Jolene" music.

In a 2016 interview with Larry King, immediately following Dolly's usual deflection on her political leanings, King asks, "Didn't you recently, though, throw your support to the LGBT community?" Dolly doesn't hem, haw, or hesitate when she says, firmly, "We are who we are and we should be allowed to be who we are." King follows up by asking how her more faith-based fans feel about her point of view, and Dolly, who in the same interview wouldn't say whom she was voting for (this was the election that resulted in Donald Trump), shoots back with, "If you are the fine Christian that you think you are, why are you judging people? . . . If you're gay, you're gay, if you're straight, you're straight, and you should be allowed to be how you are, and who you are." Although she is almost relentlessly neutral and frustratingly both sides of the fence on almost all hot-button issues, queer rights, it seems, is the hill Dolly will die on. Dolly recorded a track called "Travelin' Thru" for the 2005 movie *Transamerica*—a flawed but progressive-at-the-time film starring cis woman Felicity Huffman as a trans woman on a cross-country road trip—and the song was nominated for an Academy Award, losing to "It's Hard Out Here for a Pimp" from *Hustle & Flow*. In 2005, and in the country music world, that was a deeply bold thing to do; trans rights (and the denying of these) as a movement didn't enter the larger public consciousness until almost a decade later.

Dolly's "Two Doors Down" episode of *Heartstrings*— intended, like the rest of the series, to be family fare, releasing on Netflix around the holidays—is about conservative southern parents learning to accept their son's queerness. Introducing the episode, Dolly explains, "Being gone all that time from my home and family, well, that was tough. But what I found out on the road was a whole new family with bands and crews that were made up of all kinds of people who were different colors, gay, lesbian, transgender, and all different faiths. But it didn't matter as long as we all loved each other and got along. And we did, and we still do. Because what it all comes down to is love is love, in road families and in real families." Dolly appears in the story itself (as herself) at the end to sing "Two Doors Down" and promote acceptance.

I might argue that Dolly's done more for queer acceptance among certain communities than almost anyone else. In the documentary *Hollywood to Dollywood*, a young gay man, traveling with his brother and his partner to meet their hero, says, "I think she would embrace that one part of us in our lives that our mom doesn't embrace." Brilliant queer comedian

Tig Notaro, who does a hilarious bit called "Three Friends Down" in which "Two Doors Down" features prominently (I implore you to google it), says, "My love for Dolly Parton comes from being a human being on this planet. If you don't love Dolly Parton then you are not a real human being." In 2020 the "Two Doors Down" episode of *Heartstrings* won a GLAAD Media Award and I just felt so fucking proud of Dolly as she came onscreen to accept it.

When she was in middle school, Ada liked to brag to her friends about how sex-positive I am, and it's true that it doesn't surprise me at all that adolescents want sex and have sex. When she texted me in sixth grade that she thinks she's bisexual, I texted back, "OK, great! Let's talk about it later, I'm in a meeting." Later that year, I sat at a McDonald's with Ada and her friends and answered their questions about the whole spectrum of gender and sexuality. Dolly, filmed talking to a bunch of teens in what appears to be the very late 1970s or early 1980s, when asked about sex by one of the girls, replies, "Sex to me is not a dirty subject. . . . Everybody's curious! I don't care what prude is watching this show. They're either no good at sex or they're so good they're ashamed for anyone to know how bad they like it." The teens all giggle. Dolly giggles. Recently, Dolly told *People*, "I'm a very passionate person in everything that I do, and I think passion has great sex appeal. I think people are drawn to that because it's a magic. It's an energy. And I've always been a great lover because I'm passionate. I just feel my sensuality, my sexuality, my passion, and I don't have to apologize for any of that."

During my stay in rehab in 1988, a young assistant counselor—she was a student at UCLA—sat in the teen patient lounge with me and got me to talk about my experiences with sex. The lounge in the Glen Recovery Center was decorated with kitten posters and uplifting slogans about sobriety. Listening to me speak about sex, the counselor realized I'd never really enjoyed it. She was a small woman with short, blond hair and white plastic squares dangling from her ears. She brought me to the bathroom connected to the shared therapy office, gently took my pants off, and proceeded to teach me better ways of masturbating than I'd figured out on my own the few times I'd actually tried. I'd been so disconnected from my body and its feelings. I didn't enjoy food or even, most days, the sunlight on my skin. I'd pushed my body away from myself—dissociation is criminal that way—and so, although I suspected it was inappropriate, given that I was fourteen and the counselor's hands should have been nowhere near my vulva, I felt grateful for the connection. I came a lot, and I started to learn how to claim pleasure for myself for a change.

When I was in community college, I tried to get a job at a phone-sex line but I sucked quite badly at acting. Instead, the owner there let me write scripts for the prerecorded option, and a few months in, he also let me talk to the men who didn't want to call for a conversation about sex, just this and that, just companionship. I had regulars, middle-aged married-with-kids men or awkward loners who liked to hear about the classes I was taking at school, my opinions on the Gulf War (I kept these mild—"I wish the world could just be at peace," was the kind of shit I said—diplomatic like Dolly), my questions about crossword clues from the daily *LA Times* that I just couldn't figure out. They thought I was wonderful, virtuous, perfect. We'd chat for a while and then inevitably they would get quiet and I would have to fill the silence with chitchat while listening to their staggered breathing. After they came, they hated me. I'd betrayed them by being the kind of woman who could get them off. Their voices would get clipped or they'd just hang up. I'd always feel a little humiliated then.

In 2018, I gave a reading at the Poetry Project in the East Village, and afterward a friend told me that when I perform my poems I make everyone in the room want to fuck me. I don't do it on purpose, I said, ashamed and confused by the shame. Later that winter, I was invited to a dinner party at Lewis B. Cullman's house—he was in his late nineties and had funded the New York Public Library fellowship I was enjoying—and one of the other fellows, a frequent writer for top-tier magazines, found out I'd be seated next to her male partner, a noted academic, and suggested I show a lot of cleavage because he likes cleavage. I'd been spending the academic year trying to hide my sex appeal but I obliged her, and him, and was quite a hit.

While a lot of Dolly's early songs have that midcentury habit of punishing a woman for giving in to her desire, Dolly also has a lot of songs where desire is celebrated and defended. It is her refusal to let her capital be dimmed, no matter how she plays up her sexuality and her body, that makes Dolly—despite whatever hang-ups she has about her body—a third-wave feminist icon, even though she would likely never claim that particular label. Her songs are feminist as fuck. In 1968's "Just Because I'm a Woman"—written after her husband, Carl, expressed alarm that she'd had sex partners before him—she sings against that old double standard where slutty men are heroes and slutty women are trash, and she encourages men to imagine the shame they place on women just for having the same desires they themselves have.

Scholar Leigh H. Edwards observes "two notable recurring critiques" of gender depictions in Dolly's songs from the '60s and '70s: "She decries double standards for women, and she questions mountain girl idealizations while reframing the hillbilly tramp positively." Singer Brandi Carlile recently said of Dolly, "She's as pure as the driven snow and dirty all day long and I love everything about her." At the Newport Folk Festival in 2019, joining Carlile's feminist country supergroup, the Highwomen, onstage, Dolly gives the background to "Just Because I'm a Woman." She recounts what she replied when her husband asked her why she was finally telling him she'd had prior sexual partners: "Because you asked me, dumbass!" The glee with which she tells this anecdote and the joy with which she presents female sexual autonomy are palpable, as if she's been waiting years to live in a climate where such is possible.

In Dolly's 1974 song "You're the One That Taught Me How to Swing," the protagonist's boyfriend encourages her to be more wild and then complains when she's more wild. The B side to "Two Doors Down" (actually another A side) was "It's All Wrong, but It's All Right"—basically a "U up?" in a classic-country-song package. In Dolly's 1978 song "Baby I'm Burnin'," the singer is horny as hell for her lover, joyously giving in to her sexual urges. Dolly is ready to claim sexual pleasure. You might recall "Steady as the Rain," that sad-banger breakup song where the singer misses the sex as much as anything else. For a woman who sometimes seems so at odds with the fact of her body, Dolly sure does enjoy enjoying it.

I can relate to this. While my body has been the site of so much violence and pain, sex allows me to let that go. My head leaves my body. Poet Emily Dickinson once wrote in a letter, "If I feel physically as if the top of my head were taken off, I know that is poetry." Good music does that too. Those two notes at 2:58 and 2:59 in "Little Sparrow" do that.

Living in a body that is a site of unease or trauma is exhausting every day. Looking for ways to set it free can be harmful—you can wind up in rehab or in the wrong love affair—but it can also be a lifeline. I have been to the depths, I have done destructive things to my body, punished it, used it in reckless ways, but I've learned that sinking into the pleasures of the senses is a resistance against a rape culture that would prefer to keep us as commodity; having fun despite rape culture is an act of rebellion. What do clam strips have to do with phone sex? It's all connected, somehow, to the body and what it wants and what we grant it and what we withhold. Sex is fun! Fried clams are fun! "Two Doors Down"? Extremely fun.

CHAPTER EIGHTEEN

Put a Little Love in Your Heart

Slow Dancing with the Moon, 1993, 2:27

"IF MADONNA IS THE WICKED Witch of pop music," novelist and sometime music critic Stacey D'Erasmo wrote in *Rolling Stone* in July of 1993, "Dolly Parton is surely Glenda the Good Witch. Buoyant and glitteringly white, Parton radiates good-heartedness and the conviction that what you really want is not sex but love—a love she, more than any other woman, is equipped to give you." These sentences are vexing not just because they take powerful, astute, iconic women and reduce them to convenient stereotypes—Madonna and the Madonna complex, as it were—but also because they couldn't be more wrong about Dolly and sex. Not only did she write and record songs like "You're the One That Taught Me How to Swing" and "It's All Wrong, but It's All Right," but the very album D'Erasmo is reviewing, *Slow Dancing with the Moon*, contains a song called "I'll Make Your Bed," which is sung from the point of view of a woman who's like, look, I can't bake or sew, but you're really not gonna care about that once we get between the sheets, I promise. D'Erasmo seems to be writing the review from a more second-wave feminist standpoint than third wave, which was starting to come into its own right about when *Slow Dancing with the Moon* appeared.

Hugely influenced by Anita Hill's 1991 testimony, during US Senate hearings to confirm Supreme Court justice Clarence Thomas, about Thomas's sexual harassment of her (a devastating precursor to the Kavanaugh confirmation hearings decades later, in September 2018), the third wave of feminism also reclaimed the notion of being a girl and being feminine as a strength. We didn't want to be one of the guys, we wanted to be girls, and we knew girls could be badass. Constance Grady explained in *Vox* that "third-wavers liked being girls. They embraced the word; they wanted to make it empowering, even threatening—hence *grrrl*. And as it developed, that trend would continue: The third wave would go on to embrace all kinds of ideas and language and aesthetics that the second wave had worked to reject: makeup and high heels," among others. D'Erasmo, meanwhile, has a hard time imagining that someone can be soft and traditionally feminine but also sharp and horny. She can't resist objectifying a woman who dares to objectify herself, referring to Dolly's "much bandied about" boobs as "holding up the weight of the world."

It was this wrong interpretation of who and what Dolly is that made me shy of proclaiming my love for her in the '80s and early '90s. How does the trauma of misogyny play out among generations? Sometimes we unwittingly train it on ourselves. Still, D'Erasmo is not wrong when she talks about the music on *Slow Dancing with the Moon* being mediocre. She's also not wrong when she describes Dolly's rendition of "Put a Little Love in Your Heart" as "mighty." Yes. One hundred percent. Dolly's rendition of that song is exceedingly mighty.

"Put a Little Love in Your Heart," composed by Jackie DeShannon, Randy Myers, and Jimmy Holiday, was first a hit in 1969 for DeShannon. That same year, it also appeared on albums by country singer Susan Raye, rock and roll band the Dave Clark Five, singer Andy Williams, and soul musician David Ruffin, formerly of the Temptations. It has since been recorded and performed at concerts by more disparate artists than seems reasonable: Annie Lennox and Al Green, Mahalia Jackson, Leonard Nimoy, Ella Fitzgerald, Anne Murray, Sonny & Cher, and Circle Jerks. I watched a live performance of a 1979 UNICEF telethon in which ABBA, John Denver, Donna Summer, the Bee Gees, Olivia Newton-John, Andy Gibb, Rod Stewart, Rita Coolidge, and Earth, Wind & Fire perform the song for the big finale. It was Jimmy Holiday's biggest hit as a songwriter. His daughter Harmony Holiday is a poet. She was Lucie's and Timothy's student at Columbia some years ago. On a *Poetry* magazine podcast in 2018, she talked about her poem "What Jimmy Taught Me" and the domestic violence she witnessed from her father growing up. "It's not that big a skeleton in the closet to have had domestic turmoil," she says. "It doesn't define your whole narrative. For a while it does and then you get to a point where it doesn't."

I first heard the song "Put a Little Love in Your Heart" in 1989 via the famous Jackie DeShannon version, which was used in the movie *Drugstore Cowboy*, a movie I saw many times in the movie theater in the mall where Jason worked. I loved the song's groovy hippie vibe; I didn't shave my armpits then (still don't, actually) and I wore billowy flower-print dresses. I was happy and in love. Jason wrote poems about me and played songs for me and touched me in ways that felt great, that could bring me back to my body. Jackie DeShannon was in a relationship with Jimmy Page for a while in the 1960s, and he wrote the Led Zeppelin song "Tangerine" for her. If you had told me as a teenager that I'd grow up to have a super acclaimed poetry book dedicated to me—Timothy's *The Cloud Corporation*—I would have felt a satisfied success. Being a muse seemed like the best thing one could hope for sometimes, and I didn't really know how to dream further than that in my younger years. I'd been objectified for so long, I wanted to put that to artistic use.

The man who threw the bookcase on me was not an artist and I was not a muse and when we fucked it was almost always with my face held down into a pillow. By the time we were living together, I was writing as if my life depended on it, because it did. If a body was all I had when I was younger, words would save me then. I was still in that moment Harmony Holiday speaks of, where domestic turmoil defines your whole narrative. I wore drab, oversized outfits that the man who threw the bookcase on me felt comfortable with me leaving the house in. In college, my male poetry professor asked me to stop writing poems about abuse; I was getting repetitive. Some of the other women in my class gathered around me after the workshop to share their outrage over his comment, an outrage that none of us would dare to have expressed in class. I was the best poet in that class and I knew it, even as I accepted that my voice maybe didn't mix with the kind of work we were encouraged to write. My professor called me a "militant feminist" because I wrote poems about hands around throats, about choking and unconsciousness. I was baffled at the time—also still between the second and third waves in my feminism and not sure how to define my belief system—but now I would say, sure, if believing in the rights and dignity of women and femmes is militant, then I'll enlist.

Another of Jimmy Holiday's daughters is a musician. On her 2017 album, *Free2B*, all of the compositions are hers, except for her silky cover of her dad's most famous song. In a video of the raw studio recording of the song, Debby Holiday says, "This song has been done so many times, so well, by so many people. Oddly enough, one of my favorite versions is Dolly Parton's, 'cause, I mean, she's such a phenomenal songwriter, that if she chose to sing it . . ." Of course, I get a thrill out of any nod to Dolly's songwriting, and especially after reading the D'Erasmo review and pretty much anything else about *Slow Dancing with the Moon*. The album went certified gold in April of 1993 and certified platinum that October, and reached number four on the *Billboard* country chart—despite having no big hit singles to come out of it—but by Dolly's standards it didn't do very well, and it's as frustrating an album to listen to for a Dolly fan as 1987's *Rainbow*, because it's so devoid of her personality, her resilience, and vulnerability.

Certainly, though, the message of "Put a Little Love in Your Heart" is a Dolly-esque one, and as with Led Zeppelin's "Stairway to Heaven" and Collective Soul's "Shine," she takes a well-known rock or pop hit and gives it a religious flare. The backing vocals by Nashville's Christ Church Choir on Dolly's "Put a Little Love in Your Heart" ooze ecstatic faith. Where a lot of critics seem to read Dolly's version of the song as "Let's all get along!" and an upbeat nod to the Golden Rule (do unto others), I hear more defiance than anything else, an acknowledgment that, sure, we could wallow, but why? I love Dolly's "Put a Little Love in Your Heart" for its absolute enthusiasm and its refusal to wallow; it demands you do the work of uplifting yourself. In this way it reminds me of "Two Doors Down," among other Dolly songs.

In her 1979 *Cosmopolitan* interview with Dolly, the year after "Two Doors Down" was released, journalist Laura Cunningham notes that Dolly's voice goes flat when she talks about her childhood. Peering into the re-created two-room cabin at Dollywood, I couldn't help but marvel that this small space once contained what would become all that is Dolly. "I am a happy person," she tells Cunningham. "I am a positive person. The only thing I hate is negativity. That's the one thing I won't put up with . . . negativity." Cunningham also notes a bit of anger here.

In the video for 2008's "Better Get to Livin'," Dolly basically lectures a room full of drably dressed, middle-aged, white women to get their shit together and stop whining about the small stuff. The mega-best-selling 1997 book *Don't Sweat the*

Small Stuff . . . and It's All Small Stuff, by Richard Carlson, was one of the first books I worked on at my job at Bennett Book Advertising, when I was having frequent flashbacks and panic attacks and trying to hide it. In 2012, the year my first poetry book came out, a book largely about trauma, there was a trend of articles about the positive effects of trauma. I read as many as I could find. I couldn't understand why I was still suffering. People with PTSD, these articles seemed to suggest, come out the other side having grown emotionally and spiritually. First, unfortunately, is the trauma, but then is the growth! "Toxic positivity," some have called this pressure to get to living.

In an article in *Psychology Today* in 2016, Anthony Mancini notes that while there are some positive results from adversity, "just because someone believes that they are better off does not mean that they are. In fact, it may very well mean that they are not." In a 2015 news story for KERA public radio, Courtney Collins states, "Some experts consider childhood poverty a form of trauma. Counselors and directors with a Dallas nonprofit say growing up poor can impact everything from impulse control to anxiety." The trauma responses from poverty—being on high alert, catastrophizing (i.e., sweating the small stuff), having a pounding heart rate—are like the trauma responses I've experienced from violence. There is a kind of desperation in the need for positivity.

"When something doesn't go my way or I stumble," Dolly writes in her book *Dream More,* "I pick myself up, make sure I brush the disappointment off my rhinestones, and try not to harden my heart over it. Instead, I set about trying to strengthen the muscles around it."

In a 2020 interview in the *Advocate* about her uncle Donald, Mary Trump talks about her grandfather's toxic positivity: "He believed in the power of positive thinking to such a degree that it wasn't positive at all. Because if you are required to think that everything was great all the time, that there was no room for mistakes, and that there was no suffering or pain or any emotion . . . it was severely damaging." Toxic positivity is everywhere on social media, lots of talk of positive vibes and seeing the glass half full. Lots of better get to living. Lots of drying useless tears. Jews have their own particular phrase for it: "It could always be worse."

In 2018, Ada suffering, Lucie dead, my grandmother dead, my whooping cough–affected lungs gasping for air, my PTSD triggered by retraumatizing myself at so many book events, I probably had that phrase from my childhood running through my head even more than "The only way out is through," which has peppered my adult coping strategies for as long as I've been an adult. It isn't wrong. Things could have been a lot worse. Still, it might be useful to acknowledge pain. "Grandma and her dad and so on were so determined that we would not experience pain that they made no place for the sorrow that's necessary to living joyfully too," my aunt Barbara wrote to me when I asked her about this phenomenon.

When Ada was four and found out she'd be going to pre-K without her best friend, Julian, she was deeply disappointed and terribly down. Being a Melnick, I tried to talk her out of it, to explain why it wasn't sad, and I talked up all the good that could come of making new friends. Ada said, very earnestly, "Why don't you want me to feel what I feel?" Stella, when she was eight, scolded me: "You're not in charge of my emotional system!" My girls are saving themselves from this generational pitfall; by not acknowledging the range of truth in one's emotions, a high-wire act of lies has to ensue. I spent years trying to hide anything negative about myself so as not to upset anyone, including myself.

When asked about Dolly in an interview, musician Mac Davis describes her as intimidating and says her strength comes from her tough background. I'd say, she's a ray of sunshine but don't fuck with her, and I get why Dolly's voice might go flat when she talks about her childhood. And I get, too, how the sheer force of the music in songs like "Two Doors Down" and "Put a Little Love in Your Heart" propels her vocal performance into celebration. One of the reasons these songs endure is because of the possibilities of a happily ever after, the notion that humans are basically decent. This is when Dolly's positivity soars. "Put a Little Love in Your Heart," when sung with Dolly's unmatched ability to inject emotion into words, feels like an irrepressible smile, a hug from a friend whom you've been running toward down a sunny block. There is a hint of what might have come before the hug, but we're not going to focus on that.

Dolly's "Put a Little Love in Your Heart" starts relatively simple, in the world of the *Slow Dancing with the Moon* album. There is a generic drum downbeat and a kind of goofy but crucial backing harmonica that starts us off but disappears fairly quickly as the choir builds. Dolly's voice at first promises she'll be gentle with us. "On the benevolent planet from which Parton seems to hail," D'Erasmo writes in her review, "breast size must be indicative of the size of the heart underneath." The mistake here isn't just the reductive and misogynistic obvious, but also the "benevolent planet." For a critic, very little time seems to have been spent with Dolly's catalog, a catalog that includes silver daggers, stillbirths, complaints about the sexual double standard, and a workers' anthem. How does someone come out of poverty and violence with a completely benevolent heart? Dolly's heart has seen things. Dolly's heart is weary, steely, and as hopeful as any I've met. True, *Slow Dancing with the Moon* is an album full of forgettable and sometimes even insipid songs that might have been recorded by Lite FM consensus, but her "Put a Little Love in Your Heart" is sneaky, the way Dolly is sneaky, the way she scolds us to remember that wishes aren't dreams and to get off our asses and live life fully. By the end of the song, her voice has risen. It isn't gentle. It's demanding.

"The thing that's always worked for me is the fact that

I look so totally artificial," Dolly writes in her book *Dream More*. "It gives me something to work against. I have to overcome myself. I have to prove how good I am." Remember Dolly fending off Barbara Walters's question, "Do you feel like you're a joke, that people make fun of you?" in her 1977 interview? In other words, Dolly was likely unsurprised by D'Erasmo's review, if it ever found its way to her. Recently John Cleese, longtime British comedian of Monty Python fame, tweeted, "The wondrous, life-enhancing Dolly Parton says she's 'bustier than ever' / Sorry! / 'Busier than ever,'" and Twitter got so angry at the objectification that "Dolly Parton" and "John Cleese" were trending all that morning on the site.

It's fascinating to observe a generation that didn't grow up with Dolly's being the butt of her own and others' boob jokes on talk shows, a generation that sees her as an artist, an activist, a whole, sometimes even nonobjectified, person. Meanwhile, my friend Ashley, fellow Gen-Xer and my partner in all things Dolly, responded when I sent her Cleese's tweet, "She's probably jealous she didn't come up with it!" As Rob Harvilla said in a recent article for the *Ringer*, "She can be both the punch line and the icon; one role can strengthen the other. She has to look like this; it's one of her crucial superpowers, even if it still distracts from her various other superpowers. And she's never not joking, no. But she's never *just* joking, either." If some people can't see past Dolly's boobs, Dolly doesn't seem to care. She just keeps moving ahead with kindness, talent, and, yes, that tremendous rack.

"True happiness comes not when we get rid of all of our problems, but when we change our relationship to them, when we see our problems as a potential source of awakening, opportunities to practice patience, and to learn," Richard Carlson wrote in *Don't Sweat the Small Stuff*. "Do things for people not because of who they are or what they do in return, but because of who you are," Harold Kushner once advised. "Don't ever let me hear you say you don't care," Dolly's mom scolded young Dolly. "I didn't put you on earth to just suck up the air and not care."

I added "Put a Little Love in Your Heart" to the playlist a couple years after I created it, because it was Stella's favorite Dolly song. She was about to turn five. It was maybe the song on the playlist to which I was least connected, but with every listen my connection grew. Nothing has changed me quite so much as Stella's fierce love. She's that emoji with the hearts in its eyes. From her first day on earth, I could feel her love and forgiveness, her patience with me. Plus, her constant presence in the rooms I'm in has resulted in her extensive knowledge of the Dolly deep cuts, the remakes, the songs that sound like other songs. She's older now, taller than I am, and doesn't want to tell me what her favorite Dolly song is these days, though my hunch is that it's 1977's "Light of a Clear Blue Morning," a Dolly-penned song about hope and new beginnings. I know Stella is on the cusp of that necessary pushing me away, but I also know that she'll be back. You've never met a heart with more love in it.

CHAPTER NINETEEN

Blue Smoke

Blue Smoke, 2014, 3:34

SONGS THAT PACK WORDS INTO musical lines—songs where, when you're singing them, you're thinking there's no way all these words will fit into this music, and then they do—songs like that delight me. Bruce Springsteen's "Thunder Road" does that. Mary J. Blige's "Family Affair." And Dolly's "Blue Smoke," from her 2014 album of the same name. Her prior two full-length releases—the soundtrack to the movie *Joyful Noise* and the album *Better Day*—were both albums of inspirational music, and while I am frustratingly optimistic and inclined to tap my toes to songs like "Better Get to Livin'" and "Two Doors Down," a whole album that's supposed to lift me up often leaves me empty.

I remember exactly where I was when Dolly released the song "Blue Smoke." The album dropped first in Australia and New Zealand in early 2014, in anticipation of her Blue Smoke World Tour, and the single arrived on YouTube in March. I sat on my couch in my previous Brooklyn apartment and listened several times in a row. It hooked me immediately. Stella, then only four, listened with me. The song's energy is peppy and the lyrics are kind of sad and defiant, and this is apparently always going to be a style that grabs me.

On the surface of things, it kind of sounds like a song for

kids; it's got a lot of clickety-clack and choo-choo. The first book Dolly gives out in her Imagination Library is *The Little Engine That Could* because Dolly, as the little engine that did, feels a connection to the story: "Didn't know it couldn't be done til I'd already done it," Dolly once told British talk show host Gloria Hunniford. "Blue Smoke" obviously evokes the landscape of Dolly's youth, the ever-present Smoky Mountains not even in the distance but floating just right there. This song isn't for kids though. "Blue Smoke" conveys assuredness, defiance, and getting the hell out of town. The singer packs up her stuff and heads to the train station. Here's a woman who is done with your shit, and she's pissed and she's sad, but it's also a celebration. For a clickety-clack song, it's got very sophisticated lyrics, snappy rhythms, and internal rhymes I envy as a poet: "In a trail of blue smoke with my heart broke / Said goodbye to you." Dolly's poetry makes it impossible not to want to sing this song. Stella and I have been singing it all week because I've been playing it so much again, but also because it's immensely enjoyable to sing along to; you always wonder if this time the words will spill out of the music measure, but they never do. It's intoxicating to head from one verse to the next without even a pause between words.

When I prepared to skip town and get away from the man who threw the bookcase down on me, I sat in our bedroom and watched the Harrison Ford and Annette Bening movie *Regarding Henry* over and over on VHS on my wonky television. I could only see about three-fifths of the screen (the rest was snow) but I paid very close attention to each viewing as I made secret piles of what I absolutely needed and what could be left behind. When we'd moved in, I'd placed a little basket of butterfly soap on the toilet tank. It felt homey to me, it felt like what adults did, it felt like what Dolly would do. The soaps were never used and grew dusty and almost hostile in the way they pointed to the misery and failure of my life as it was. I packed letters that were important to me. I packed some outfits. There were some clothes I missed, but mostly I regretted nothing I left; it had all been tainted by my unhappiness. I never actually caught the ending of the movie—something always distracted me—but it was about a long-cold married couple finding their spark again. Decades later, Bening's plea to Ford, "Please don't walk away. Not now," pops into my head and I think about leaving that shitty little apartment and that shitty TV and that shitty man behind. I think about being alive.

"In this CD," Dolly told talk show host Wendy Williams about *Blue Smoke* in 2014, after talking to her about shoes and boobs and diets, "is some of the colors of all the music I've done throughout my career." Though the title song didn't get much traction, the *Blue Smoke* album earned Dolly some of the best reviews of her life. *Country Weekly* said, "On *Blue Smoke*, the country legend travels many different paths and sounds only like herself." Herself is a very complicated thing. Music scholar Lydia Hamessley writes that the phrase "blue smoke" "plays with multiple associations: train smoke, the color and name of the mountains (Blue Ridge, Smoky Mountains), bluegrass music, and sadness." Later that year, Dolly headlined the famed—and long male-dominated—Glastonbury Festival in Somerset, England. At age sixty-eight, it was the biggest audience of her life, two hundred thousand bodies packed around the stage. "I told you we'd be doing some of your favorites," she tells the very hopped up crowd, "but as usual we're out on a tour, so we're promoting something new!" She launches into "Blue Smoke." Her voice, and I can't overstate this, is *perfect*. The crowd of mostly young people is clapping along, and "you were singing it like you knew it and thank you so much," she tells them after the song ends.

In the parking lot of the otherworldly beautiful Great Smoky Mountains National Park in July of 2018, Stella and I spotted license plates from all over. We'd been trying to col-lect—since earlier that year back in Brooklyn—sightings of plates from all fifty states. We probably caught a dozen in that parking lot, from Alabama to Indiana to South Dakota. I took some silly photos of the girls at a scenic point before yielding our spot to others. It's never New York crowded in East Tennessee, but the national park is one of the more popular attractions—the most visited national park in the country, the information sheet said. I stood by the Appalachian Trail marker and asked Ada to take a photo of me in my sundress and rainbow wedge heels.

The next day we'd visit Dollywood and ride the Dollywood Express train and many of the other rides. "Dollywood is," writes Helen Morales in her book *Pilgrimage to Dollywood*, "the only amusement park in the world to be themed around a woman." "I don't ride the rides. I never have," Dolly told the *New York Times* in 2019. "I tend to get motion sickness. Also, I'm a little bit chicken. With all my hair I got so much to lose, like my wig or my shoes. I don't like to get messed up. I'm gonna have some handsome man mess it up, I don't want some ride doing it." I cosign the motion sickness and the chicken. I spent a lot of my visit to Dollywood waiting on a bench for the others. When I went on a relatively gentle water ride, my kind nephew Jake, then thirteen, kept turning around to see if I was okay. The Dollywood Express was supposed to be gentle too. "Our authentic 110-ton coal-fired steam engine takes you on a breathtaking five-mile journey through the foothills of the Great Smoky Mountains," sings the Dollywood website, "where you'll enjoy pastoral scenery and some of the most beautiful views that nature has to offer. Close your eyes and enjoy a fascinating trip back in time." What they don't tell you is that because it's so authentic that it runs on coal, the coal dust is gonna blow back into your eyes and mouth and lungs.

The Dollywood Express was originally an army train from World War II that came down from Alaska with the name Klondike Katie in 1961. It was renamed the Rebel Railroad in time to celebrate the centennial of the Civil War, and several YouTube videos are dedicated to old footage and to people fondly remembering the ride from their youth, when they were given cap guns to shoot at "Northerners" trying to attack the train. By the mid-1960s, interest in the Civil War anniversary was dying down, and the train and its surrounding Old West attractions were renamed Gold Rush Junction and then Silver Dollar City, which is what they were still called when Dolly bought them in the 1980s and renamed the train Dollywood Express. To celebrate a coal-run train when we're in a climate crisis is a definite *move*, and within and surrounding the old-timey-ness and deep-white nostalgia in Dollywood, one can find a lot of things that are ruining the planet. "Dollywood helped to spark an explosion of tourist attractions," wrote Jessica Wilkerson in 2018, in a critical piece in *Longreads*, "cheap amusements, chain restaurants and outlet malls that litter the path to the Great Smoky Mountains National Park."

In her 2020 article "Redneck Chic: Race and the Country Music Industry in the 1970s," Amanda Marie Martinez writes, "As the bicentennial lingered and Americans of all backgrounds showed interest in reclaiming ethnic identities, country music and the trend of 'redneck chic' were celebrated as symbols of whiteness and invoked as mythic but accepted evidence of a purely white American heritage. The country music industry . . . sold country music fans on the optics of white rusticity." I wonder, looking back to my week in East Tennessee, how much of this romanticized whiteness I was buying into. I feel like I've been trained by the United States to find the Cracker Barrel country store wholesome and to enjoy the Main Street feel of Dollywood, like I'd always lusted after Disneyland's Main Street as a kid. Everything did seem slower and simpler.

Speaking recently on her podcast *Hear to Slay*, Roxane Gay said, "I think a lot of times people want to see country music as the purview of whiteness, and I understand why, because they want to be comfortable and say, you know, we're just good old aw-shucks down-home people and this is what we do, but guess what? Black people are too. And frankly country music would not exist without us. It's not a window into whiteness, it's actually a genre which has historically marginalized Black talent if not completely erased it." On an episode of *The Phil Donahue Show* in the mid-'80s, when Dolly is asked by a Black woman, an aspiring musician, whether there is a place for Black people in country music, Dolly responds that she thinks things are changing because of the success of country legend Charley Pride, and far be it from me to agree with that showboating blowhard Phil Donahue, but he's not wrong when he responds, "But that's an isolated example, Dolly. We're not blaming you for this but the point is, the business does not appear to be very receiving." Her exception proves the rule.

The dearth of Black country musicians in the national consciousness is not because they don't exist and haven't existed and aren't recording—the banjo is descended from West African lutes made from gourds and was a key instrument in the music of Black people in the United States before it was picked up by white traveling musicians. Many early white country artists appropriated songs by Black musicians, who were then ignored by white record executives. Black artists built country music, and then country music shut them out. On *Hear to Slay*, Rissi Palmer—whose 2007 single "Country Girl" made her the first Black woman to chart a country song since 1987—spoke about Lil Nas X, the queer Black Gen-Zer whose "Old Town Road" was everywhere in 2019. He got there, says Palmer, "by circumventing all the systems." The systems, as ever, are on the side of white supremacy. Dolly, on the line with the caller to *The Phil Donahue Show*, reminds the audience that the country music business is based in the South and that the South has a difficult history with race. She then talks of her own struggles and perseverance despite the odds and expresses hope the caller will follow her same trajectory. The next question is about her relationship with her brothers and sisters, and so that was the end of that.

"The ability to sell a version of the South, even one that chafes at some sensibilities, is precisely why Dollywood matters," writes Graham Hoppe in his book *Gone Dollywood*. In *Pilgrimage to Dollywood*, Helen Morales describes the success of Dollywood as "fusing the fantasy and the everyday." Jessica Wilkerson, in her *Longreads* piece, writes that Dolly's "Appalachia is pure and white and heroic; her Appalachia is drained of white America's sins." In other words, Dolly's Tennessee mountain dream is what a Trump supporter might imagine it means to be great again. Traditional values, better jobs (East Tennessee was hit particularly hard by plant closures and jobs going overseas in the early 1980s), and a solid white majority. I'd say, for the most part, in East Tennessee, they've still got the latter.

"The lack of diversity was pretty startling," my niece Annie recently wrote to me about East Tennessee. She's eighteen as I write this and was sixteen—born and raised in California—when we visited Dollywood together. "I remember vividly that I only saw one nonwhite family the entire time we were there." Coming from California and then New York, I, too, was startled by the whiteness. On the other hand, Vermont, for example, is whiter than Tennessee, and I wonder if I notice blue-state whiteness less than red-state whiteness, and what that says about the lies I tell myself about race and the North. I've been to enough towns in Vermont maintained to look like villages out of a toy train set to know that the South hasn't cornered the market on romanticizing the simpler (white) times.

In 1981, at the height of Dolly's crossover, performance artist and musician Laurie Anderson released her most well-known single, "O Superman," which also appeared on her album *United States Live.* The song is concerned with communication and technology and it arches an eyebrow toward US imperialism. I was obsessed with this song in 1989 when I was fifteen and in love with Jason and writing my first poems and feeling very artsy and newly politically aware. I didn't completely understand it—my struggle to be avant-garde in my tastes remains to this day wildly unachieved—but I could feel in my bones a critique of the country I had only begun to question. The B side to "O Superman" is "Walk the Dog," which I didn't know about then because it's not on the album and was only released with the single, when I would have been about seven. In it, Anderson makes fun of country music's woe-is-me tropes and mocks Dolly for singing songs like "My Tennessee Mountain Home" when, suggests Anderson, we all know Dolly's not going to return home now that she's fled the backwoods for Hollywood.

The song is a critique of MAGA before MAGA was a thing, a decent critique of nostalgia and its more racist, sexist times, but also a phenomenal misread of who Dolly is as a person. Being away from home for so long is part of what led to Dolly's suicidal crisis in the 1980s; her love for the Smoky Mountain landscape is earnest and unflinching. Perhaps Dolly was, coming off five hugely successful years, a good stand-in for someone forsaking one problematic America for Hollywood, another problematic America. It also reads to me like an Ivy League–educated woman from a blue state crapping on a woman the same age who was the first in her family to ever graduate high school. In her article, Amanda Marie Martinez writes, "The [country music] industry's efforts to target a large white and affluent audience came at the expense of not only non-white listeners, but also actual Southerners and low-income whites, who were harmed by the stereotypes and widespread appropriations perpetuated by 'redneck chic.'" Anderson's song's assumption that Dolly wouldn't want to go home, that she was happy to be out of there, is perhaps why blue states are so easy to resent. For better or worse, metaphorically or not, Dolly goes home regularly.

In one of her earliest appearances on Johnny Carson's *Tonight Show* in the 1970s, Carson asks Dolly a stereotyped question about her region of origin and the making of moonshine—those illegally concocted, high-proof spirits—and instead of taking the bait, Dolly explains why people in her region make the illicit alcohol in the first place; she turns her reply into a lesson on the socioeconomics and poverty of her home county, and she does it with a smile on her face and a pleasant lilt to her voice.

I've talked already about how Dolly is all things to all people, how she's brilliantly able to skirt the line, able to be—as former president George W. Bush once wished (quite unsuccessfully) for himself—a uniter, not a divider. But whiteness doesn't like to be crossed, and in 2018, a controversy erupted when Dolly changed the name of her Pigeon Forge dinner-theater attraction—the most visited dinner attraction in the country—from Dolly's Dixie Stampede to Dolly Parton's Stampede in an effort to, she says, streamline all the many Stampedes she had hoped to open across the country (as of my writing this, they only exist in Pigeon Forge, Tennessee, and Branson, Missouri), but more likely to erase the racism and the white supremacy inside the notion of Dixie. Quoted in the *Knoxville News Sentinel*, Dolly's press release says, "Our shows currently are identified by where they are located. Some examples are Smoky Mountain Adventures or Dixie Stampede. We also recognize that attitudes change and feel that by streamlining the names of our shows, it will remove any confusion or concerns about our shows and will help our efforts to expand into new cities." She frames it as a business decision, but people on both sides of this suspect differently.

When my sister-in-law, Jessica, and I were planning our Dollywood trip, we stumbled onto the Dixie Stampede in the guidebooks and our jaws dropped at the description.

Apparently, you show up and you have to choose sides, North or South, so you're advised to get there early (although it seats about one thousand), lest you have to cheer for the North. It sounds like the dinner-theater chain Medieval Times, but with the Confederacy. You even get a whole chicken! This would never be something I could attend, simply because of my inability to handle crowds and noise, but the whole thing seemed icky at best. "It is an inconvenient truth," sociologist Tressie McMillan Cottom has written, "that no one gets as rich as Dolly Parton in this country without trading in some aspect of our worst impulses. It simply cannot be done, not even by Dolly Parton."

"It's a lily-white kitsch extravaganza that play-acts the Civil War but never once mentions slavery," wrote culture writer Aisha Harris in *Slate* in 2017, not long after the removal of a statue of Robert E. Lee led to white-power marches and the death of counterprotester Heather Heyer in Charlottesville, Virginia. "The Dixie Stampede has been running for nearly 30 years, but some informal straw-polling suggests that many casual Dolly fans (including black fans like me) have never heard of it. They might also be surprised to learn," Harris continues, wryly, "that the Union vs. the Confederacy was just the Lakers vs. Celtics of its time."

History books have long been whitewashed, and many people would like to keep it that way; laws are currently being enacted to that end all over the United States, from Arizona to New Hampshire. In May of 2021, Tennessee passed a law that would withhold funding to schools that teach about white privilege. In 2018, Knox County mayor Tim Burchett said he was disappointed that the Dolly's Stampede show yielded to "political correctness": "What's next? Are we going to change the name of Dixie cups and the Dixie sugar company? You know, I just hope they don't change their Christmas program."

When asked about the Stampede brouhaha on the podcast *Dolly Parton's America*, Dolly says, "A lot of my things that I do wrong are just out of pure ignorance, really. Because you grow up a certain way and you don't know." I often say, in and around my work as an activist for women's safety and equality, "You don't know what you don't know." Oprah Winfrey says, quite famously, "When you know better, you do better." Still, I think many people would suggest that knowing, in 2018, that a Confederate-themed dinner theater is a bad idea, is, well, a low bar, even for a woman who grew up in the backwoods of Tennessee in the 1940s and 1950s. "I never thought about it being about slavery or any of that," Dolly says, "but when it was brought to our attention . . . I thought, Lord have mercy, I never really want to hurt anybody." She goes on to say, "If I've offended one person, as a businesswoman, I don't want to do that." Dolly always seems to weigh heart against wallet.

Standing in line for the Smoky Mountain River Rampage at Dollywood, we—my family and Cliff's family—were subsumed by whiteness, more or less complicit in this lucrative fantasy. We were also subsumed by heat. A recording of the country classic "Rocky Top"—one of Tennessee's state songs, the fight song of the University of Tennessee, and a song that Dolly often sings in concert—was piped into the line (a line long for Dollywood but short for anyone who has ever lived in New York City), along with mists of water meant to cool us down as we waited to get into our circular raft. Timothy was not on board with everyone's hands and faces reaching up to the spray, and when someone lifted a diaper-clad baby into the mist, he began to sing his own "Rocky Top" lyrics: "There's a mist that blows through hordes of strangers / Landing all over my face / It's full of feces and other dangers / I'm gonna die in disgrace." Two years later and we still sing this around the apartment. Yet, when we were talking about what was so startling to us about Pigeon Forge and Dollywood, the girls and I mentioned how unbusy and uncrowded it had been, and Ada mentioned all the strip malls, and Timothy pointed out that none of this startled him at all, perhaps because he's the only one of us who didn't grow up in a city; he grew up with the woods as his backyard.

The "smoke" of the Smoky Mountains is almost literally the mountains exhaling at the end of the photosynthesis process. The many trees and plants give off a vapor that creates the fog that looks like smoke. It's astonishing. Standing on the porch of our cabin in Dollywood every morning of our visit, I realized I'd never spent that much time just contemplating nature before. Flora was a backdrop growing up—Los Angeles has astounding plants and flowers—yet always the bits of scene I would ignore for crisis or file for poetry. The light of the Smokies, though, the fog, the endless green, it just took me with it. Not in sadness, or urgency, or anything but beauty. The gift is that I realized that beauty is sometimes enough.

I mostly didn't go to high school, and I didn't take science past the eighth grade, and so learning that the molecules that make up the gas released from East Tennessee's vegetation are what scatter blue light from the sky—it feels like a poem. "It is this phenomenon that creates what the Cherokee called 'blue smoke,'" explains the area's tourism web page, in a nod to the mostly erased history of the indigenous population of the area. When I asked Ada what she enjoyed about the region, she said she liked living in a house with her cousins, the slower pace, and that it was nice to be in such a grand national park. It was a huge relief to be with Ada then, and all of us, okay for a moment inside that beauty. On my laptop's desktop, I still display the photo of my girls making ridiculous poses at the park and in front of a landscape that is an astonishment of trees.

When I asked my nephew Jake what stood out to him about Dollywood, he mentioned all the old people, and that's something that stood out to me too. Particularly all the elderly people working very physical service jobs. In Wilkerson's *Longreads* piece, the angle is that Dollywood is not a good place to work, generally because of the structure of labor in the United States, the seasonal nature of theme-park employment, and the fact that Dollywood doesn't pay what the disappeared factory jobs would pay. Most employees, though, seem to rate the work average or above average in polls, particularly in regard to their hours, flexibility, and benefits.

Job postings describe the work as physically laborious—many hours of sitting or standing, long hours, hot hours. When we visited, our waitress at lunch, in a white bonnet and old-timey dress, had to have been in her seventies, carrying to us a full tray of mediocre sandwiches and soft drinks. At the Waltzing Swinger ride in the Country Fair section of Dollywood, a slow and slightly hunched elderly man was in charge of making sure each kid, and their grown-up, was secured in the ride. It was like watching one of those slow and surreal scenes in a David Lynch movie; it took almost a half hour for the attendant to check every seat belt, for which I'm grateful, because Stella and Timothy were in line for those seats next. That work is hot and grueling, and much of what I thought about—as I sat at a picnic table under an umbrella—was how so many of these elderly people had probably, based on election-board statistics, voted for politicians whose policies make it that much harder to retire from this kind of labor, and who pay no mind to what the fallout from climate catastrophe and rising temperatures might be for all of us.

I don't think Dolly is unaware of her environmental impact, or, at least, of climate change. In 2011, on her inspirational gospel album *Better Day*, her song "In the Meantime" implores us to "lead the good life, just treat this planet right." A 2014 article in *Yes!* magazine headlined "Where Does All the Trash from Dollywood Go?" begins, "When you think about progressive composting and recycling programs, big cities such as Seattle, San Francisco, and Los Angeles might come to mind—yet one of the most efficient composting facilities in the world is in Appalachian Tennessee." Tom Leonard, the general manager at Sevier Solid Waste, is quoted as saying, "I just don't like the word 'forever,' because that's a long time. So what we're doing is, we're stabilizing the material back down to its form, and our ultimate goal is not to put anything from this plant into a landfill."

In 2016, when wildfires—brought about in big part, concluded the National Park Service, by climate change—swept through Gatlinburg, Tennessee, Dolly created a fund that sent $1,000 a month to local families to help them rebuild. "Preliminary results of a study of that funding indicate it provided the right money at the right time," the *Knoxville News* reported the next year, a nod to the success of universal basic income programs. Giving this money, of course, is not in and of itself a recognition of climate change. What Dolly was responding to was personal: these were her people in need. When Jane Fonda kept getting arrested in 2019 protesting the climate crisis, Dolly went on *The View* and stated her support for her longtime friend. This did not please a lot of right-wing fans, some of whom, on an online *Fox News* story, commented things like, "Dolly knows she's endorsing a traitor to the U.S.," and misogynistic things like, "All that plastic surgery has affected her brain," and more speculation about her intelligence and reducing her to her breast size, and then somehow the Jews get roped into this, and then comments like, "Climate change has become a dangerous religious cult." And this is with Dolly staying pretty neutral!

"Do you think she's wasting?" Stella asked recently, when we were talking about the Dollywood gift shop as we opened the box of a jigsaw puzzle I'd purchased on Dolly's website. The puzzle features a wistful-looking Dolly against an artfully smudgy all-white background. "Yes," I answered. "Anyone who makes money selling cheap, often plastic crap is wasting." Other items in the online store have included tees and totes, umbrellas, and beer koozies.

"Were you more offended by the taste level of the stuff or the environmental catastrophe of the stuff?" I asked Timothy recently about the Dollywood gift shop. "Both," he replied. Like the possible stretch of Wilkerson's criticism of Dollywood for not having the same wages and working conditions as the area factories that had moved operations to Mexico, I recognize that Dolly can't be held responsible for the worldwide proliferation of mediocre *stuff* and the not-unrelated environmental collapse. Peering into Dolly's re-created childhood home attraction at Dollywood at a time when small homesteads are disappearing across East Tennessee, I still felt the intended nostalgic wistfulness. "I just wanted people to come visit the area," Dolly told the *Pittsburgh Post-Gazette*, "and we're just blessed that all these years later we're getting folks from all over the world coming to visit this beautiful place." That Dollywood made her one of the richest self-made women in the world is the bonus.

Last night, Timothy, always a night owl, finished the new Dolly puzzle for me. My eyes aren't sharp enough to make out differences in what was a pretty homogenous set of pieces, and I was going to just pack it in and give up, but I woke up to Dolly's face smiling at me from the dining table. It didn't matter the quality or risk or site of the manufacturing, it brought me joy, which is both the point and the problem.

CHAPTER TWENTY

The Bargain Store

The Bargain Store, 1975, 2:42

I'VE BEEN HANDCUFFED AND PLACED in the back of a police car exactly once in my life. I was fifteen, it was December 1988. My friend Kimmy and I were on a street in Hollywood when we should have been in school. We were being goofy kids, laughing about something, feeling happy just to be alive, despite everything, in a way only a kid can. We somehow, despite the shit, hadn't shaken the wonder. Kimmy was a year or two older than me; we'd met in rehab. She'd been selling sex for a while. We were not dressed like you might imagine—I was wearing a long white T-shirt and white leggings and knockoff Keds—but I guess this was a *corner*, and a man slowed and asked how much we charged. I've always been a lightweight drinker, and I think I'd had one beer, maybe two, and I was tipsy and I don't remember any of what we said to that man but he was an undercover cop and off Kimmy and I went to the police station. I was terrified; I imagine she was too.

When we got there, it had the same cinder-block bleakness as rehab, as my middle-school cafeteria, as the basement bathroom of my parents' shul. Kimmy, whose mother had brought her from Mexico into California as an infant and then worked impossible hours at a manufacturing business

downtown, was put into a holding cell. It was a small pre-
cinct, and I could see her in there staring at me. It was literally the first time it occurred to me that my whiteness had
benefits. Kimmy had committed a crime, whereas I had made
a mistake. A white female cop brought me a can of Coke,
which I sipped slowly, not looking up at Kimmy or anyone
else. Eventually, a male cop came over to me, told me to leave,
get my act together, and he didn't want to see me back there
ever. You've got your whole life ahead of you, he said, echoing what the rabbi whose dick I jerked for money told me
a year or so before. Having my whole life ahead of me was
far too abstract. I didn't think past the next day. I never saw
Kimmy again.

Dolly often tells a humorous story of being mistaken for a
sex worker when she was on her first trip to New York City
with her childhood friend Judy Ogle in the late 1960s. Always
up for an adventure, Dolly and Judy decided to check out one
of the porn theaters on Forty-Second Street. This would have
been in the '60s, well before Times Square was turned into
what Hollywood Boulevard also turned into, an overdeter-
mined gathering of chain stores mixed with whatever life was
left gasping in a storied history. Somewhat mortified once the
porn started—supposedly because it turned them on and they
weren't with their partners—the two women left the theater.
One of Dolly's recurring bits is that she modeled her look on
the town tramp, trollop, prostitute. She uses different words
for sex workers depending on the interview. She loves to tell
the story of how her parents, when she asked them about
a woman who stood all dolled up on a street in her small
town, replied, oh, she's just trash. And Dolly thought, that's
what I want to be when I grow up! Trash! Dolly thought
the sex worker was beautiful, and still does. "I had never seen
anybody, you know, with the yellow hair all piled up and the
red lipstick and the rouge and the high-heeled shoes, and I
thought, 'This is what I want to look like.'"

Dolly has told this story in more interviews and talk shows than I can sensibly list here. She told this story at her well-loved (turned into a book!) University of Tennessee commencement address in 2009. She included this anecdote in her Hallmark Channel movie *Christmas of Many Colors*, in which she herself plays the woman whose style she most admired. "I'd never seen a painted angel up close before," says Dolly in a voice-over. "Especially not one driving a red Thunderbird. But I never stopped dreaming of looking just like her." (Wink, wink.) By the time Dolly and Judy got to Times Square, Dolly says, she hadn't realized that prostitutes ran in pairs for their own protection, and men kept coming up to the two of them, thinking they were available. "They thought we were for sale," she told *Playboy* in 1978, looking back a decade earlier. "You can imagine how ridiculous I looked, I would look like a streetwalker if you didn't know it was an image. I would look like a total whore, I suppose. . . . But I had a gun. I never traveled without a gun, and don't. I always carry a gun." She ended up having to threaten a man with that gun because he "kept pullin' at me and I was getting furious." "By now, the man was grabbing at me in places I reserve for grabbers of my own choosing," recalls Dolly in her autobiography. "I became irate. I pulled out my gun and said 'You touch me one more time, you son of a bitch, and I'm gonna blow your nuts off.'"

Several years later, in January of 1975, just before Dolly's twenty-ninth birthday, her song "The Bargain Store," from the album of the same title, was released. Presumably the song positions Dolly as a thrift store: worn, but if you search you find treasure, love, and satisfaction, and, what's more, it comes cheap. Likely meant more as an analogy for older or divorced women—women who had been through some stuff, who were not virgins, who might have been thought of as used goods—it was interpreted by many country radio stations as a song about sex work and was banned from the airwaves.

While the meaning of "The Bargain Store" was miscon-strued, I can't think of a single celebrity who has been so openly supportive (and sometimes even celebratory!) of sex workers; certainly none of Dolly's icon status. Dolly has written and recorded songs explicitly about prostitution, including 1969's "Mama Say a Prayer," about a lonely girl who moves to the big city and falls into sex work, and 1982's "A Gamble Either Way," about a girl abandoned by her parents who feels unloved and unnoticed until she has a body to use for the pleasure of others. In a 1983 London-filmed TV special called *Dolly in Concert*, Dolly was asked about sex work in regard to her second film, *The Best Little Whorehouse in Texas*. She gives her usual answer about loving everyone and not judging, and at the tail end of her answer she asks the questioner, "Are you a prostitute?" And the woman seems embarrassed. It's hard to tell how much Dolly meant to say with that question, but certainly she is reminding us that sex work is work and sex workers are people who matter, like all people.

Dolly isn't always great on this subject. Using words like "trollop" and "trash" throughout her career to talk about the sex worker who inspired her look isn't exactly unharmful, even when the words are said with love. She can be a little judgmental, as in her 1981 cover of "The House of the Rising Sun" and her 2019 collaboration with Christian alternative rock duo For King & Country on "God Only Knows," for whose video Dolly plays what she would call a "trollop" or "fallen woman." The message of both of these is that God forgives but sex work is a sin. Yet even this notion, the for-giveness, is a radical statement in some communities.

The 1982 movie musical *The Best Little Whorehouse in Texas*, adapted from the 1978 stage musical, is based on the true-life story of sensationalist investigative journalist Marvin Zindler's 1973 takedown of the Chicken Ranch, a brothel that had operated somewhat openly and without incident since the mid-nineteenth century near La Grange, Texas—located

kind of in the center of a Houston–San Antonio–Austin tri-
angle. Coming off the success of *9 to 5*, Dolly's first film, *The
Best Little Whorehouse in Texas* was also a hit, knocking *E. T. the
Extra-Terrestrial* out of the number-one spot at the box office.
I was eight when those movies came out and spent almost the
entirety of *E. T.* crying.

I wasn't aware of *The Best Little Whorehouse in Texas* at
the time, even as it enjoyed the biggest opening weekend
for a movie musical ever up until that point and went on to
be the most successful movie musical of the 1980s. It also
scored Dolly a Golden Globe nomination despite its mixed
reception. In a review in the *Chicago Sun-Times*, Roger Ebert
complains how unsexy Dolly is in the movie. There is zero
chemistry between Dolly and Burt Reynolds—they apparently did not get along well in real life—and Dolly lobbied
to add an actual kiss between them. For the fans, she said. It
all seems perfect on paper, two huge sex symbols in a movie
about sex. But there's no accounting for chemistry.

"There are a few funny jokes, some raunchy one-liners,
some mostly forgettable songs set to completely forgettable
choreography," notes Ebert at the end of his review, "and then
there is Dolly Parton. If they ever give Dolly her freedom
and stop packaging her so antiseptically, she could be terrific."
He's right. Most of the time, Dolly seems too reined-in in the
movie. It is during the moments where she is off the cuff—
when she's Dolly—that she truly shines. There's a scene where
Dolly and Reynolds go out to the country to get drunk on
beer and they have a conversation about Jesus being good to
fabled biblical prostitute Mary Magdalene and it was ad-libbed,
which isn't a surprise, because not only does Dolly seem the
most natural in this scene but her politics come out whether
she likes it or not. "That's funny now how God can forgive
you, but people can't," Dolly, as the madam, Miss Mona (Miss
Edna, in real life), says to Reynolds's cop character.

"She liked her ladies to treat her customers real good, but

never in an unladylike way," the movie's narrator tells us in the beginning of the film, and that is certainly the scrubbed-down version of a brothel. Still, the movie was hard to market because "whorehouse" was considered a dirty and taboo word in many places at the time. In a recent interview, actress Kristin Chenoweth says of *The Best Little Whorehouse in Texas* and Dolly's part in it, "She managed to make a movie, a story about a whorehouse okay, acceptable, hilarious, and heart-warming. Who else could do that but Dolly Parton."

The movie is surely hokey, corny, predictable, and super '80s-tastic, with the women (besides Dolly, who is always in Dollywear) in off-the-shoulder blouses and clashing Lycra ensembles that look like they'd make a lot of sense on the VHS of *Jane Fonda's Workout*, which came out the same year. It's also kind of progressive. At one point there's a conversation about whether brothels are obsolete because of the sexual revolution. After the scene where Dolly and Reynolds fight and he calls her a whore, we hear an instrumental version of "I Will Always Love You" and then it cuts to a news report about decriminalizing sex work, which even uses the word "feminist." "You can't legislate morality," Reynolds's character argues to the governor of Texas.

Edna Chadwell, on whom Dolly's character is based, hated the movie. "There was nothing about it right except that it happened in a whorehouse," she said. In *Dolly Parton, Gender, and Country Music*, Leigh H. Edwards writes, "On one level, it cites feminist arguments for the decriminalization of prosti-tution. It rewrites a familiar, gendered Hollywood film script by widening the definition of who can count as a heroine . . . Yet, on another level, the resolution reiterates a common film trope in which the male character legitimates and reforms the female 'hooker with the heart of gold' by marrying her, restoring a gender hierarchy within a romance plot." It still seems like a victory for sex workers that the story was told with such an absence of shame or squeamishness. I wonder if such a movie could be made today; later in the same recent interview, Chenoweth talks about how the movie *9 to 5* supported a change for working women, "and not the bad kind," she says, tellingly, "not the one in the whorehouse. The one in the office buildings."

In 1973, ZZ Top recorded a terrible song about the Chicken Ranch called "La Grange." In general, though, the 1970s were a good moment for thinking about sex work (even badly, I guess). The Sunset Strip music scene, as I experienced it in the 1980s, featured a lot of songs about strippers and strip clubs, songs that confused my young friends and me about a woman's worth, but the 1970s were kind of a golden era for songs about prostitution. Lou Reed's 1972 "Walk on the Wild Side" (about queer and trans sex workers associated with Andy Warhol), Steely Dan's 1973 "Pearl of the Quarter" (about a man in love with a sex worker in New Orleans), Labelle's 1974 "Lady Marmalade" (which Patti LaBelle claimed she didn't know was about a prostitute when she recorded it), Queen's 1974 "Killer Queen" (about a high-end call girl), Leonard Cohen's 1975 "Don't Go Home with Your Hard-On" (about being raised in a brothel), the Ramones' 1976 "53rd & 3rd" (about male sex workers in Manhattan), Blondie's 1976 "X Offender" (in which the sex worker falls for her arresting officer), Kenny Rogers's 1977 "The Son of Hickory Holler's Tramp" (about the grateful son of a single-mom sex worker), Nick Gilder's 1978 "Hot Child in the City" (specifically about walking the streets of Hollywood), the Police's 1978 "Roxanne" (inspired by street sex workers near Sting's hotel in Paris), and Donna Summer's 1979 "Bad Girls" (about street sex workers on the Sunset Strip) are truly just a selection of the many 1970s songs about this subject. Many of these were hits.

On the second episode of Dolly's ill-fated 1980s talk show, when asked what she would be if not a performer, she replies, "I might have been a beautician. Or a madam." Everyone claps. Meanwhile, Dolly was already receiving complaints about the "Dolly's Date" feature of her show, where she goes on pretend dates with hunky men; many viewers felt uncomfortable with the segment because Dolly was a married lady. The high wire she was always walking was tricky. "Sex work is not simply sex," writes journalist Melissa Gira Grant in her book *Playing the Whore: The Work of Sex Work.* "It is performance, it is playing a role, demonstrating a skill, developing empathy within a set of professional boundaries. All this could be more easily recognized and respected as labor were it the labor of a nurse, a therapist, or a nanny. To insist that sex work is work is also to affirm there is a difference between a sexualized form of labor and sexuality itself." She goes on to say, "When anti–sex work activists claim that all sex work is rape, they don't just ignore the labor; they excuse the actual rape of sex workers."

When I was still fifteen and wore vintage hippie-style skirts with frayed edges and a few remaining beads, a man slowed his car and said to me, exactly, "Say yes." He was in Hasidic garb—the hat, the tzitzit, the peyos, the long, black, wool winter coat even though it was an LA winter and the temperature likely in the sixties—and he pulled up to where some friends and I were hanging out one Sunday morning, just kicking around because we had no money. The man drove a black pickup truck with a Confederate flag decorating the back, which was confusing, but he looked like something out of *The Chosen*—that book my dad loved and, to be honest, so did I—and I felt kind of chosen, really, as I was raised to think of the ultra-Orthodox as in some ways better than the rest of us Jews.

He put a twenty-dollar bill on the dashboard and I said, "Just my hand, right?" And then he was driving and driving out of the city and into the mountains. I regretted my impulsive decision as soon as I made it. I didn't know where I was. He was skinny and his clothes were too big and he was sweating so much. I didn't say anything, I don't think, or else I only replied to questions he asked me. I was nervous because I'd read somewhere to never let yourself be driven to a location you're not familiar with, but I had gotten myself into a hole of bad choices and worse luck, starting, perhaps, with the rape or cocaine or with my hand around the rabbi's dick, so I was used to getting myself into and out of bad situations all by myself. At that point, I kept everything about my life a secret from anyone who could help me.

Eventually the truck stopped on the side of a dirt path and the man motioned for me to get out and to climb up into the truck's flatbed. I did and then the next thing I knew he had forced me onto my stomach with my skirt hiked to my waist and then he pushed his penis inside of my vagina. He had, I'd seen first on the steering wheel, very long, unclean fingernails, and as he raped me he dug them into my back until he drew blood. It was so unexpectedly painful, it distracted from the pain of the rape. There were spools and spools of wire in the flatbed, and cases of Pepsi. It took maybe about five minutes, maybe ten, maybe twenty. When he was done he looked at me with utter disgust and told me to walk home.

"That's what I want to be when I grow up! Trash!" I was disposable. I did walk home, the cuts on my back stinging, my vulva swollen with trauma. Miles and miles, through scrubland whose landscape felt like all those hikes I went on with my family as a younger kid, and then the posh part of town past the Beverly Hills Hotel and then finally a crisscross of city streets and the RTD number-twenty bus to take me east down Wilshire. The light of Southern California was at first very sharp and then retreating and then gone. It was near the solstice, the darkest day of the year, the day after which everything begins to get brighter again. I thought, I need to find a better way to survive. I thought, I need to tell my secrets. I couldn't tell them yet though. I couldn't even acknowledge to myself my body as a site of violence and I certainly couldn't

bother anyone else with it. It's not unusual for a trauma survivor to disproportionally focus on the needs and comfort of
others, and keeping my secrets felt like a kindness.

"As long as you keep secrets and suppress information,
you are fundamentally at war with yourself," Bessel van der
Kolk writes in *The Body Keeps the Score*. "The critical issue
is allowing yourself to know what you know. That takes an
enormous amount of courage." Almost three decades later, I
published a poem about that flatbed rape in the *New Yorker*.
For weeks after the issue came out, I felt angry with the con-
straints of linear time. What would it have meant to the girl
in that pickup truck to know how it all turned out, that she
learned to do the work of truth telling against silence?

"There is so much pain in the world. What does it mean
to have to suffer so much if our lives are nothing more than
the blink of an eye?" Chaim Potok wrote in *The Chosen*. "Pain
is the price we pay for being alive," Harold Kushner explained
in *When Bad Things Happen to Good People*. "Dead cells—our
hair, our fingernails—can't feel pain; they cannot feel anything. When we understand that, our question will change
from, 'Why do we have to feel pain?' to 'What do we do
with our pain so that it becomes meaningful and not just
pointless empty suffering?'" Publishing my poem about the
rape in such a high-profile place made my pain meaningful—
especially when I received grateful letters from survivors—
although not gone, never gone.

Despite being banned from some radio stations for its
supposed allusion to prostitution, "The Bargain Store" still
reached number one on the country chart in early 1975 and
stayed on the chart for nine more weeks. It also reached number thirty-five on the adult contemporary chart. The tone of
"The Bargain Store" is different from that of many of Dolly's
other hits. I could easily imagine Mary Travers or Judy Collins
singing it. There's no twang, and the bounciness is definitely
in a more self-serious folk way than a sad-banging country

way. It feels old, like "Little Sparrow" or "Silver Dagger." "I like doing old-timey songs," Dolly said, responding to a question about the word "unto" in "The Bargain Store." "It's in that minor key, which sounds old world to me, that lonesome drone." It's in A minor, the same key as "Aint No Sunshine" by Bill Withers and the opening of Led Zeppelin's "Stairway to Heaven." In "The Bargain Store," Dolly uses a lot of vocal embellishments, a quivering vocal on an already gentle path. The song has a relentless urgency, not unlike "Jolene." It has a bewitching quality.

The question that might haunt this chapter is, When a person makes their body into a commodity, how can they stop others from regarding it as one, and treating it as disposable? When you put yourself forward as an object, how can you control how you are consumed? Dolly carried a gun on her Times Square adventure with her friend Judy perhaps because she was so on top of this question and so many steps ahead. As Bessel van der Kolk says, it takes an enormous amount of courage to know what you know. Sex work isn't like any other work, because sex isn't like anything else, but sex work is still work, and sex workers' rights are still human rights. Which is to say, sex workers are people and not trash. "The Bargain Store" doesn't end so much as it moves away with the promise it will continue. It's a song whose speaker hasn't given up. It feels like someone spinning away in circles, or refusing to stop spinning in the face of a world that would demand conformity or defeat. It is a refusal of secrets.

CHAPTER TWENTY-ONE

The Story

Cover Stories, 2017, 4:17

ALMOST TWO DECADES AGO, AND about a week or so after Paul and I encountered him on Madison Avenue near our office, I saw the man who threw the bookcase on me for the very last time. I had exited the back of the building—a quieter Forty-First Street to the chaotic Forty-Second Street out the front—and stood in one of the doorframes smoking during my afternoon break. Out of nowhere, my ex came up to me with malevolent eyes, as if he'd been waiting there all week to see me. But now that I was there he seemed befuddled. "You fucking that white guy?" he asked, meaning Paul, his body trapping me in the doorframe, my heart beating so strong it escaped onto the street, where it pulled me toward it. "I have to go," I said, ducking under his arm. He grabbed mine and held it and then I don't think he knew what to do after that, trucks rumbling, people shouting, New York City continuing on.

He let me go. I went upstairs, put on *The Grass Is Blue* or *Little Sparrow*, and kept on going. I probably joked around with Paul and wrote some ad plans and window-shopped for heels online. I probably counted my breathing to slow the tremble inside my body. George Bonanno, who heads the Loss, Trauma, and Emotion Lab at Columbia University's

Teachers College, found in his research that how we conceptualize traumatic events—traumatic as an end stop versus traumatic as a learning experience—may be what does and doesn't get us through. When I showed this chapter to a friend, he recounted the preceding events as "freaky and scary," when to me they seemed like just a thing that happened. What I did know was that I didn't want to feel that fear ever again, nor despair, nor powerlessness. I was in New York City. I had a fine job. I had love and friends and poems. As life continued I got a better job and more love and friends and poems. Each day that I wake up is a step away from despair and a step toward hope. Here we are at the last chapter, the last song on my Dolly playlist, but not *my* last chapter. Writing this book has been an act of defiant joy, despite all the sadness.

I've been writing most of this through a worldwide pandemic, one that I don't have to tell you about, because you've lived through it too. Being in New York City brought a particular pain to spring of 2020. Like 9/11, I feel the wound to the city in a personal way. I've lost work. I lost a friend to COVID-19. I lost my beloved everyday routine of writing in coffee shops or the library. I developed a cat allergy—two years after testing negative for cat allergies—from being indoors with them so much more frequently; now I get weekly shots to try to reverse my body's response.

As I first typed this, New York City was still under pretty serious lockdown, it was summer, and as I revise, it was fall, then winter, then spring again, and I can still walk through the city—in my mask—and dream of its full return. In Los Angeles and Rhode Island, my parents and my in-laws grow restless indoors, and my brother, Cliff, texts me that working from home is a necessary drag but they're all hanging in there, and what new country music have I been listening to? He recommends Kelsey Waldon and I listen and she's great. As ever, my friends are a lifeline, and I've been spending more time with Timothy and the girls than we ever get to spend together and that's been a blessing. Right now, Ada and Stella are playing some game they invented and I don't understand and they're giggling. We are, it seems, somehow, often content, and fortunate, and while social media is constantly scolding people for being productive because—and I get it—the pressures of capitalism are harmful, having these pages to return to every morning has been what has gotten me through.

When I hadn't left the apartment in many days and the bustle of my Brooklyn block was replaced with the endless sounds of sirens screaming toward the overfull hospitals; on days when four of us were trying to work or go to school in an apartment not built for that, I planted myself in the corner of the girls' bedroom, or in the hallway, or on the couch, or at the kitchen counter, or wherever I could find a bit of even the illusion of space, and wrote the first drafts of this book. "I can write anywhere, anytime, any place," said Dolly recently. "Noise or anything else around me can't stop me. On my tour bus, on an airplane, in the bathtub, or just about anywhere." Early in the pandemic, Dolly released all her albums for streaming so I no longer had to listen to "Seven Bridges Road" via YouTube, although I never really minded. Earphones in, Dolly ringing through, the banging of words up one against the other saved me, as it always had, since I wrote my first poem after my second abortion. And Dolly saved me, truly, as she always has, since her radiance piped into the hospital speakers on March 3, 1988. I have been writing a book about how Dolly has gotten me through trauma, and the writing of it has gotten me through trauma.

In an interview for LA's PaleyFest, celebrating the Emmy nomination for her Netflix *Heartstrings* series, when asked what TV shows she's been watching recently, given that the majority of us have been homebound, Dolly answers, "Well, I am home, but I'm not watching TV! I'm writing songs, I'm writing songs about what's going on. . . . I don't have much time to watch TV. I watch the news in the morning to see if the world's still standing." Later she told *The Today Show*, "We can't save the world, but we can save the world we're living in." She added, "Maybe I'm dreaming. But I don't think so."

So, I mean, what all has Dolly been doing during the pandemic? Well, she's recorded a whole Christmas album; she released a single, "When Life Is Good Again," to cheer us up and ask us to be better to one another, and then she shot a touching video for it that ended with a reminder to wear our masks; she recorded a web series of herself in light-blue moon pajamas in bed reading bedtime stories for children, which was broadcast every Thursday, as part of her Imagination Library, to give parents a small break in the evening; she recorded a song with Jordin Sparks, Monica, and others to benefit a breast cancer awareness organization; she landed the cover of *Billboard* for the first time in her career; she became the first country artist to chart a top-twenty single in the 1960s, 1970s, 1980s, 1990s, 2000s, 2010s, and 2020s; she received her fiftieth Grammy Award nomination, won an Emmy for her deliciously cheesy TV movie *Christmas on the Square* (which is, in part, about an unwed mother—very on-brand), and won a GLAAD Media Award; she inked a deal with American Greetings cards; she developed a perfume called Scent from Above; she partnered with Jeni's Splendid Ice Creams to create a special flavor, Strawberry Pretzel Pie, which would benefit her Imagination Library, and the rush of fans crashed the Jeni's website within minutes of it becoming available; she partnered with Williams-Sonoma to sell kitchenware to benefit No Kid Hungry; she cowrote a novel with James Patterson and wrote an entire album of songs to go with it; she donated $1 million to Vanderbilt University in Nashville for COVID-19 research; she offered up Dollywood as a mass vaccination site and filmed herself getting her vaccination ("Vaccine, vaccine, vaccine, vacciiiiine") to encourage others to do so; she finally, during a *Time* magazine interview, outright identified as a feminist and was, in 2021, named one of their most influential people; and, in the *Billboard* cover-story interview, when asked how she feels about the Black Lives Matter movement, she answered, "I understand people having to make themselves known and felt and seen. And of course Black lives matter. Do we think our little white asses are the only ones that matter? No!"—an answer that, you might imagine, sent shock waves through social media and beyond.

I'd been so disappointed with Dolly because of her total silence during all the weeks of the marches for racial justice after George Floyd was murdered by police in Minneapolis in May of 2020. I'd even tweeted as much, which felt like a betrayal but also entirely and urgently necessary. And then, to my relief, Dolly stated her unequivocal support for Black lives. "All these good Christian people that are supposed to be such good Christian people, the last thing we're supposed to do is to judge one another," she told *Billboard*. "God is the judge, not us. I just try to be myself. I try to let everyone else be themselves."

Like after her much-milder explanation of the change from Dolly's Dixie Stampede to Dolly Parton's Stampede, the trolls came out. One, a comic named Stuart Baker, found himself fired from his TV show after posting on Facebook, "So, now this freak tittied, old Southern bimbo is a BLM lover? Remember, slut, Rednecks made you a Millionaire!" Ah, the heady mix of racism and rape culture! Other outraged fans vowed never to buy Dolly's music again, and still others patronizingly worried that Dolly just didn't understand that the Black Lives Matter organization is, in their minds, communist and a bunch of other things they find undesirable (like Jewish).

It used to really matter to Dolly what people thought of her; she wanted everyone's love. Yet, in 2020, when she took a stand for right, something else happened besides the once-feared derision, something that hadn't happened with the Dolly's Stampede brouhaha: Dolly was lauded as a hero. Social media flooded with excited celebration that a white woman in her seventies from the South could and would say out loud that Black lives matter and would do it in a way that would slam shut the "all lives matter" retort. Author and sociologist Tressie McMillan Cottom celebrated the white woman who hadn't let her down: "Dear god she is hanging in there," she tweeted. "Oh god I might make it to my grave with one true thing being true my god keep going Dolly." Someone put up a mural in Nashville with Dolly's smiling face amid flowers and the words, "Of course Black lives matter." Seventy-seven percent of Sevier County, home to Dollywood and Dolly's entire childhood, voted for Trump in 2020, voted for hate or fear or whiteness or nostalgia, or all of the above. Dolly would never say for whom she voted, but 2020 was the year she stood behind justice, and the country—and the world—has been very grateful.

Suddenly Dolly went from resurgent cultural icon to someone whom the *Washington Post* said was "the super-hero America needs in 2020." "The one good thing in our empire's twilight," wrote Cottom. When the medical trials Dolly funded through Vanderbilt resulted in a reported 95 percent effective vaccine, social media went wild over the "Dolly Parton vaccine." Dolly's sister Stella—with whom there'd been tension around the #MeToo movement and Stella's wishing Dolly would say more—tweeted, "My sister Dolly has 'put her money where her mouth is' look out, a vaccine is on the way!!!"

Dolly herself found out about the results of the vaccine trials when the rest of us did. "I just felt so proud to have been part of that little seed money that will hopefully grow into something great and help to heal this world," she told the BBC. "I'm a very proud girl today to know I had anything at all to do with something that's going to help us through this crazy pandemic." In an interview on a local Knoxville television station, Lance Kinney, a public relations professor at the University of Alabama, called Dolly Parton the ideal crisis manager. The key is consistency. "You think of each time you see Dolly Parton, she is always Dolly Parton." A Dolly-themed bar, White Limozeen, opened in Nashville in the summer of 2020, and later that fall, scientists named the 460-million-year-old fossilized moss *Dollyphyton boucotil* in honor of her. "Just Let Dolly Parton Rule the World Already," a CNN headline declared. Former president Barack Obama recently admitted to talk show host Stephen Colbert that he made a mistake in not giving Dolly the Presidential Medal of Freedom. "I'm sick of Dolly, ain't you?" Dolly joked to a *New York Times* reporter in December of 2020. Never. We need Dolly.

Dolly talked a few times about maybe posing for *Playboy* for her seventy-fifth birthday in January of 2021, full circle from her delicious interview and bunny-eared cover photo in the magazine in 1978, but instead, on her seventy-fifth birthday, Dolly released a statement via her website calling for people to practice kindness: "My wish is that everyone does something a little different today. Let's call it a call for kindness. If you want to donate to your favorite cause, then donate. If you want to give an old friend a call during these lonely times, give them a call. If you can safely volunteer, then raise your hand and do so." Later in 2021, for her husband's birthday, she did re-create her photo shoot in *Playboy*, just for him—but also for the rest of us, as Dolly in bunny ears was plastered all over the internet and print media that week.

When I was a little girl, before I could read or write, I composed a poem. "Past the trees / Past the snow / Past the things I used to know." My mom quickly wrote it down. She was very proud. When Dolly was a little girl, before she could read or write, she composed her first song, called "Little Tiny Tasseltop," named for a beloved corncob doll. Her mother, Avie Lee, also wrote down the words. Dolly hasn't stopped writing or performing since. In recent years, Dolly has laid down hours of vocal tracks so that after she's gone people can still use her voice and release her songs. Dolly wouldn't let a pesky thing like death get in her way, and while her Christian idea of heaven is so much more promising than my secular Jewish skepticism of anything actually being on the other side, the idea of an eternal Dolly is one literally almost everyone can get excited about. And they do! Endlessly. The world seems to be discovering what I've known since March of 1988 and what many have known since the 1960s: Dolly is both what we all could be—kind, creative, sexy, relentless—and what we are—flawed, frustrating, hurt, enigmatic. There are hundreds of recordings to accompany us in this knowledge. Hundreds more written and waiting.

In 2017, Dolly released a cover of singer-songwriter Brandi Carlile's song "The Story" as part of the ten-year-anniversary cover album of Carlile's *The Story*, called *Cover Stories*, and as a benefit for child refugees around the world. I'd been listening to Carlile since Timothy's best friend from college, Holden, sent me *The Story* on CD when Ada was quite small. When the album first came out, the BBC reported that "most of *The Story* is filled with gentle, loping acoustic folk country. [Carlile's] use of the country singer's accented break between upper and lower ranges adds depth and nuance." It was the first album to enter my regular rotation since Dolly's *Little Sparrow* in 2001. Carlile sings the title track, written by her longtime bandmate and songwriting partner Phil Hanseroth, with tremendous power and conviction. The song suggests that each of our lives—even the hard parts—are a progression of exhaustions and triumphs that hopefully brings us to fulfilment.

When it came time to find someone to cover the song on the benefit album, Carlile wrote to Dolly. She suggested to Dolly, then seventy-one, that she'd be happy to drop the key for her—it's a very wide-ranging song that starts soft and then builds impossibly and yet necessarily high—and in a show supporting *Cover Stories* in 2017, Carlile recounted for her audience how that request went. "There are hard notes to sing in that song," she tells the crowd, while laughing at her miscalculation. "And I just hadn't heard her sing full voice in a while." Dolly wrote her back, told her of course she wanted to do something to help the children, and very sweetly suggested that she would be just fine hitting the high notes. "Honey," she wrote back to Carlile on butterfly letterhead, "don't worry about changing that key. I intend to Dollyize it."

And Dollyize it she does. When done by Carlile, "The Story" is an affecting notion sung by a young woman finding her footing in life and love. When done by Dolly, it's a story of survival, a remembrance of all she's been through and all the pain she's had to stuff down and plow through to get here. It's the story of an everlasting love, and that kind of love deserves might. Not grandiloquence, but toughness. That kind of strength that recognizes its own pit stops and heartbreaks along the way. Vocal powerhouses Kelly Clarkson and LeAnn Rimes have both covered the song, and, much younger than Dolly and with uncommonly stout lungs, they can push harder and go louder, but they can't Dollyize it—which is to say, they can't make each word so crushingly human that it hurts and soothes at the same time.

I'm ending this book on a song Dolly herself didn't write, even as I insist to you repeatedly that Dolly is one of the genius songwriters of American history, and it's because I've been following the progression of my playlist but also because of Dolly as an interpreter of songs. She doesn't just sing someone's song. She reimagines it, sometimes even re-creates it. She is a light, deepening the humanity of each word, each sung note. She meets us where we are, where the song is, and then shows us where more is possible.

Writing for NPR about the *Cover Stories* album, music critic Ann Powers says, "Dolly Parton's climb to the heights of her vocal range on the title track reminds listeners that Carlile can [create] a blockbuster." Like Whitney Houston taking "I

Will Always Love You" from achingly beautiful to stop-every-thing-and-listen insistent, Dolly takes "The Story" and finds more there than perhaps was even intended. This is her gift for singing many emotions into whatever limitations a single song presents. Dolly is the authority on this move. From her earliest hits, like "Mule Skinner Blues" and "Dumb Blonde," Dolly knew how to surpass what a song's dreams proba-bly even were for themselves, written by her or not. Dolly knows about the power of the sublime, or maybe it moves through her organically, but quite likely both. "She takes me to school!" Brandi Carlile exclaims when she describes the reach of Dolly's voice in her cover of the song.

When Dolly sings the pivotal words from "The Story" about the lines on a person's face becoming their biography and how being meant for someone means knowing them in their entirety, it's an ode to longevity and survival and to hav-ing a partner with whom you go through life. "Like every-one else," Dolly wrote about her husband, Carl, "we have our ups and downs, but we have always been and will always be committed to our love for each other. I do not easily cut and run. If something is broken, then let's fix it. If it's wrong, then let's make it right." When the song first came out, I felt like it existed not for Hanseroth or for Carlile and not for Dolly and Carl, but for me and Timothy, and the unmatched intimacy of long-term relationships in general, the freedoms and restric-tions afforded by the safety in knowing someone knows your head and heart by the tone in your voice or the fleeting look on your face.

On our first date, in a denim and floral outfit that I prom-ise you made sense in the 1990s, after we'd gone to a bar and then a diner and then found ourselves back on the steps of my apartment building on 112th Street, talking until dawn, I kept asking Timothy, "Does that make sense?" as I poured out my ideas and feelings and what suddenly seemed possible to pour out to another person. He kept answering, "Of course!" How many ideas and feelings and how much of my constant questioning of the world, like a toddler's has Timothy endured now, decades later? He always stops to listen. As fragile as I sometimes feel or imagine myself, Timothy sees me as tough and practical and razor-sharp. I think it took me a while to see that too. It took me a while to really see myself at all, from the steps of my building on 112th Street through decades existing in the city's energy, always in my armor of a dress and heels.

Sometimes I spend all day fielding other people's worries and tending to the kids and pushing through work and I think, Timothy is the one who knows what I'm pushing through. No one knows how far I've come like Timothy; he knows me at my darkest and loves me anyway. Recently my friend Carley said I have forgotten to own all the caretaking that I do for others. I am, in fact, probably juggling more people's secrets and emotional weight and practical needs than might be tenable, but I don't think to flag it; it feels like what we're supposed to be doing. This is how I love.

Early on in my writing this book, Carley also gently suggested, after reading a chapter draft, that I try to recount stories where I'm not the asshole; I have tried here to see myself as others see me, worthy of the enormous love I get from Timothy, from my family and friends. If, in a pandemic, under cruel government, in the midst of a rape culture that would render so many of us in harm's way, I can still thrive; if, from the time I sat in rehab waiting for the beauty of Dolly's voice to tell me what to do, tell me what to live for until I discovered what to do and what to live for; if, as I struggled for years to put my story onto paper and then I finally did; if I am this lucky to have all my mailboxes filled with love—then I want for little.

For years I talked about writing a book about Dolly Parton. For years I said I could never write my life in prose. Yet my dearest friends, my aunt Barbara, Timothy, all said, "Of course you can." Find people who see your survival before you can see it yourself.

A lot of people say to me, "There are so few worthwhile people in the world," and I say, "That's the biggest crock of shit I ever heard." I don't ever meet a freak. The biggest freaks in the world for me are my favorite people, like you, like me.

DOLLY PARTON

You don't become happy by pursuing happiness. You become happy by living a life that means something.

HAROLD KUSHNER

Resilience. Longevity. Outlast those who would doubt you. Just keep going. In my darkest moments, that's been the light she shone on me.

ME, ON DOLLY, TO ME—TO US—AT THE START

OF THIS BOOK

I began this book thinking that despite my nearly lifelong fandom, Dolly and I didn't have much in common at all. The more I wrote, though, the more I grew to understand just the opposite. I've been way overdressed for the pandemic we're in; I step onto the street in my purple velvet coat with fauxfur trim and my high-heeled boots just to walk to my weekly allergy shots and I feel *good* and I have always gotten Dolly in that way. But there's more. I've learned that the struggles that bring the smile lines and the heartbreak lines to our faces are in fact one story, and they are the story of humanity, of this connection that keeps my loved ones, and the beauty of the world, and Dolly close to my heart. I've never felt more seen than in the path Dolly's music laid out for me, and all of us.

Now, as I sit here in my apartment in Brooklyn, the city I love buckled but not broken under the weight of the pandemic, feeling too homebound and yet at the same time heartened to be at home so much with my family, I imagine myself at once walking lightheartedly through the loud and smelly streets of the city I love and also returned to that back deck in East Tennessee, taking in the scope and low bustle of animal life under blue smoke over the landscape. Sometimes you have to survive by leaving, but it all comes with you every day.

In a book Dorothy Allison published in 1995, the year I met Timothy, she wrote, "When I began, there was only the suspicion that making up the story as you went along was the way to survive. And if I know anything, I know how to survive, how to remake the world in story." There is such power in telling our stories. For all there is yet to accomplish, think of how much the world has changed since #MeToo broke. The stories I told in my book of poems about trauma, launched the day that famous hashtag flew wide on Twitter, are now a blip in a pile of stories, all terrible, but all also allowing the light in. This is how we change the culture; inch by inch we let the light in. No one knows that like Dolly.

Talking recently with my friend Ashley, she referred to Dolly as an unreliable narrator, often shifting details of, and reactions to, her own stories from her life. In interviews, Dolly sometimes even confuses a song lyric or scene from one of her movies with her own autobiography. My father recently remarked to me that all autobiography is in some way a lie, meant to fluff up the teller or at least make them more interesting. "She is essentially unknowable, like my grandmother," I said to Ashley during that recent conversation about Dolly. Maybe like me too, maybe like everyone. Dolly is, and knows she is, wildly imperfect. Yet she continuously strives to do right by, and for, others—and for herself. She consistently works to create beauty even in the darkest days. "Dreams are of no value if they're not equipped with wings and feet and hands," says Dolly. I've learned so much from that. In 2020, on my aging laptop, I listened to almost six thousand minutes of Dolly songs (and this doesn't include all the songs via You-Tube!). Timothy tells me it takes less time to get to the moon.

The night before we left Pigeon Forge in 2018, Timothy

and I laughed and talked in the gigantic wood-framed bed of the floor-to-ceiling-knotty-pine bedroom, with Stella between us sleeping. Ada was downstairs with her older cousins, feeling, at least temporarily, joyful and unburdened. Outside, the sparrows and the eagles and the myriad other wildlife were doing all the things they need to do to survive, and the trees just went about cleaning the air we breathe.

Speaking of the shame that survivors of violence experience, Dolly recently said, "It's not their fault! But also they don't have to be defined by that if they can find a light, and a way to actually brighten up their own little light." I would get up the next morning and keep plowing ahead toward meaning, toward happiness, toward ease, chasing the ineffable light of Los Angeles, or the sparkling light of the Smokies, or the promiseful light of New York City. The hard stuff wasn't all behind us, and still isn't, and never will be. Yet I have faith in the dreams and the beauty and the music ahead. Survival, like pain, lives in the body. Survival is in the telling of it. Survival is in the stories.

I Will Always Love You

Jolene, 1974, 2:56

DOLLY ENDED EVERY EPISODE OF her television shows with her iconic song "I Will Always Love You." Like so many of her songs, Dolly recorded it multiple times and in multiple ways: the 1972 mournful country ballad meant as a goodbye to Porter Wagoner; the 1982 poppier version that appeared in *The Best Little Whorehouse in Texas* during her crossover moment; the 1995 duet with then-hot Vince Gill as she tried to stay relevant in a new country era, before she returned successfully to her roots with her bluegrass/mountain trilogy.

Whitney Houston's heart- and record-smashing cover version of the song, from the 1992 movie *The Bodyguard*, is the version so many people heard first. The press often tried to create some drama between Dolly and Houston, but it seems only love ran both ways. "It's my song, but it's most definitely her record. It didn't sound like that when I had it!" Dolly has said. On *The Graham Norton Show*, Dolly recounts hearing Houston's version for the first time while driving, and having to pull to the side of the road: "It was one of the most overwhelming feelings I have ever had, to hear it done so well, so beautifully, and so big. She took it and made it so much more than what it would ever have been. It was such a joy as a songwriter. I don't think I will have a bigger thrill, ever."

At the 1994 Grammys, Dolly and producer David Foster announced the award for Best Female Pop Vocal Performance, and I tear up every time I watch the footage of Whitney Houston heading onto the stage toward Dolly; the intensity both women feel in the moment is so pure. "Dolly," Houston says, "of course coming from you this is truly an honor. You wrote a beautiful song, thank you so much for writing such beautiful songs." Almost half a century since "I Will Always Love You" was born, Dolly still ends almost all of her concerts with it. And here I turn to it in an attempt to thank those who have helped me get here, both the living and the gone.

First and foremost, an unending thank you to my editors at the University of Texas Press, Jessica Hopper and Casey Kittrell, who believed in this project when it was just an unformed idea. Thank you for your good humor, your honesty, and your faith in me. Resounding thanks to Lynne Ferguson, Abby Webber, and Wendy Moore for their sharp and kindhearted insights. To Kimberly Glyder, who designed such a magnificent cover; to Linda Ronan, who designed the ideal interior; and to Cameron Ludwick, Joel Pinckney, Gianna LaMorte, Bailey Morrison, Danni Bens, and the whole brilliant team at the University of Texas Press who champion this book in the world: my enormous gratitude.

Thank you to the uncommonly generous Hanif Abdurraqib, for literally making this book possible. Thank you to Christopher Deputato and the Café Royal Cultural Foundation for a generous grant that enabled the completion of the book. Thank you to *jubilat* and *Limp Wrist* for publishing early excerpts. Gratitude to Fred Courtright at The Permissions Company for easing my mind. Thank you to Eloisa Amezcua and the late Costura Creative for looking out for me and being a family.

Thank you to Yes Yes Books for the permission to reprint my poem "Twelve," from the book *Refusenik*, and for being a home.

Carley Moore! You already know you are the fairy god-mother of this book. Thank you and James Polchin for our small but mighty group. "It's hard to write a book, I'll tell you that," Dolly recently said to Brandi Carlile. She couldn't be more correct, but you both made it easier. What a blessing to be among your talent.

Endless gratitude and huge love to Paul Bottigliero, Kate Colby, Brett Fletcher Lauer, Melinda Moustakis, Deborah Paredez, Barbara White, and Jess Workman, who have been with me in so many entireties through the writing of this book. I couldn't imagine a better way to survive.

My grateful heart also to Melissa Febos, Hafizah Geter, Tyler Mills, Ricardo Alberto Maldonado, Ashley Nelson, Shelly Oria, Alicia Jo Rabins, Camille Rankine, Leigh Stein, and KMA Sullivan. To the ever-enduring memories of Lucie Brock-Broido and Evelyn Melnick. And to the late Phil Bosakowski, who first saw me.

Thank you to all my friends and family, who, named and unnamed here, are a crucial part of my life and became a crucial part of this book. Thank you to everyone who has sent me a Dolly-related text, email, article, message, song, gift, or comment before and during the writing of this book. Don't stop now! Thank you to Chris at *Dolly Parton News*, who somehow manages the impossible task of keeping up with Dolly. Thank you to all the superfans who put music and interviews on the internet.

To Anita and Michael Melnick. It is my great fortune to be your daughter. Thank you for all the love and all the books. To Cliff, Jessica, Annie, and Jake Melnick, who gamely went with me on the trip to Dollywood and all that came after: I love you guys.

To Dolly Parton, all of this. Thank you for the music and for these wings. To all the backing and studio musicians, and all musicians, and poets, and all artists who make beauty and get us through: my deep respect and admiration.

To my girls: my love for you is beyond measure, truly infinite. Ada Donnelly, your bravery and compassion are what inspire mine. I admire you so much. Stella Donnelly, thank you for your steadfast love, creativity, and silliness. You have cleansed my heart.

Timothy Donnelly, can you believe this life we made? Thank you for being here, in every way imaginable, the whole time. I will always love you.

REFERENCES AND RESOURCES

An enormous amount of reading, viewing, and listening went into the writing of this book. In addition to Dolly Parton's entire discography—which I listened to in chronological order several times—and filmography, here, for further exploration, is a list of sources used most directly in the making of this book.

Books

Allison, Dorothy. *Two or Three Things I Know for Sure*. New York: Plume, 1996.

Berman, Connie. *The Official Dolly Parton Scrapbook*. New York: Grosset and Dunlap, 1978.

Cardwell, Nancy. *The Words and Music of Dolly Parton: Getting to Know Country's "Iron Butterfly."* Santa Barbara, CA: Praeger, 2011.

Carlile, Brandi. *Broken Horses: A Memoir*. New York: Crown, 2021.

Carlson, Richard. *Don't Sweat the Small Stuff . . . and It's All Small Stuff: Simple Ways to Keep the Little Things from Taking Over Your Life*. New York: Hyperion, 1997.

Delffs, Dudley. *The Faith of Dolly Parton: Lessons from Her Life to Lift Your Heart*. Grand Rapids, MI: Zondervan, 2018.

Edwards, Leigh H. *Dolly Parton, Gender, and Country Music*. Bloomington: Indiana University Press, 2018.

Ernaux, Annie. *The Possession*. Translated by Anna Moschovakis. New York: Seven Stories Press, 2008.

———. *Shame*. Translated by Tanya Leslie. New York: Seven Stories Press, 1998.

Febos, Melissa. *Abandon Me: Memoirs*. New York: Bloomsbury, 2017.

Firestone, Tirzah. *Wounds into Wisdom: Healing Intergenerational Jewish Trauma*. Rhinebeck, NY: Monkfish, 2019.

Ford, Henry, and Clara Ford. *Good Morning: After a Sleep of*

Twenty-Five Years, Old-Fashioned Dancing Is Being Revived. Dearborn, MI: Dearborn Publishing Company, 1926.

Grant, Melissa Gira. *Playing the Whore: The Work of Sex Work.* New York: Verso, 2014.

Hamessley, Lydia R. *Unlikely Angel: The Songs of Dolly Parton.* Urbana: University of Illinois Press, 2020.

Hoppe, Graham. *Gone Dollywood: Dolly Parton's Mountain Dream.* Athens: Ohio University Press, 2018.

Kolk, Bessel van der. *The Body Keeps the Score: Brain, Mind, and Body in the Healing of Trauma.* New York: Penguin Random House, 2014.

Kushner, Harold S. *Overcoming Life's Disappointments: Learning from Moses How to Cope with Frustration.* New York: Penguin Books, 2006.

————. *When Bad Things Happen to Good People.* New York: Penguin Books, 1981.

Miller, Stephen. *Smart Blonde: Dolly Parton.* London: Omnibus Press, 2008.

Morales, Helen. *Pilgrimage to Dollywood: A Country Music Road Trip through Tennessee.* Chicago: University of Chicago Press, 2014.

Nash, Alanna. *Dolly: The Intimate Biography of Dolly Parton.* London: Panther Books, 1978.

Parton, Dolly. *Coat of Many Colors.* Illustrated by Brooke Boynton-Hughes. New York: Grosset and Dunlap, 2016.

————. *Dolly: My Life and Other Unfinished Business.* New York: HarperCollins, 1994.

————. *Dolly Parton, Songteller: My Life in Lyrics.* San Francisco: Chronicle Books, 2020.

————. *Dream More: Celebrate the Dreamer in You.* New York: Riverhead Books, 2012.

Potok, Chaim. *The Chosen.* New York: Simon and Schuster, 1967.

Reinhart, Mark S. *Chet Atkins: The Greatest Songs of Mister Guitar.* Jefferson, NC: McFarland, 2014.

Schmidt, Randy L., ed. *Dolly on Dolly: Interviews and Encounters with Dolly Parton.* Chicago: Chicago Review Press, 2017.

Smarsh, Sarah. *She Come By It Natural: Dolly Parton and the Women Who Lived Her Songs.* New York: Scribner, 2020.

Spitz, Bob. *Dylan: A Biography.* New York: W. W. Norton, 1988.

Magazines and Newspapers

Advocate	*Knoxville News*
American Songwriter	*Longreads*
Atlantic	*Los Angeles Times*
AV Club	*Ms.*
Baffler	*New Yorker*
Billboard	*New York Review of Books*
British GQ	*New York Times*
Bust	*Out*
Cashbox	*Parade*
Closer Weekly	*People*
Cosmopolitan	*Pigeon Forge News*
Country Music	*Pittsburgh Post-Gazette*
Country Queer	*Playboy*
Elle	*Playgirl*
Entertainment Weekly	*Prevention*
Financial Times	*Psychology Today*
Forbes	*Rolling Stone*
Forward	*Scientific American*
Goldmine	*Southern Living*
Good Housekeeping	*Tennessean*
Guardian	*Texas Monthly*
Harvard Magazine	*Time*
Houston Chronicle	*Toronto Star*
Independent	*Tulsa World*
Interview	*Washington Post*
Journal of Popular Music Studies	*Winston-Salem Journal*
JSTOR Daily	*Yes!*

Websites

albumism.com	arts.columbia.edu
allmusic.com	bbc.co.uk
americanradiohistory.com	bookriot.com

brainpickings.org
bringyouchickens.wordpress
     .com
brookings.edu
businesswire.com
catapult.co
cc.com
christchurchnashville.org
clairlynch.com
cmt.com
cnn.com
consequenceofsound.net
countrymusic.fandom.com
cvtresearch.com
dailymotion.com
discogs.com
dollymania.net
dollyon-line.com
dollyparton.com
dollywood.com
douglasjonesmusic.blogspot
     .com
eagles.org
edwardalbeesociety.org
elevationbehavioralhealth
     .com
etymonline.com
facebook.com
foxnews.com
glastonburyfestivals.co.uk
goodreads.com
grammy.com
gutenberg.org
health.com

history.com
hooktheory.com
huffpost.com
imaginationlibrary.com
keithlittle.com
learnguitartunes.com
lgbtqnation.com
lithub.com
lorareynolds.com
loudersound.com
mayoclinic.org
merriam-webster.com
muppet.fandom.com
music-illuminati.com
mykindofcountry.wordpress
     .com
mynewboyfriend.com
nbcnews.com
newengland.com
news.lafayette.edu
nickiswift.com
nme.com
nnedv.org
npr.org
nps.gov
opportunityagenda.org
ourdocuments.gov
poetryfoundation.org
poets.org
qz.com
richieowensandthefarmbu-
     reau.com
rogerebert.com
scrapsfromtheloft.com

setlist.fm
slate.com
snltranscripts.jt.org
songfacts.com
southwritlarge.com
spotify.com
stereogum.com
talkclassical.com
theboot.com
thehotline.org
theknot.com
theloop.ca
theringer.com
today.com

tonyconniff.com
tressie.substack.com
twitter.com
udiscovermusic.com
vimeo.com
visitmysmokies.com
vox.com
vulture.com
wccsevier.org
wkrn.com
worldradiohistory.com
wsmv.com
wvit.com
youtube.com

Audiovisual Sources

Country Music, directed by Ken Burns, 2019
Dolly (talk show), 1987–1988
Dolly and Friends: The Making of a Soundtrack—Dumplin', 2018
Dolly Parton's America (podcast), 2019
Hear to Slay (podcast), 2021
Imagination Library, Library of Congress award ceremony, 2018
Linda Ronstadt: The Sound of My Voice (documentary), 2019
The Porter Wagoner Show, 1967–1974
This Is Pop, 2021
The Tonight Show Starring Johnny Carson, 1977–1992
University of Tennessee, Knoxville, commencement address, 2009
Unlocking Us (podcast), 2020

Other Resources

Brandi Carlile tour, Forest Hills Stadium, Queens, NY, 2021
Chasing Rainbows Museum, Dollywood, Pigeon Forge, TN
Country Music Hall of Fame Museum, Nashville, TN

Dolly Parton, Pure & Simple Tour, Forest Hills Stadium, Queens, NY, 2016

RCA Studio B, Nashville, TN

Rock and Roll Hall of Fame Museum, Cleveland, OH